OFFENDER PROFILING SERIES: Vol III
THE SOCIAL PSYCHOLOGY

Offender Profiling Series
Series Editor: David Canter

Titles in the Series

Interviewing and Deception
Edited by David Canter and Laurence Alison

Profiling in Policy and Practice
Edited by David Canter and Laurence Alison

**The Social Psychology of Crime
Groups, teams and networks**
Edited by David Canter and Laurence Alison

Profiling Property Crimes
Edited by David Canter and Laurence Alison

Profiling Rape and Murder
Edited by David Canter and Laurence Alison

The Psychology of Rape Investigation
Margaret Wilson, David Canter and Karen Jack

OFFENDER PROFILING SERIES: Vol III
THE SOCIAL PSYCHOLOGY OF CRIME
Groups, teams and networks

Edited by

DAVID CANTER and LAURENCE ALISON
Centre for Investigative Psychology
University of Liverpool

Ashgate

DARTMOUTH
Aldershot • Burlington USA • Singapore • Sydney

© David Canter, Laurence J. Alison 2000

All rights reserved. No part of this publication may be reproduced, stored in a retrieval system, or transmitted in any form or by any means, electronic, mechanical, photocopying, recording or otherwise without the prior permission of the publisher.

Published by
Dartmouth Publishing Company Limited
Ashgate Publishing Limited
Gower House
Croft Road
Aldershot
Hants GU11 3HR
England

Ashgate Publishing Company
131 Main Street
Burlington
Vermont 05401
USA

Ashgate website: http://www.ashgate.com

British Library Cataloguing in Publication Data
The social psychology of crime : groups, teams and
   networks. - (Offender profiling series ; v. 3)
   1.Crime - Social aspects 2.Criminal psychology 3.Social
   psychology
   I.Canter, David, 1944- II.Alison, Laurence J.
   364.3

Library of Congress Cataloging-in-Publication Data
Canter, David.
    The social psychology of crime : groups, teams and networks / David Canter and Laurence Alison.
     p. cm. - (Offender profiling series ; vol. III)
    ISBN 1-84014-435-1 (hbk.)
    1. Criminal behavior–Social aspects. 2. Criminals–Social networks. 3. Social groups.
    4. Criminal psychology. 5. Social psychology. I. Alison, Laurence J. II. Title. III. Series.

HV6155.C36 1999
364.3–dc21

99-044828

ISBN 1 84014 435 1 (Hbk)
ISBN 1 84014 497 1 (Pbk)

Printed and bound in Great Britain by MPG Books Ltd, Bodmin, Cornwall

Contents

	Series Preface	*vii*
	Acknowledgements	*ix*
1	The Social Psychology of Crime: Groups, Teams and Networks *David Canter and Laurence Alison*	1
2	Culture and Crime *Gerald Mars*	21
3	The Structural Analysis of Criminal Networks *Duncan McAndrew*	51
4	Investigating Fraud *Alan Doig*	95
5	Rules and Roles in Terrorist Hostage Taking *Margaret Wilson and Alaster Smith*	127
6	Riot by Appointment: An Examination of the Nature and Structure of Seven Hard-Core Football Hooligan Groups *Lynne Johnston*	153
7	Ram Raiding: Criminals Working in Groups *Ian Donald and Angela Wilson*	189
8	The Social Structure of Robbery *Karyn McCluskey and Sarah Wardle*	247
9	Criminology, Desistance and the Psychology of the Stranger *Shadd Maruna*	287
10	Destructive Organisational Psychology *David Canter*	321

Series Preface

'Offender Profiling' has become part of public consciousness even though many people are not really sure what it is and the great majority of people have no idea at all of how it is done. This ignorance is just as prevalent in professional circles as amongst the lay public. Psychologists, psychiatrists, probation officers and social workers all have an interest in how their disciplines can contribute to police investigations, but few practitioners are aware of exactly what the possibilities for such contributions are. Others, such as police officers and lawyers, who seek advice from 'profilers' often also have only the vaguest ideas as to what 'profiling' consists of or what scientific principles it may be based on. The army of students who aspire to emulate the fictional activities of psychologists who solve crimes is yet another group who desperately need a systematic account of what 'offender profiling' is and what the real prospects for its development are.

The public fascination with the little understood activity of 'profiling' has meant that no fictional account of crime, whether it be heavy drama or black comedy, seems to be complete without at least one of the protagonists offering as a 'profile' their opinion on the characteristics of the perpetrator of the crime(s) around which the narrative is built. This popular interest combined with widespread ignorance has generated its own corpus of urban myths: such mythical 'profilers' produce uncannily accurate descriptions of unknown killers, solve cases that had baffled the police and seem to know before the criminal where he would strike next.

Sadly, like all myths not only do they only have a very loose connection with reality but they also distract attention away from a range of other significant and more intellectually challenging questions. These are the important questions that are inherent in the processes of criminal behaviour and its investigation. Such considerations include assessments of the quality and validity of the information on which police base their decisions and subsequent actions. This also involves assessing the possibilities for detecting deception. There also exist questions about the consistencies of a criminal's behaviour and what the crucial differences are between one offender and another.

Group processes of criminals raise other questions, which surprisingly are seldom touched upon by 'profilers' in fact or fiction. These ask about the form such groups take and the influence they have on the actions of the criminals, the role of leaders in crimes or the socio-cultural processes of which they are a part. There are also important issues about the implications and use of any answers that may emerge from scientific studies of crimes and their investigation

These and many other questions are raised by the mere possibility of psychology being of value to police investigations. To answer them it is essential to go beyond urban myth, fiction and the self-aggrandising autobiographies of self-professed 'experts'. A truly scientific stance is necessary that draws on a wide range of social and psychological disciplines

Many of these questions relate to others that are central to any psychological considerations of human actions, such as the nature of human memory, the processes of personality construction, group dynamics and interpersonal transactions. Therefore the systematic, scientific study of the issues relevant to 'offender profiling' are recognisably part of a burgeoning field of psychology and related disciplines. In an attempt to make this point and distinguish the steady accretion of knowledge in this area from the mythology, hyperbole and fiction of 'offender profiling' I labelled this field *Investigative Psychology*. This term seems to have taken root and is now evolving rapidly throughout the world.

Yet in the way that labels and terminology have a life of their own 'offender profiling' and its variants will just not lie down and die peacefully from a robust youth and dissolute old age. So we are stuck with it as a somewhat unhelpful shorthand and therefore the term has been kept for the title of this series in the hope that we may gradually re-define profiling as a systematic and scientific endeavour.

The books in this series provide a thorough introduction to and overview of the emerging field of Investigative Psychology. As such they provide a compendium of research and discussion that will place this important field firmly in the social sciences. Each volume takes a different focus on the field so that together they cover the full range of current activity that characterises this energetic area of research and practice.

David Canter
Series Editor

Acknowledgements

We are grateful to Anthony Lundrigan, Julie Blackwell and Cathy Sanders for the level of organisation, commitment and precision they have brought to pulling these volumes together and to Steve Deprez and Julia Fossi for their help in compiling the volumes.

1 The Social Psychology of Crime: Groups, Teams and Networks

DAVID CANTER AND LAURENCE ALISON

In recognition of the fact that criminal activities and the processes that sustain them are embedded in the transactions between individuals this volume examines the social and organisational aspects of crime. Such an examination is of particular benefit to police investigations. It strengthens the abilities of law enforcement agencies to incapacitate criminal networks and to weaken the social interactions between criminals. Understanding the nature of a criminal organisation also has value in providing guidance for how the investigative team should be organised.

Studies show that criminal networks, teams and groups and their associated social processes are not limited to tight, confined social clusters but are a mixture of different types of organisation running the full range from the anarchic to the strictly hierarchical. These social psychological processes influence criminal activity in three broad ways. First, they have a profound influence on the way in which the criminals' self-identity is determined. Second, the form of the organisation of which they are a part shapes the roles and rules of criminal activity. Third, these organisational processes will define the 'career' paths through which criminals may move, in part at least.

For police investigators these findings imply that they do need to identify the criminal teams, networks, cliques and groups that offenders move within, as well as the likely consequences of isolating any individual from his criminal network. This leads to an investigative emphasis on the way criminal activity extends beyond the boundaries of the specific individuals involved in the immediate features of the offence itself. This in turn requires improvements in investigators own processes of networking and acting as teams.

David Canter is Director of the Centre for Investigative Psychology at the University of Liverpool. He has published widely in Environmental and Investigative Psychology as well as many areas of Applied Social Psychology. His most recent books since his award winning *"Criminal Shadows"* have been *"Psychology in Action"* and with Laurence Alison *"Criminal Detection and the Psychology of Crime"*.

Laurence Alison is currently employed as a lecturer at the Centre for Investigative Psychology at the University of Liverpool. Dr Alison is developing models to explain the processes of manipulation, influence and deception that are features of criminal investigations. His research interests focus upon developing rhetorical perspectives in relation to the investigative process. He has presented many lectures both nationally and internationally to a range of academics and police officers on the problems associated with offender profiling. He is affiliated with The Psychologists at Law Group - a forensic service specialising in providing advice to the courts, legal professions, police service, charities and public bodies.

1 The Social Psychology of Crime: Groups, Teams and Networks

DAVID CANTER AND LAURENCE ALISON

Criminal activities and the processes that sustain them are embedded in the transactions between individuals. They may therefore be seen as social psychological phenomena. Indeed, many of the social mechanisms relevant to conventional psychological explanations of behaviour are also important for understanding the actions of criminals. Yet curiously, attempts to draw upon psychological theories and methods in order to contribute to police investigations – often referred to as 'profiling' – have almost universally ignored the social dimension. The present volume fills this gap and considers the implications of social psychology for both the understanding of crime and its successful investigation.

The absence of the social psychological dimension in 'offender profiling' has largely been because 'profilers' have commonly focused on bizarre individuals, drawing upon models of individual disturbance to account for offence behaviour. We have shown in earlier volumes in this series the weaknesses of approaches that rely upon pathogenic models of immutable deviant dispositions (Canter and Alison, 1999). One failing of such models is their inability to account for the many aspects of offending that necessitate and are actually defined by socially functional behaviour.

Many aspects of offence behaviour require interpersonally 'successful' transactions. For example, the financial exchange between burglar and handler may require appropriate negotiation tactics; armed robbers may benefit from interpersonal behaviour that avoids violent transaction but nevertheless gains compliance through social manipulation; individuals who are members of a robbery team have to function effectively as a group to rob specific targets; crime syndicates rely on co-ordination between skilled individuals in order to be able to manipulate the system to their own ends. Even in some cases of rape and murder there are instances where offenders gain control over their victims through socially skilled processes of persuasion and deception.

A second and related set of issues concerns the group structures, social and cultural networks, that form the context within which many offences occur. Few offences involve a sole operator and, instead, often consist of groups or teams of individuals that, to a greater or lesser extent, have to interact to make the offence possible and for criminals to benefit from it. This is most obvious in what is known as 'organised' crime, typically dealing with the purchase and sale of illegal goods, but it is also a part of all crime that has some financial component to it from burglary to major frauds. To understand how these crimes are possible the implicit and formal organisational networks of which they are a part, have to be understood.

The recognition of the social and organisational aspects of crime offers a particular perspective for police activity. Social and organisational psychologists devote their time to considerations of how social transactions can be facilitated and how organisations can be made more effective. Yet in the criminal context the very opposite is the objective. Individuals involved in the process of investigation are attempting to incapacitate criminal networks and to weaken the social interactions of criminals. There is a sense in which such investigators need to turn organisational theory on its head, learn what factors make an organisation efficient and then see whether the same factors used 'in reverse' can render that organisation unworkable. Many examples of the possibilities for this are given in the following chapters.

The social environment is also relevant, though, even for the allegedly 'alienated' offender. Indeed as discussed by Canter (1995) the bizarre thought patterns, self images and extreme behaviours that help to distinguish offenders are likely to be a product of a personal narrative of alienation, nurtured and fuelled by comparisons to the groups that the individual no longer feels part of. The increasing distance created between such offenders and these groups can only occur as a product of interacting increasingly poorly with them. Thus, to understand this alienation the social psychological process that engenders it also needs to be understood.

Cultural Ideologies and Criminal Networks

Mars [2][1] provides a particularly helpful framework for examining the social psychology of crime by drawing on cultural theory that has its roots in anthropological considerations. Mars emphasises two underlying dimensions that help to distinguish between the various criminal cultures that exist. One dimension is the extent to which a culture imposes rules and classifications on its members. The other is the strength of the group of which a person is a member and how much of the person's life is tied into that group. Combinations of these distinctions help to draw attention to important differences in the social context of which a criminal may be a part.

For example; Chinese *triads*, a group that is suggested to have a high degree of classification, and clearly defined ranks, requires the person to be strongly committed to that group whilst providing for all aspects of his life. Such a group is thought to be less vulnerable to police informants than an *ad hoc* gang of armed robbers who only come together to carry out one particular crime. It follows that one task for a police investigator is to determine where on these dimensions any criminal network actually resides. From such examinations the vulnerabilities of those networks can be revealed.

McAndrew [3] describes in detail the mathematical possibilities that now exist for describing criminal networks. In doing this he shows that some of the central concepts for describing groups can be very ambiguous unless given mathematical precision. Such precision then allows sensible consideration of crucial investigative questions. For instance, where the vulnerabilities really are in any networks or if the criminal organisation really will be fatally wounded if its apparent leader is removed. These analyses also facilitate the monitoring of changes in communication networks and the revelation of just how fluid they are and how difficult it may be to specify their structure. Likewise, Johnston [6] uses particular analyses to draw out the structural details of football hooligan networks and the relationship between a person's position and their individual background.

---

[1] Numbers in [ ] refer to chapters in the present volume.

Criminal Activity as Evolving within Social Contexts

Mars' model of criminal cultures helps to show how it is also the case that it is the very lack of group strength and clearly defined rules and roles that creates the context in which some crimes occur. These tend not to be crimes in which illicit goods and services are bought and sold but those in which individual offenders, who see themselves as autonomous and free from the rules that bind others, take advantage of the organisations of which they are a part to perpetrate frauds. Not surprisingly, then, these types of crime require rather different investigative strategies. For organised crime the nature of that criminal organisation needs to be understood, as it is the key to the criminal's actions. For business related fraud it is the nature of the organisations that suffer the crimes that needs to be understood. They facilitate offences that are typically perpetrated by criminally minded individualists who are exploiting vulnerabilities in the systems of which they are members.

As Doig [4] points out, the losses incurred by fraudulent behaviour have a far wider impact than all those incurred by theft, burglary and robbery together. Yet fraud is low on the priorities for the police and not generally considered as a particularly heinous crime. In fact some varieties of fraud are able to exist 'disguised' as legitimate practices simply because they can easily go under the camouflage or extensions of more conventional behaviours. This indicates that the socio-cultural processes that define what is criminal may under-emphasise the significance of fraud and thereby contribute to its prevalence.

The Social Landscape of Offending

We have discussed before the neglect of contextual features within the investigative literature in our discussions of the information gathering stage of enquiries (Canter and Alison, 1999). There we noted that the collation of worthy information was highly influenced by the confines within which it occurred. For example Koehn, Fisher and Cutler (1998) noted how important re-constituting context is in helping to elicit photofits. Kebbell and Wagstaff (1998) noted how the cognitive interview relies heavily on its success in reconstructing context. Aked et al. (1998) also emphasised that forensic assessment of linguistics needs to take very careful notice of the contextual effects upon the writing of documents. Context is also poorly understood and little researched in relation to criminal action. Indeed, as van Duyne (1999) states with some authority, having worked closely within the remit of investigations into organised crime, merely examining the profile of the criminal entrepreneur is not sufficient unless one also has a grasp of the entrepreneurial landscape.

van Duyne's work is also important in outlining not just the social landscape of the criminal domain but also of the investigative team. Networks, teams and groups and their associated social processes are therefore not limited to tight, confined schematic representations of social clustering but rather, the social fabric between the investigative team and the offenders is often intertwined - they do, after all, have some overlapping social concerns. Thus, whilst van Duyne credits the criminal intelligence systems that represent individuals and their links with some worth, he is dismissive of the idea that these 'bubblegrams' can ever hope to represent the complexity of the social processes between offenders. In fact van Duyne suggests that these can misrepresent the links between offenders, pointing out that they make the links more overt than they may in actual fact be. This is a point that McAndrew outlines more fully in his chapter in the present volume by drawing attention to the weaknesses of the sources of information on which such diagrams are often based.

Few crime entrepreneurs, as van Duyne points out, recognise such corporate reconstructions, noting instead that often times these seemingly highly organised, supposedly meticulously planned operations are far more labile, spontaneous and risky than sociograms, network analysis or any other visual representation may indicate. They are less highly placed on Mars' structural dimensions than certain journalists would have us believe. McAndrew [3], Donald and Wilson [7] and McCluskey and Wardle [8] all found differentiation in roles and levels of individual power, but no rigid hierarchies. As a result, a systematic approach to the social organisation of the enquiry team itself is required to take into account such flexibility. Much of this work points out the limitations of the military model of policing noted by Franz and Jones (1987) suggesting, instead, that certain types of criminal social structure may be better dealt with by different types of investigative social structure. In other words, although the military model may be efficient in some phases of an investigation it may not be well suited to other aspects of the enquiry.

The importance of considering the social transactions and parallels between the investigative team and the groups that they are dealing with is nowhere more important than in hostage negotiation situations where the subtleties of the dynamics between hostages, terrorists and the negotiation team must be observed to avoid potential catastrophe. Wilson and Smith [5] emphasise that these processes, even though they occur in high stress situations, follow surprisingly conventional social roles and rules.

As Donald and Canter (1992) have previously shown in their work on behaviour in fires, though potentially high stress situations may lead us to believe in more chaotic behaviour being a product of traumatic conditions, actually the contextual features result in surprisingly rule bound behaviours. This, as Wilson and Smith argue, is primarily a function of the social dynamics that evolve between the parties involved in the hostage situation. Negotiation strategies appear to follow processes similar to normal equity situations with totally unreasonable demands rarely being made and even the most extreme agendas being flexible enough occasionally to result in compromise.

Wilson and Smith point out that both parties often make concessions. Holding to absolute values, i.e. no concessions, can be very dangerous for government policy and particularly unfruitful for the terrorists. Thus, whilst undoubtedly there are occasions where the behaviour of terrorist groups appear irrational, uncompromising and brutal, such occasions are rare. Perhaps this is because terrorists do not see themselves as deviant or as offenders. Their actions may be more likely to conform to what they see as their own ideology, seeking justice, equity and freedom. They often see themselves as acting out an historic episode that gives meaning to their actions. Living a narrative that assigns them heroic roles.

Social Narratives of Crime

In order to understand the actions of many criminals it is useful to consider the self-created narratives that help to give shape and significance to their actions. It seems plausible that it is not only terrorists who structure their lives around key episodes and particular patterns of transaction with others. This process of embedding the view of the self in an unfolding personal story, called by Canter (1995) an "inner narrative", helps to explain many aspects of criminal activity. It is especially helpful in explaining those crimes that are not of obvious financial benefit or are extremely high risk. The white-collar criminal may see himself as obtaining redress for earlier slights; an unwilling victim rather than a manipulative villain. The member of a criminal gang may view himself as a dashing leader or professional 'hard-man' rather than the dishonest bully that others may recognise.

The roles that are drawn on to give meaning to offenders' lives are embedded in a social matrix. They are supported and refined in the contacts the criminal has with other criminals. They also connect with the notions of antagonist and protagonist that are present in the larger culture of which the criminal partakes. This enables the criminal to legitimise, in his own eyes and those of his associates, the acts he performs and to neutralise in his mind their destructive consequences.

Criminal Identity and Socialisation

Maruna [9] argues that a true understanding of criminal behaviour can only come through indepth analysis of such narratives, and connecting those narratives to roles and behaviours. The criminal narratives to which offenders subscribe may lead them to consider their actions as acceptable and not 'criminal'. Or they may revel in being part of an 'outlaw' group that lives by rules that break conventions. Thus these narratives of offending can be seen as a product of social processes. This 'evolution of identity' accords with social constructionist perspectives:

> *"Identity is formed by social processes. Once crystallised, it is maintained, modified, or even reshaped by social relations. The social processes involved in both the formation and maintenance of identity are determined by the social structure. Conversely, the identities produced by the interplay of organism, individual consciousness and social structure react upon the given social structure, maintaining it, modifying it, or even reshaping it"*
>
> Berger and Luckmann (1981, p. 194)

Vygotsky (1978) noted that mental functioning is shaped by and situated within social life. This socio-cultural approach to mind emphasises how interpersonal contact shapes individual and mental processes. This can also be seen as a natural psychological consequence of the Sutherland's seminal argument that criminality emerges out of differential association (Sutherland and Cressey, 1974). To the psychologist Sutherland's criminology implies that it is not just the actions of the criminal that are shaped by his social network but the whole way in which the criminal sees his world and makes sense of himself. Like all cognition, criminal cognition is socially situated. The social context of any criminal therefore has a profound relevance for the way in which that criminal's self identity is determined. The organisational structure of criminal groups may therefore be examined to reveal the varieties of roles available to offenders and the implications they carry for any offender's identification with criminal activity.

Studies of the organisational structure of criminal groups show the many levels of and varieties of involvement in offending that are available. For example Johnston's [6] examination of the structure of football hooligan groups shows there are differences in levels of 'commitment' to offending depending on the extent to which the individuals identify with the hooligan group. This is manifest in such differences as, for example, the extent to which individuals are prepared to travel to organised fights. The more committed members travel further. So strong are these group processes that fighting is often dictated by the extent to which the individuals feel a part of the 'in' or 'out' group. As Johnston points out, two groups that have recently fought one another may form into a larger group to fight against a jointly perceived more dissimilar, and therefore 'threat' group. Thus persistence and the severity of offending appears to be a product of subtle social processes.

Criminal 'Careers'

The organisational processes that Johnston indicates can be seen in many other forms of offending and have been explored at least since the early ethnographic studies of the 20s and 30s (cf Thrasher, 1927; Whyte, 1965). Many of those studies and more recent explorations, such as Marsh et al. (1978), have demonstrated the existence of role differentiation and consequent organisational structure within gangs and teams of offenders. Donald and Wilson's [7] study of ram raiders shows that the different roles within a team are derived partly on the basis of the different skills available to and necessary for the purpose of carrying out ram raids. In fact the authors argue that the offence requires such a level of skill that it can only be effectively carried out if it is considered and planned as a professional activity. Donald and Wilson see no need to draw upon diagnostic or pathological models to explain behaviour but instead develop an argument for group processes as evolving from principles of organisational and social psychology. They draw heavily upon Guzzo's (1996) research on work groups. These are defined by the existence of social entities within a larger social system, where tasks are performed as a product of the group not by discrete individuals. Moreover, they note that in ram raiding there are specified roles that the offenders appear to be well aware of.

Indeed McCluskey and Wardle [8] reveal from interviews with members of armed robbery teams that these criminals have a clear conception of roles amongst their members and they appear to enjoy these self descriptions. Katz (1988) has pointed out the value in examining the 'seductive' qualities of the image that certain criminal lifestyles promote. Thus, in denying a belonging to the conventional, non-criminal group, some offenders define themselves as members of an 'out group'.

If such roles can be found in groups of criminals, and those roles relate to the offence histories of the offenders, as indicated for example in chapters [8] and [9], then the question arises as to what paths lead criminals into these different positions in criminal organisations. Are there any parallels here to the 'careers' that people follow in legal organisations?

The idea of a criminal career, in which offenders take on different roles in an illegal enterprise and possibly move through those roles over time, is rather different from the notion that, for example, Blumstein et al. (1988) offer. They merely consider the temporal progress of serial criminals in order to establish if there are any defining consistencies to that progress. From a social psychological perspective a career implies changing relationships to the other people with whom the person is working. Therefore understanding where an offender is on his career path can assist in understanding his current actions and criminal history, both matters of great significance to police investigations.

This development in a criminal's involvement in crime, as Johnston has illustrated for football hooligans, may involve more commitment to the 'job' being carried out. For an offender this would imply that they identify with the life of crime, becoming a 'career criminal'. They can come to see significant aspects of themselves as defined by the 'job' they do, namely committing crimes.

Maruna [9] develops the implications of this social construction of criminality a stage further. He contends that proposals for the existence of criminal 'genes', neuro-physiological damage, traits or any other pathogenic explanation of criminal behaviour must deal with the fact that the overwhelming majority of individuals stop offending. He emphasises that there is nothing stable about most criminals' careers.

The fact that so many individuals desist from crime presents a serious problem for the stable trait theory. Instead, Maruna asserts that a narrative perspective, which is a social process model, helps to explicate the changing dynamic features of the individual's life - the way in which identity is formed as a product of each individual's 'story-line'. This internalised autobiographic narrative is continually evolving to help promote coherence and meaning in individuals' lives. These processes of 'self-telling' (Bruner, 1987) have the capacity to shape events and therefore result in a dialectic process between the individual and his social environment. This joint construction of identity, as shaped by the social environment, clearly does not involve pathological diagnostic criteria though the routes through which individuals develop their identities may be deviant and destructive. Criminogenic socialisation processes therefore are not, as Maruna puts it, "created in a vacuum" but are shaped by the opportunities of each individual's social world. Such developments have implications for our understanding of the development of these life stories and the social context from which they evolved.

Implications for Police Investigations

There has been little direct application of social psychological concepts and findings to police investigations. As a consequence, the ways in which the results reported in the present volume can be utilised by police investigators have still to be explored in practice. However, various possibilities for making police investigations more effective are indicated in the following chapters. Four main aspects will be summarised here of the social psychology of crime that have broad ranging implications for police investigations.

The Criminal's View of himself is Socially Constructed

It is often assumed that a criminal's view of himself can only be determined by asking him directly. The social psychological perspective emphasises how much that view is influenced by the contacts the offender has with many other people. So, although the evidential constraints on hearsay are very important, for investigative purposes there is much to be gained by building up a picture of known offenders from interviewing their close associates and relatives. This can provide important information for lines of enquiry as well as insights that can help when interviewing a suspect.

If the community of which an offender is part does not see certain actions as especially criminal then it is very likely that the offender views the actions in the same way. Indeed the perpetrator may measure his own personal worth in terms of the way he contributes to criminal endeavours. This could be revealed through discussions with other members of that criminal community.

The search for 'motives' can also be seen as rather unproductive in many investigations if the actions being investigated are recognised activities within that social group. If those actions, whether it be unprovoked violence or casual theft, for instance, are 'what people do' in certain situations. It may be no easier to establish 'motivations' for those crimes than to establish motivations for why some people are altruistic, for example, and help others when there is no benefit to themselves.

Moreover the social psychological perspective helps to dispel the belief that horrific acts of brutality are simply the product of 'evil' minds, with the consequent investigative implication of searching for a person who is recognisably evil. Often, even the most macabre acts of sadism have logic to them. That is, they need not have evolved as a product of a chaotic, unpredictable and disordered mind but instead have an unfolding personal logic that draws upon accepted practices within particular sub-groups within society.

It would be useful for investigators to bear in mind the possibility that even the most deviant acts can be understood through a thorough examination of the social processes that have contributed to the behaviour. For investigative psychologists the routes through which these behaviours evolve must be understood. The challenge is to reveal these latent paths and establish lawful relations between sets of events and actions of offenders. This will only occur through the systematic evaluation and empirical analysis of the personal learning histories of offenders and the manifestations of offence actions.

Most of the features of these learning paths are likely to connect very closely with the ways in which interpersonal relations have developed over the life span. For example, an individual who is used to controlling others or gaining influence through threats or acts of violence is more likely to be violent in a robbery than one who has learnt to control others by planning and determination. The means by which offenders control their victims may be revealing about their personal histories. In order to explore such issues, greater attention must be paid to the social landscape within which offence behaviour occurs.

Criminal Groups will have Varying Degrees of Group Structure, which carry Implications, Relating to Specialism in their Roles and to the Predictability of their Actions

From the labile networks that burglars exploit to sell stolen goods to the organised hierarchies within professional robbery teams, the notion of role and the contextual features that surround it carry many implications for criminal behaviour. Roles may be socially rule bound and occur within more or less strict contextual parameters. Moreover, more explicit rules may be employed in more overtly 'managed' groups in order to guide behaviour. In all cases, however, knowledge of the social process that shapes these behaviours may prove invaluable to investigators. It may help guide both the enquiry team's social structure as well as impose frameworks within which to examine and narrow down particular behavioural 'paths' of offending. This may even be useful for the prediction of certain forms of criminal behaviour.

Investigations into criminal teams and networks do need to identify the cliques and groups that offenders move within. Tightly bound cliques will create their own internal pressures on individuals to perform in certain ways, whereas more labile structures take on their own momentum. The issue is then that the genesis of much behaviour lies within the different structural properties of groups rather than 'inside' the criminal mind. The studies that are presented here demonstrate that a clear understanding of the ways in which groups influence individual behaviours has great relevance for the way in which crime might be investigated. The identification of structural properties of the group may lead the investigator to make reliable assumptions about the likely characteristics of offenders within that network. It will also help the investigator to understand the likely consequences of isolating any individual from his criminal network.

At a Larger Scale the Organisation of Criminal Networks will take on Many Forms, but often they will not Reflect Legal Organisations as Readily as is Sometimes Assumed

Investigators should not assume that the organisational processes within criminal networks, groups or teams reflect perfectly the types of legitimate institutions upon which they may be distortedly modelled. Although the present volume points to the many overlaps between legal organisations and criminal activity, there are many levels and qualitative variants of organisation that, although conforming to generalisable social processes, do not necessarily depend upon the structural properties within conventional organisations. As one might intuitively anticipate, many features of criminal activities reflect a weaker allegiance to an organisational structure than do non-criminal activities. They sometimes more readily reflect expressions of anarchy.

If investigators can identify central figures in the criminal network and establish if there are any cliques that support these central figures then the investigation has a firm basis for planned actions to weaken that network. The further identification of peripheral but potentially knowledgeable members of the network could also open routes to informants or forms of access for undercover agents.

It is also worth noting that there may be particular forms of social behaviour that are peculiar to the realm of offending. Thus, although it is unlikely that criminals operate within entirely alien social systems that bear no relationship to legal society, there remains the possibility that we still do not have a clear understanding of the peculiarities of criminal social behaviour. The identification of its unique features is best discovered by relying on the careful collection of intelligence, guided by hypothesis testing based upon current knowledge. Through a number of iterations, these processes may reveal those particular features and, in turn, have a significant application to investigations. This volume is just one example of how researchers can work with material that reveals these patterns.

Criminal Actions Need to be Understood in their Cultural Context

One further point is the impact of the overall culture in which crime occurs on the criminal culture itself. Leyton (1997), for example, looks at the way in which the nature of murder can be understood as a product of the cultural processes within which it occurs. He suggests that murder rates and the subsequent responses to murder by the murderers themselves may be understood as a product of the overall societal perspective on murder. Leyton's view that murder manifests itself in different ways according to cultural parameters is rarely considered in the criminology literature. But Cooke's (1996) studies of psychopathy indicate that the trans-cultural perspective can have significant implications for understanding the actions of individual criminals. Cooke has argued that UK psychopaths reveal the features of their disorder in markedly different ways to American psychopaths. In essence, Cooke reports that UK psychopaths reveal more muted versions of processes of manipulation and selfishness than do the more 'florid' and blatant strategies of the American psychopaths. If substantiated this claim would have major implications for the investigation of crime as well as its treatment and punishment. In particular any readiness to adopt American practices in the investigation and treatment of psychopathy would have to be cautiously considered.

Thus in terms of understanding criminals we should raise questions about how much of the explanation should be sought within the individual and how much is the product of what people absorb from their culture. However, there has been little systematic analysis of criminal social roles. For example what is expected of a leader in a gang may vary considerably according to the role structure of the gang and the general cultural attitude to leadership. There is even likely to be variation in the extent to which labelling of that role occurs; with some groups studiously avoiding such labels.

Many of the social networks of criminal activity extend beyond the boundaries of the specific individuals involved in the immediate features of the offence itself. For example, 'handlers' who purchase stolen goods are not necessarily involved in the details of the offence but are, for example, concerned with the products of a burglary. McAndrew [3] points out that investigators have long been aware of the importance of the links that are external to the crime scene. They are, increasingly, developing systems to help identify relative positions, roles, subgroups and communication methods within the criminal network. McAndrew illustrates how social network analysis has been employed to examine relational and position features of such networks, outlining how various patterns and structures impact upon the means and methods of engaging in crime.

As a developing area of criminal intelligence, a wide range of systems are being created to handle a whole variety of information across different modes of contact - from analysis of surveillance observations to the documentation of phone calls amongst offenders. However, as with all statistical summaries, care has to be taken to avoid the assumption that an organised group necessarily exists as a distinct sub-set of the population just because an intelligence analyst can produce a striking diagram indicating links between the individuals concerned. At both the individual and group level it is clear that the social boundaries are far less clear than many of these structural diagrams may suggest. Future research does need to explore the relationship between representations of criminal group structure and coherence and the actual experience of being members of those hypothesised groups.

The Future

With the increasing capacity of communication systems and with the breakdown of geopolitical barriers, many and varied contacts between criminals are more feasible than ever. Changes in the national and international market places have made old types of crime more global and more part of world wide communication systems. This widespread communication network also opens up many opportunities for new types of crime. For example fraud is more possible now with international banking, internet sales, and the free flow of goods across international markets. Academics and investigators are likely to find themselves concentrating more closely on the social processes that afford opportunities for offending. In turn, they must develop improvements in their own processes of networking and acting as teams to work effectively in understanding the processes of criminal behaviour.

One direct investigative implication is that the police may have to develop structures that mirror those they are studying and see if loose networks of crime are better examined through a more loosely coherent investigative team. There may be many disadvantages to the military model of policing - particularly in relation to certain types of offending. These problems may be overcome by examining differently structured investigative teams for different types of problem. Attempts to develop different combinations are likely to be merely a process of trial and error unless based on studies of the ways in which behaviour is affected as a product of context. For investigators this is true both in terms of the group that they are studying as well as the groups of which they, themselves, are a part. Increasing knowledge of these social processes is therefore the first step in tackling many forms of present day crime as well as being in a position to deal with new forms of crime in the future. The examination of criminality as a product of the transactions between people is likely to be far more productive for investigators than delving ever further into the supposed 'internal chaos' of individual criminals.

This examination of criminals in what is, in effect, an organisational context opens up the possibility of a rather new form of organisational psychology. In a concluding chapter, written as a sort of Epilogue to the present volume, Canter [10] has called this "Destructive Organisational Psychology". He offers the prospect of utilising what is known about the vulnerabilities of organisations to seek out the weakness in criminal groups, teams and networks. These weaknesses can then be the target of police activities. He points out, though, that one of the greatest potential weaknesses is that members of criminal organisations may not get the benefits from them that they desire. If these dissatisfactions can be encouraged the whole basis of the criminal network is thereby challenged.

The social psychological perspective on crime thus does take account of what may loosely be referred to as the 'motivations' for crime within the individual, but looks for the support of those motivations within the social, organisational context of which the criminal is a part. A fuller understanding of how criminal groups, teams and networks operate will therefore be of immense value in understanding those experiences of individual offenders that keeps them criminally active. It also provides new possibilities for the reduction of crime.

References

Aked, J., Canter, D., Sanford, A. and Smith, N. (1999), 'Approaches to the Scientific Attribution of Authorship', in D.V. Canter and L.J. Alison (eds), *Interviewing and Deception, Offender Profiling Series*, I, Aldershot: Dartmouth.

Berger, P.L., and Luckman, T. (1991)[1966], *The Social Construction of Reality. A treatise in the Sociology of Knowledge*, London: Penguin.

Blumstein, A., Cohen, J., and Farrington, D.P. (1988), 'Criminal Career Research: Its Value for Criminology', *Criminology*, 26, 1-36.

Canter, D.V. (1995), *Criminal Shadows*, London: Harper Collins.

Canter, D.V. and Alison, L.J. (1999), *Profiling in Policy and Practise. Offender Profiling Series*, II, Aldershot: Dartmouth.

Cooke, D.J. (1996), 'Psychopathic personality in different cultures: What do we know? What do we need to find out?', *Journal of Personality Disorders*, 10, 23-40.

Cooke, D.J. (1995), 'Psychopathic disturbance in the Scottish prison population: Cross cultural generalisability of the Hare PCL', *Psychology, Crime and Law*, 2, 101-118.

Donald, I. and Canter, D.V. (1992), 'Intentionality and Fatality During the King's Cross Underground Fire', *European Journal of Social Psychology*, 22, 203-218.

van Duyne, P. (1999), 'Mobsters are Human Too'. in D.V. Canter and L.J. Alison (eds), *Profiling in Policy and Practise. Offender Profiling Series*, II, Aldershot: Dartmouth.

Franz, V. and Jones, D. (1987), 'Perceptions of Organizational Performance in Suburban Police Departments: A Critique of the Military Model', *Journal of Police Science and Administration*, 15, 153-161.

Guzzo, R.A. (1996), 'Fundamental Consideration about Work Groups', in M. West (ed.), *Handbook of Work Group Psychology*, Chichester: Wiley.

Kebbell, M. and Wagstaff, G. (1999), 'The cognitive interview: An analysis of its forensic effectiveness', in D.V. Canter and L.J. Alison (eds), *Interviewing and Deception, Offender Profiling Series*, I, Aldershot: Dartmouth.

Koehn, C., Fisher, R. and Cutler, B. (1999), 'Using cognitive interviewing to construct facial composites', in D.V. Canter and L.J. Alison (eds), *Interviewing and Deception, Offender Profiling Series*, I, Aldershot: Dartmouth.

Leyton, E. (1995), *Men of Blood: Murder in Modern England*, London: Constable.

Marsh, P., Rossee, E. and Harre, R. (1978), *The Rules of Disorder*, London: Rouledge & Kegan Paul.

Sutherland, E.H., Cressey, D.R. and Luckenbill, D.F. (1992), Principles of Criminology, 11th edn, Dix Hills, NY: General Hall.
Thrasher, F. (1927), *The Gang: A Study of 1,313 Gangs in Chicago,* Chicago: Chicago University Press.
Vygotsky, L. (1978), *Mind in Society: The Development of Higher Psychological Processes*, Cambridge: Harvard University Press.
Whyte, W. (1965), *Street Corner Society,* Chicago: Chicago University Press.

2 Culture and Crime
GERALD MARS

This paper introduces four suggested archetypal categories of criminal organisation, each with its own different and distinct cultural characteristics. It then assesses the interactions between these and the strengths and vulnerabilities of each. It concludes with a brief assessment of the organisation and varying cultural characteristics within law enforcement agencies and considers in their turn, their interaction strengths and vulnerabilities when dealing with different kinds of criminal organisation.

Gerald Mars is an applied anthropologist. His first degree was in Economics and Social Anthropology from Cambridge and his PhD is from the London School of Economics. He is currently a part-time Professor at Bradford University's Management Centre, and has been Visiting Professor at Cranfield and at The University of Hong Kong. He has published five books, with four more in press, and over forty papers. He is joint general editor of the International Library of Criminology, Penology and Criminal Justice.

2 Culture and Crime
GERALD MARS

Introduction

It is not possible in the space available to discuss the various types of classifications that have emerged within criminology. It was observed, however, as long ago as 1975 by Mary Mackintosh, that most attempts at classifying types of criminal organisation have chosen lay categories, been dominated by correctional concerns and been overly influenced by the psychological characteristics of offenders. There has been little change since then. Two exceptions are D. R. Cressy's approach (1972), and the work of Mackintosh herself. Both authors treat the organisation of professional crime as "geared to the conduct of the criminal activities in question" an approach further developed here through the application of what has been termed 'Cultural Theory'. This author has previously applied Cultural Theory to the classification of workplace crime, the amateur crime of ordinary people in ordinary jobs (1982); an area that, too, had been dominated by lay definitions, correctional interests and an overly influential concern with the psychological make-up of practitioners. It is believed that the application of Cultural Theory to crime more widely interpreted, will bypass these partial truths and that its understanding will benefit from the further uses and developments to the theory that have occurred since 1982.

The categories that emerge in this analysis encompass four 'ideal types' of crime. I do not discuss types of law breaking that are categorised by their legal definitions. Where examples of criminal behaviour are discussed, they are offered to illumine types of organising (Thompson, 1996, ch.4) and not criminal categories. For this reason I have combined some aspects of the normally separate categories of terrorist and organised crime, and have subsumed them both under the description: 'Criminal Hierarchies' while other aspects of terrorism are discussed under "Ideological Crime".

A Brief Account of Cultural Theory

Cultural Theory originated with the need of anthropologists to classify the myriad of cultures that had been recorded since 'hands on fieldwork' became established in the 1920s. Unless any one culture can be meaningfully compared to another there can be no science, no matter how accomplished the description and analysis of individual cultures may be. Various attempts to construct classifications offering synthesis and comparison were attempted but were sequentially doomed. They each breached the first requirements of valid classification: that categories must be both exhaustive and exclusive. Mary Douglas' Cultural Theory,[1] originally called Grid/Group Theory, overcame these difficulties. Considerable development and work since then has demonstrated its applicability to, and within, western industrialised societies. (Thompson et al., 1990, and Appendix).

Cultural Theory's categories are based upon the way people are organised 'on the ground'. In our own society it can and has been applied to study how people relate to each other to do a job, that is to their task-based social organisation; the behaviours considered appropriate to it, and the different views of the world they use to justify such behaviours. These different worldviews, behaviours, ways of organising and the values, attitudes and justifications they customarily use, are what is here meant by 'culture'.

There has been substantial debate amongst scholars about the definitions of culture. Rather than getting drawn into this debate Thompson et al. (1990), who are Cultural Theorists clarify matters by distinguishing three terms: cultural bias; social relations; and way of life. "Cultural bias refers to shared values and beliefs [and] social relations are defined as patterns of interpersonal relations... a viable combination of social relations and cultural bias is a 'way of life'". Cultural Theory posits four archetypal ways of life.

Cultural Theory is based on the argument that there are two dimensions by which all cultures can be classified.

a) The first is the extent a culture imposes rules and classifications on its members and therefore limits their ability to transact freely. These limitations are called GRID. At one extreme, for instance, we find the caste societies of India. There, rules and classifications governing gender, age and family tightly define how people can relate to each other and in doing so thus limit their life chances and opportunities. These are strong grid cultures. At the other extreme we find weak grid cultures such as our own in western industrial society. Here fluidity is more pronounced and life chances are less influenced by pre-set classifications. Jobs, for instance, are able to be filled more on merit and contacts, than through pre-set classifications. This distinction between strong and weak grid can be usefully set out as a continuum showing strong grid at one extreme and weak grid at the other. Wearing uniforms, badges and other indications of rank are indications of strong grid cultures. Membership in an egalitarian commune, on the other hand, would be demonstrated by weak grid indicators such as an absence of uniforms and attempts at negating differences in rank and in function.

b) The second dimension, GROUP, emphasises collectiveness among people who meet face to face and "refers to the extent to which an individual is morally coerced by others, through being a member of a bounded face to face unit" (Thompson et al., 1990). Living and working in a total institution such as an army barracks or being a member of a Chinese lineage are both examples of strong groups. Such groups offer members a total life support system. On the other hand, being housebound and living alone in a high rise apartment block, are examples of weak group, especially if the people related to, do not relate to each other. Our own society is, on the whole, an example of a weak group culture. This is not to suggest that groups do not exist in our society. On the contrary, it asserts that most individuals, being likely to belong to several groups, find that none of them is able to exert a dominating influence. Like grid, group characteristics can also be set out as a continuum showing strong group at one extreme and weak group at the other.

Cultural Theory Applied to the Organisation of Crime

When we consider these two dimensions together, as continua, we can construct a simple 2 x 2 matrix to obtain a four-fold topology of ways of life that will form the bases of our fourfold categories of criminal organisation (fig 2.1). Each involves a characteristically cohesive and coherent cluster of values and attitudes, beliefs and pattern of relationships. Thus, each criminal way of life is the product of, and in turn supports, a value system and a pattern of social relations that can be classified by reference to the relative strengths of grid and group. These criminal ways of life inform the perceptions of the participants, determine their behaviours and are used by them to justify the validity of their social situations. In effect, and to simplify, Cultural Theory says: "Tell me how you are organised and I will be able to deduce your values and attitudes and allocate you to your criminal archetype. Not only this but I also possess a lever that will help me understand your vulnerabilities". The reverse also applies: "If I know your values and attitudes I am able to deduce the dominant form of your social organisation". The four archetypal ways of life can be depicted as follows:

Where both dimensions are weak, as at *A*, we find neither ranking nor boundary. These are the free-booting individualists, the entrepreneurial criminals – innovative schemers, fixers and opportunists. An individualist way of life is characterised by networking, aspiration and competition.

Our second category, the Criminal Isolates, at *B*, lacking membership in a significant group, therefore lack group support. And, being strongly constrained by lack of both social and material resources they are therefore, subject to manipulation by the law and by other criminals. Isolates are the failures of most systems. In criminal terms they are the lower level 'hangers on', petty criminals who are likely to act as 'fall guys' for their more organised colleagues.

Where both dimensions are strong, as at *C*, we find both ranking and boundary. Operating together these offer an original and hierarchical way of life marked by a strong boundary that differentiates the inside from

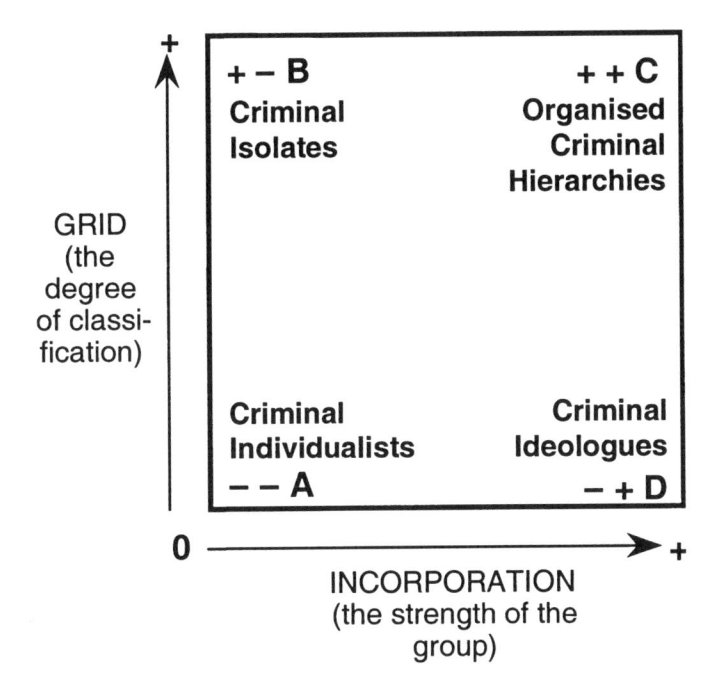

```
                    +
                    ▲
                    │  + − B              + + C
                    │  Criminal          Organised
                    │  Isolates          Criminal
                    │                    Hierarchies
        GRID        │
       (the         │
       degree       │
    of classi-      │
     fication)      │
                    │
                    │  Criminal          Criminal
                    │  Individualists    Ideologues
                    │  − − A             − + D
                    │
                    0 ─────────────────────────▶ +
                            INCORPORATION
                          (the strength of the
                                group)
```

Figure 2.1 Four-fold Categories of Criminal Organisation

the outside. These organising principles fit both the organised criminal gangs that are engaged on regular throughput activities and also the administrative levels of terrorist organisations. These are the Organised Criminal Hierarchies. Both, according to the tenets of Cultural Theory, would be expected to operate with set procedures and to prefer the comfort of established routines to the excitement of innovation.

Where classification is weak but group is strong, as at D, we find a well-defined boundary but little internal ranking. These organising principles are appropriate to Ideological Criminal Groups. Comparative experience of this kind of social organisation, suggests a commitment to egalitarianism and, applied to criminal organisation includes terrorists who operate at the active base. Ideological Criminals, it would be expected, should find difficulty in maintaining internal order since they would not readily allow their members to arbitrate or practise other managerial functions. They would thus find difficulty in resolving their internal disputes and, as a result, like similarly organised entities, be noted for a liability to fission. Where such groups do cohere, they do so by

28 *The Social Psychology of Crime*

mobilising a unifying and often paranoid opposition against what they see as evil and controlling influences outside their organisation. This may also be directed against their own formal or aspirant leaders.

Classification and rules governing the allocation of:

Space	Autonomy
Time	
Objects	Insulation
Resources	Reciprocity
Division of labour	
Information	Competition

A Individual networking
B Isolated and atomised
C Bounded and ranked
D Bounded and egalitarian

| Frequency | Mutuality |
| Scope | Boundary |

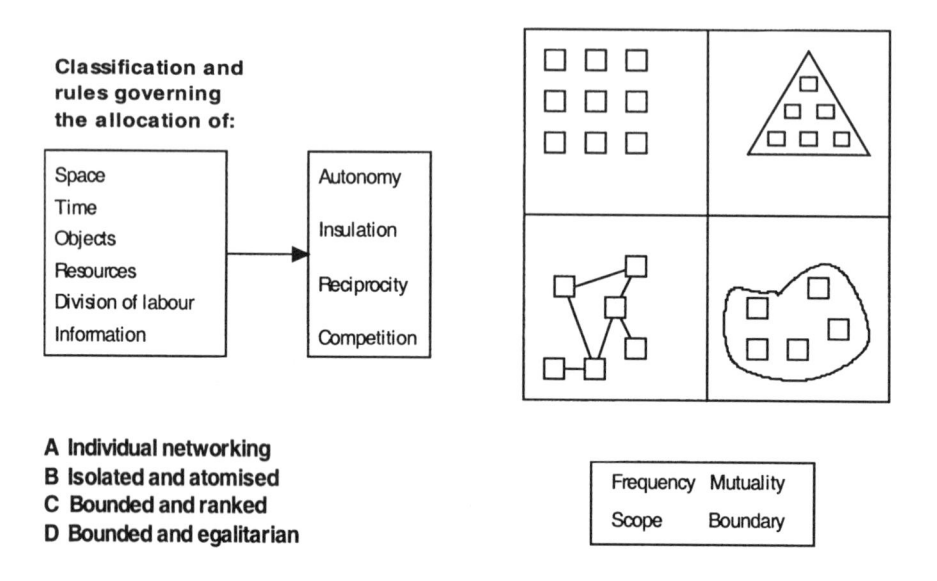

Figure 2.2 Components Comprising Analytical Framework

Figure 2.2 illustrates in more detail the components which together comprise this analytical framework. The relative strength of the grid aspect can be derived from an analysis of the use of space, time, objects, resources, labour and information. The way these six assets are used is indicative of the tolerated strength of autonomy, insulation, reciprocity and competition. An individual's autonomy in a specific milieu – how (s)he is allowed to carry out tasks in ways defined by themselves – is the first indication of grid. Low autonomy is found where classification and constraining rules are strong: high autonomy, where they are weak. The insulation of people from others is also a feature of strong grid. A ranking system, for instance, insulates people – that is, it separates them from others: its absence more readily permits links between people.

Reciprocity, the third indication of grid, has to do with how much a job allows its incumbents to offer others and how much they can accept in return. Strongly gridded petty criminals can offer very little; weakly gridded gang leaders can offer a lot. Competition is the final indicator of grid, with high constraints or competitive strategies being evident at strong grid and where few such constraints indicate weak grid.

Aspects of group are assessed by the frequency and mutuality of contact, the scope of activities under the aegis of the group and the strength of its boundary. Repeated face-to-face contacts with the same people indicate that both frequency and mutuality are strong. Group strength increases further as the scope of group activities extend. Sharing a common residence, working and taking recreation together, as with terrorist cells, for instance, all increase group strength. The strength of a group's boundary is also indicated by the distinctiveness of its internal behaviours compared to those considered appropriate to outsiders. Another indicator of the strength of boundary is the ease or difficulty of entry. The more difficult to enter, the stronger the group. Elaborate recruitment procedures thus indicate strong group.

These four categories are essentially archetypes and, as indicated, are rarely found in their pure form. Most social situations comprise 'regimes' (Thompson, 1996), combinations of archetypes though usually with a dominant bias of one or two. Most criminal activity thus involves a mixture of interdependent cultures. Even the most ideologically oriented, spontaneous and egalitarian of groups, need, for instance, at least a minimum administrative structure, that is, a degree of hierarchy. As an example, spontaneous grass root protesters such as the heavily ideological 'Eco Warriors' have to co-ordinate their activity, obtain and distribute equipment and arrange for minimum budgeting. These are all grid requirements covering the control of space, time, objects, resources, the division of labour and information. In increasing order of hierarchic sophistication we may rate the Animal Liberation Front and the Irish Republican Army. Both nonetheless have a strong overall cultural bias toward Ideology, though the latter in particular, has an extensive hierarchic command structure.

Like all cultures, Cultural Theory categories practise their own version of ethnocentricity – it is difficult for members of any one culture to see the validity of the other three points of view. As a result, collaboration between them is a source of tension and the implications of these mixtures for the functioning of their organisations and the different vulnerabilities they display can be considerable.

This model is essential sociological; it argues that behaviour is primarily a product of the social situation in which people operate.

People can shift between different contexts and behave differently in each because it is the context that primarily determines behaviour. Members of an IRA Active Service Unit, for instance, are careful when in the field, to maintain weak grid characteristics and to enjoy living conditions and spending that are essentially egalitarian. This is despite their differing specialist skills or even their formal military ranking in the IRA.

The Four Criminal Cultures and Their Organisation

Organised Criminal Hierarchies (Strong Grid/Strong Group)

Criminal Hierarchies, as indicated, are marked by a strong boundary that essentially differentiates the inside from the outside and which encompasses an unambiguous system of classification and ranking. As used here, the term 'criminal hierarchy' necessarily assumes a degree of organisational stability and continuity.

Aspects of the organisational mode and vulnerability of Organised Criminal Hierarchies may be better assessed by considering two examples of the Mafia: one from Italy, one from the United States. Set as they are in different contexts, their vulnerabilities are shown also to be different but both derive from weaknesses in the structure of hierarchy. The first concerns the accidental discovery of an extensive Mafia scam based in South Italy which came to grief in Milan in the early nineties.

Originally reported and researched upon by David Nelken (1993) from a report by an investigating judge, this first short account nicely reveals some of the vulnerabilities of hierarchy: a reliance on records, necessary dependence on alliance with a service provider when out of its 'home' area of competence, and in this case, a recourse to draconian punishment. This is often counterproductive because it tends to demotivate those who think they might well be next. The account also demonstrates the interdependence and built-in conflict that is always at least latent between any two cultural theory constituencies, in this case Hierarchic organisation on the one hand and Individualistic endeavour on the other.

This Italian account records how, one evening, police were called to an apartment in Milan to what initially appeared merely a noisy, out-of-hand drugs party. This apartment belonged to an accountant, Bruno, the party's host, who worked as a management consultant and spare time facilitator of documentation to the Mafia. At the apartment, police noticed two large suitcases and these, when opened, were found to contain a mass of forms. They were the paperwork by which claims were made against Italian government ministries for refunds of payments to be set against spurious exports of EC agricultural products. It was noted that the quality of the paperwork was extremely poor and though names of legitimate firms had been used, the notepaper was obviously forged and had been carelessly completed.

It was soon apparent to the investigating judge that Bruno was running a paper factory that was integral to achieve frauds against the EC and that the venture had extensive ramifications covering much of Italy. It was also revealed that this scam had its origins in an organisational centre that was based in Sicily and was run by the Mafia. Under police interrogation Bruno quickly confessed to his part as consultant to the scam and it was this confession and evidence from the false records that led to an uncovering of the role of his Sicilian principals. As a result of the machinations of his principals Bruno was granted bail and was promptly murdered soon after his release.

The second case also involves the Mafia but operating in North America. It derives in large part from the 'Valachi Papers' (Maas, 1969), the product of the confessions of a 'foot soldier' in New York's Mafia. The American Mafia is organised differently from that in Sicily. This is hardly surprising since the social and economic context in which they are set are vastly different. In the United States, Mafiosi run their own businesses and operate more autonomously than do their compatriots in southern Italy, though they also operate collectively for mutual support as members of 'The Mob'.

Valachi, 'the canary who sang', sang because he had a grudge, or rather a compound grudge and because he was frightened. It appears that the New York Mafia at this time had shifted from hierarchy to a greater degree of individualism. Valachi's (crooked) business, he felt, had been intruded upon by senior Mafia members and he believed he was being ousted from control. As is usual in hierarchies, there existed a legitimised system of arbitration for settling disputes but Valachi was not happy with the impartiality of the arbitrator. He was aggrieved, too, that because of political shifts and resultant reorganisations, he had lost his patron and the replacement was, in his view, unsympathetic to his interests. Further, when he found himself threatened by law enforcers he felt that he had not received the protection that was his due. Faced with the shift of organisational values, with the possible loss of his business and his liberty, and finally, fearing for his life in the new, more cut throat environment, he decided his interests would best be served by singing to the law enforcers. And he backed his testimony with damning documents. It was the first such case in North America of any significance and one that led directly to the significant findings of the Kefauver Commission (1978) and a serious weakening of the Mafia.

In both cases internal reaction followed turbulence in the environment. The New York Mafia, set in a sea of North American individuality, was more likely to shift down grid than in the Sicilian case and it more readily submitted to the pressures of short-term competitive manipulation that negated Valachi's ideal of impartial arbitration. The Sicilian Mafia, on the other hand, more secure in the stability of its own hierarchy, offered less alternative opportunities to its members and suffered less damage.

Sixteen 'Ideal Type' Characteristics of Organised Criminal Hierarchy

1) Formalised recruitment processes. These are often 'stepped' so that people are required to prove themselves by performing 'ordeals'.
2) A division of labour and provision of training for specialised roles, with all roles graded in a system of understood ranking.
3) An accepted system of promotion to posts of increasing responsibility and rewards, both material and symbolic.
4) A respect for authority with authority primarily linked to office rather than function.
5) An emphasis on ritual and ceremonial with close attention, for instance, likely to be paid to anniversaries that are significant to the group and rites of passage to mark entry to, and departure from, the group and its constituent sub-groups.
6) An expectation of loyalty to the group linked to a strongly defined conception of the inside/outside boundary.
7) The existence of an ambiguous entity of boundary straddling supporters (Mars 1988) – often consultants or experts who mediate between the organisation and its outside.
8) An emphasis on tradition, the importance of precedents and generally understood rules as a way of governing and justifying current action and the legitimacy of authority and office.
9) An approved and generally acceptable process of arbitration for dealing with disputes.
10) An unambiguous and understood scale of punishments that

emphasise the importance of the group at the expense of the individual.
11) An adherence to long-term time spans (since individuals may pass through but the group itself has a longer life). This facilitates planning, investment and task consolidation at the expense of the quick fix and the quick profit.
12) A conservative attitude to risk. This allows new ventures but attempts to have them validated by traditionally tried and tested means and approved by appropriately senior members of the hierarchy.
13) A relative slowness in adapting to change, especially sudden, unprecedented change.
14) A dependency on record-keeping that supports the maintenance of procedures and especially those governing the movement of resources both in and out of the organisation.
15) An emphasis on vertical communication by which information flows to and from approved sources, through appropriate conduits. This leads (a) to the operation of implicit (and sometimes explicit) 'need to know' criteria, and (b) to negation of information from non-approved sources.
16) A system of insurance and welfare that operates beyond the participant's operational life and can cover payments during sickness and prison terms as well as covering the care of families and the provision of pensions.

The Strengths of Organised Criminal Hierarchies

Of the four archetypes of criminal organisation, Organised Criminal Hierarchies are the most stable and the most likely to adapt and survive over time. They can institute administrative procedures, plan and carry out research and operate internal political checks and balances. They benefit from the specialisation that comes with a developed division of labour, the long-term frameworks they employ and their ability to shift resources to investment.

The mutual support, career structures and welfare facilities they offer their members, and the ability to operate sanctions and distribute rewards all contribute to their effectiveness. And if the strengths of these groups are further enhanced by the bonds of ethnicity then they are particularly difficult to penetrate.

Because Organised Criminal Hierarchies are essentially bureaucracies, they develop routine and regular activities. They therefore tend to develop high levels of expertise, albeit in a limited range of activity. They are less well adapted to change in routines.

Eight Vulnerabilities of Organised Criminal Hierarchy

The vulnerabilities of Organised Criminal Hierarchy can be seen as potential 'fault lines'. Many fault lines represent the mirror images of hierarchic strengths. They are liable to exploitation by rival organisations and opposing law enforcers.

1) To maintain the morale and commitment of their members, a Criminal Hierarchy needs a constant throughput of resources. It has therefore to continually adapt and to operate where its expertise and experience are not most developed. This may involve geographic expansion as well as a different area of crime. Both are likely to involve adaptation of its internal organisation and assessments of the new forces operating in its wider environment (Porter, 1980) – actual or potential competitors, predators and law enforcement agencies. In expanding, a criminal organisation faces more than just the vulnerability that in the business world is associated with making strategic alliances (Falkner). Intelligence would find it fruitful, therefore, to concentrate upon monitoring and anticipating potentially expanding areas as well as merely concentrating on existing ones.

2) An appreciation of the dependence of Organised Criminal Hierarchies upon externally recruited specialists will focus on a perception of their compromised loyalties. Specialists like Bruno are more likely to sing when threatened than are internal experts. They lack the social support that group membership involves, as well as ability to benefit from the insurance and welfare services not normally made available to consultants and experts. They are also more insecure than regular members because they typically lack information about the hierarchy's collective memory, political structures and power shifts. There is a parallel here with legitimate businesses' treatment of their consultants who also are considered a source of insecurity. It follows that outside experts are likely to be

more responsive to law enforcement pressures and to be potentially more fruitful as sources of information than regular, full time members.

3) A further vulnerability derives from the necessary dependence of organisations upon effective records, and therefore, in the case of Organised Criminal Hierarchies, of incriminating records. And, like other organisations, criminal hierarchies are as liable to have their computer systems entered by their opponents' hackers.

4) A fourth vulnerability is the ever-likely emergence of what are perceived as divergent interests between the hierarchy and its lowerarchy. These can derive from any of the whole area of potential resentments felt by lowerarchs over matters such as lack of promotion, unfair rewards, unjust payments of welfare benefits and dispute settlements. Intelligence that focuses on these potential 'fault lines' can therefore target likely sources of information and subversion.

5) Organised Criminal Hierarchies are prone to the instabilities of succession crises. It is not easy for them to institutionalise procedures to appoint replacements or arrange for orderly retirements. Not only do these crises leave a vacuum in control at the top; the resultant insecurity is likely to have unstable repercussions throughout.

6) Because of limits these organisations place on validating information from the outside, there is a tendency to negate such information especially, if it comes via unapproved sources. This makes adapting to change much more difficult and slower than it need be. It also means that care in the planting of misinformation may fail if not preceded by sound intelligence about the location of validated sources of information.

7) It has been shown how Organised Criminal Hierarchies, like non-criminal ones, typically need to combine two different cultural categories — hierarchy to ensure effective administrative procedures and individualism to ensure adaptation and flair. This is a common source of strain, with hierarchs seen as orientated

primarily to the organisation and its internal world and with individualists spending energy, resources and time, networking beyond the boundary. In criminal hierarchies information tends to be even more insulated and boundaries are usually stronger than in legitimate organisations. Here, the tendency of internal Individualists to network externally is a marked source of tension, suspicion and therefore of potential exploitation by opponents.

8) Finally, all organisations need to recruit. Recruits to Organised Criminal Hierarchies, however, are particular sources of instability, partly because they are unsocialised on entry, partly because even their initial dealings with the organisation will give them information of use to opponents. Because recruitment, at least to some degree, has to be routinised and involves the organisation dealing outside its boundary, the 'planting' of informants is more readily effected at the recruitment stage.

Ideological Criminal Groups (Weak Grid/Strong Group)

Ideological Criminals are marked by a strong boundary but, unlike Hierarchs, they eschew classification, and in so doing embrace an egalitarian approach to their world and an absence of institutional controls. In so-called 'simple' societies, these structures are the home of witchcraft accusations and of scapegoating. The same mechanisms operate among Ideological Criminals.

The Strengths of Criminal Ideological Groups

The purer ideological groups have few strengths except the dedicated involvement of their members. To mobilise this asset, however, requires them to have a buttressing of hierarchic organisation if they are to achieve their aims and not dissolve into factional in-fighting. They also need a limitation of their size to reduce the likelihood of factional splits. Criminal Ideological Groups, therefore, and particularly the more successful terrorist groups, are invariably found to be small and controlled, at least to some extent, by aspects of hierarchy. The Criminal

Ideologists who make up the IRA's Active Service Units, for instance, could not operate without the backup and control of the Central Command institutions – not only for supplies of arms and resources but for training facilities and the provision of systematised information.

An IRA blueprint made public in 1977 nicely revealed how reorganisation was necessary because their purely military structure, based on the hierarchic battalion, was too easily infiltrated. They moved instead to a cellular structure based on groups of four, which has proved much more effective – the new system thus combining and maximising organisational finesse and commitment, the attributes and benefits of both hierarchy and ideology.

> CELLS: As we have already said, as from now, all new recruits are to be passed into a cell structure.
> Existing Battalion and Company Staffs must be dissolved over a period of months with present Brigades then deciding who passes into the (reorganised) cell structure and who goes into the Brigade controlled and departmentalised Civil Administration (explained later).
> The cells of four volunteers will be controlled militarily by the Brigade's/Command's Operations Officers, and will be advised by Brigade's/Command's Intelligence Officer.
> Cells will be financed through their cell leader, who will be funded through the O.C. co-ordinator. That is, for wages, for running costs, financing of operations (expenses etc., will be dealt with through the O.C.).
> Cells must be specialised into I.O. cells, sniping cells, executions, bombings, robberies, etc.
> The cell will have no control of weapons or explosives, but should be capable of dumping weapons overnight (in the case of a postponed operation).
> The weapons and explosives should be under the complete control of the Brigade's/Command's Q.C. and E.C. respectively.
>
> (quoted by Coogan 1993)

Note how the IRA blueprint emphasises the necessity of centralised control.

Eight 'Ideal Type' Characteristics of (the purer) Criminal Ideologues

1) A suspicion of the outside, regarded as the source of all evil, with the inside seen as holding a monopoly of virtue.

2) A fear of internal contamination – manifest as tendencies to exert grid differentials – ranking, records, authority, classification, and indeed any system of controls, over the use of space, time, objects, resources, labour or information.

3) There is a tendency to periodic turbulence, factionalism and shifting alliances among their memberships because of the focus of these fears on particular people or factions, and especially on leaders or aspirant leaders or those so perceived or suspected. A senior member of the security forces opposing the IRA explained that when they aborted an action or picked up a suspect, they would then exploit this suspicion: "We'd suggest we had a source by telling them we were 'acting on information received' or that 'we have reason to believe...' They often think the leak comes from above".

4) Because of the refusal to legitimise authority, it is difficult to apply arbitration to disputants.

5) Thus the only effective ways to resolve disputes are by ejection or withdrawal. There is therefore always the likelihood of schism involving the formation of rival break-away groups. Coogan (1993) in his book on the IRA has a chapter (13) entitled 'Splits in the Ranks'.

6) A liability to rumour because, rejecting specialised roles, information has no approved conduits.

7) A belief in total 'whole life' commitment to the group.

8) A belief in the eventual perfectibility of human beings if only the ideologists' view can be extended beyond its boundary.

Seven Vulnerabilities of Pure Criminal Ideological Groups

Note these vulnerabilities are able to be reduced if there is a developed external source of hierarchical control and if the ideological groups are kept small.

1) Criminal Ideologue Groups are relatively easy for their opponents who have good pedigrees to penetrate, since, rejecting administrative processes, their checking procedures are unlikely to be effective or indeed developed.

2) Criminal Ideologues, rejecting administrative procedures as they do and having no effective sources of agreed precedents, accordingly have to 'reinvent the wheel' each time an administrative decision has to be made.

3) Their resultant lack of administrative continuity is increased because administrators are prone to be deposed. They therefore find difficulty in developing strategic plans.

4) Since legitimacy is not readily granted to leaders it is difficult for them to negotiate meaningfully with the outside, particularly because agreements may not be ratified, or if ratified may be subsequently reneged by a newly emergent faction.

5) Fault lines are easily apparent if not from without then certainly from within. Their exploitation can be effected by the planting of rumours.

6) Their externally defined boundary and fear of internal factionalism make them extremely vulnerable to suggestions of a 'sell out' by their colleagues and, particularly, by their own leaders: there is always a potential divorce from the centre.

7) Because Criminal Ideologues are reluctant to judge or discipline their members, they are vulnerable to the actions of their more maverick members – deviant individualists. I am told that such maverick liability to excessive risk-taking has, for instance, been responsible for the demise of several IRA Active Service Units.

Criminal Individualists (Weak Grid/Weak Group)

Criminal individualists are competitive freebooters, marked by a reluctance to accept the constraints of either grid or of group. They do not sit happily in organisations, though they often find themselves within or on the periphery of them. Assiduous networking is an activity on which they are likely to spend considerable assets, time and effort. Their cultural collateral (Hobbs, 1988) depends upon the extent and potency of their network. Like entrepreneurs in the straight world, they operate by linking opportunities to resources, particularly by using their networks to bring together information, specialists and markets. They are concerned to mobilise and plan one-off project crimes, or, like Bruno, as discussed in the section 'Organised Criminal Hierarchies', they carry out similar activities as members or consultants to criminal/terrorist groups. They are valued as sources of ideas as well as contacts, and they are the recruiters of specialists who form 'one-off' teams for specific jobs which are typically dispersed at completion.

Dan Lee, in his late forties, is a typical entrepreneur – not because of what he deals in but in how he deals. He is a solicitor with a practice in a smart part of town – but claims "I'm mostly interested in property deals, my own or on behalf of other people, and I arrange things for commission". His solicitor's practice is largely limited to dealings in property and finance.

As well as earnings from these sources, Dan also owns a small hotel and has an interest in a couple of apartment houses that are occupied by prostitutes. He is also believed to have some ongoing connections with the security services – a follow-through of his time in the armed services, and currently as an officer with the Reserve. "I couldn't stand a nine-to-five job – no two days are the same for me", he notes with satisfaction.

His leisure and work lives overlap almost completely. He entertains and is entertained a good deal in the way of business, and this often takes him and his wife to expensive restaurants. Sometimes Dan will entertain at his smart, large and heavily mortgaged home in a very good part of the city, which he owns on a very short lease. His entertainment there borders on the lavish. Dan's main asset is the extent and strategic significance of his network: "Life is about who you know as much as what you know." He is careful however to insulate the different categories of who he knows.

Shortly after this account was taken, Dan's world collapsed. His property empire, which was heavily mortgaged, was subject to a savage recession. His assets were over-stretched and, unable to pay his creditors, he hanged himself.

Ten 'Ideal Type' Characteristics of Criminal Individualists

1) A reluctance to accept organisational constraints that inhibit their autonomy make Individualist loyalty suspect to Hierarchists. This increases the more their networking takes them outside the organisation (Gouldner, 1957-8).

2) Individualists, being competitive as well as networkers, are prone to embrace the latest fashions and fads. Associated with conspicuous display and consumption, they demonstrate status and success to existing members of their networks and serve to impress new and potential ones.

3) Rejecting the constraints of procedures and due process, Individualists emerge as pragmatic short-termists, willing to bend rules and more concerned with taking shortcuts than the strategic long view.

4) Accordingly, Individualists tend to a robust and optimistic view of their world, and therefore, readily take greater risks than other constituencies. This leads to conflict with hierarchs who treat risk as calculable and subject to the constraints of due procedures and process.

5) Criminal Individualists are like to over extend their credit – both social and material – to and beyond their limits.

6) Information is hoarded, bartered for personal benefit and passed along networks that negate or short-circuit an organisation's approved conduits.

7) Short time spans mean a lack of regard for tradition and, if employed in an organisation, lead Individualists to ignorance of their organisation's collective memory.

8) Individualists, being active networkers, with adherence to short time spans and enthusiasm for the one-off project, tend to use people as means to ends. They are accordingly subject to accusations of treachery in their personal relationships.

9) Since a Criminal Individualist appears only as successful to his network as the demonstrated success of his projects and since only a minority of projects can come to fruition, an Individualist will, of necessity, have to allocate time (and resources) on a variety of projects that might never materialise. Time is accordingly weighed as the scarcest of resources, and its expenditure is costed against possible returns. This care over the allocation of time to projects applies also to its allocation to people: the attention they receive is usually related to their likely benefit potential.

10) Criminal Individualists deal in information as much as products or services, and they guard and hoard information as a valuable resource. This means both arranging strategic meetings and strategic avoidances. Putting the wrong people together can have disastrous consequences, just as the reverse can be highly profitable. Accordingly, the insulation of different aspects of life is a characteristic of Criminal Individualists.

The Strengths of Criminal Individualists

Driven by competition and unencumbered by approved procedures or the constraints of group membership, Individualists are the most readily adaptive of the criminal categories. This is enhanced because they are active in using their networks to pursue information about matters that concern them and are alert to learn about and anticipate the activities of rivals and opponents.

Seven Vulnerabilities of Criminal Individualists

1) Their need to network, and the conspicuous consumption associated with and necessary to it, mean that Individualist patterns of spending and receipts are visible to law enforcement agencies.

2) The constant need to extend their networks makes them vulnerable to the approaches of *agents provocateurs* and to deliberately planted misinformation.

3) Because they use members of their network primarily as resources, they are liable to provoke resentment when they drop them as of no

Culture and Crime 43

further use. Resentment is often fuelled by envy at high levels of conspicuous consumption. This, presented as evidence of an unjust distribution of criminal returns, is always a possible source of schism to be exploited by rivals and opponents.

4) Never fully integrated into the organisations with which they associate, Individualists are liable to be regarded with suspicion by hierarchs particularly because they operate outside the boundary and are seen as more concerned to pursue personal rather than group ends. They are thus more likely than more integral members to find themselves potentially subject to the harsh sanctions that criminal hierarchies are prone to use. This is a source of personal insecurity, readily exploitable by law enforcers.

5) Since Individualists are continually tempted by the lure of new opportunities, they frequently have to operate with collaborators and against rivals and opponents with whom they are not familiar. They are therefore, subject to the increased 'risk premiums' involved.

6) Because they are driven by opportunity and eschew the constraints of planning, Individualists are likely to be overburdened by the number of their projects, and the often unanticipated demands these involve. They therefore, tend to be perpetually short of time and liable to skimp necessary attention to detail.

7) An Individualist's lack of group involvement not only reduces the benefits of group membership but also inhibits full awareness of the group's collective memory and the protective precedents these enshrine. This, and their relationship to events as 'one-offs' rather than as parts of sequences, involve Individualists in short-termism and an approach to enterprise that can be termed 'ad hoc' or 'anti strategic'.

Criminal Isolates (Strong Grid/Weak Group)

These are the isolated and least skilled petty criminals, who lack regular association with others, and therefore lack the support of effective group membership. Criminal Isolates are also strongly gridded. Young (1991:

158-9) gives an account of the typical Criminal Isolate in his old patch as a policemen (who turned anthropologist):

> Ill educated, socially deprived, and often in custody or prison for long periods, especially during his adolescence, he inevitably belongs to the lower socio-economic classes. Poorly educated, physically and mentally undernourished, and often living in squalid and undistinguished surroundings, he has a narrow social existence, living on what is said to be his 'regular diet of brown ale and chips'. Contrary to the moving and freedom of a wild animal, the 'prig' is always oppressed and not infrequently physically constrained. His apparently wild and undisciplined natural life is therefore illusory; indeed, it might more easily be seen to be a dull, sombre world of control and limitation.

The mode of operation of Criminal Isolates is haphazard, carried out with little competence and a minimum of planning. They have little commitment to specialisation, and move from one low-skilled criminal activity to another as events present themselves. Just as their criminality is spontaneous, so are other aspects of their lives. They spend resources as they get them (Young, 1991: 158).

Hobbs (1988: 142-7) offers an insightful case study of a typical Criminal Isolate. Keith drinks in a part of the bar of The City Arms that is restricted to petty criminals. He is "on no more than nodding terms with the con-men and 'businessmen'" who drink in another, more elevated, section of this highly stratified pub, and who hold Keith in demonstrably marked contempt.

Keith ineffectually "goes through the motions of buying and selling, conspiring to set up various schemes that could never come to fruition" and mixing socially with those who similarly "shared a lack of cultural capital". But Keith "Had nothing to trade, he was a punter, and as such could not participate in the core activities of the elite section".

Keith moves on the edges of this more organised elite world but is never of it. When his wife dies, however, the elite villains out of pity, decide to give him a number of chances and he moves over to the elite bar. His lack of ability, expertise and planning, however, and his inability to co-ordinate the work of others, ensures that he fails at everything he is offered. Eventually he infuriates the elite and is publicly shamed. He ends up back with the rest of the Criminal Isolates in the low status bar. As Hobbs (1988) remarks, "Keith had not only proved himself to be incompetent and unreliable but more importantly he had failed to trade successfully".

Five 'Ideal Type' Characteristics of Criminal Isolates

1) Isolates are outside organised criminal groups, though they may carry out actions on their periphery.

2) They are constrained by a lack of both material and social capital.

3) They are reactive rather than proactive.

4) They cannot be identified with any consistent criminal activity.

5) Because they lack the ability to plan and are reactive, they embrace a fatalist view of causality and of risk: "Life is capricious." "If you're due for bad luck, there's nothing much you can do about it."

The Strengths and Vulnerabilities of Criminal Isolates

With few choices, little autonomy and a deficiency of cultural and material collateral, Criminal Isolates are in no position to offer benefits to, or to exert claims on others. Criminal Isolates, therefore, have few strengths and are vulnerable to exploitation by other criminal categories and by law enforcers. They are disorganised, with all the liabilities this involves.

Because Criminal Isolates are essentially reactive, lack skills, and possess little capital they have fewer choices and opportunities than other criminals. They are limited therefore, to repetitiously but unsystematically committing the same kind of crime in the same contexts. Careful and systematic policing records allow them to be readily identified, and their lack of planning means that they can readily fall into any available net whenever this may be spread for 'the usual suspects'. They suffer the further vulnerability that, being on the edge of higher status crime – the Criminal Individualists and the Organised Criminal Hierarchies – they are a ready target for law enforcers seeking information. And as such they are also vulnerable to suspicion from criminal elites.

Law Enforcement Agencies

Discussions with law enforcers in the UK and Dutch police and the Army engaged in anti terrorist actions, have shown that despite their differences, Cultural Theory can reveal useful insights in understanding the workings of their agencies.

The external stereotypical view of police would identify them as hierarchists. When we examine their different elements, however, we identify four different (and again archetypal but mutually interdependent) ways of life; four cultures each with a cluster of coherent values and attitudes. In brief, and to simplify, these may be set out as follows:

1) Hierarchy (Strong Grid/Strong Group) – is represented by the senior uniformed ranks, concerned with procedures, rules, processes, continuity and discipline.

2) Isolated Fatalists (Strong Grid/Weak Group) – are represented by the disenchanted stereotype of 'PC Plod', who has little autonomy, frequently feels let down by his hierarchy, can see few prospects in his present role, and looks forward to little else but an early retirement.

3) Entrepreneurial Individualists (Weak Grid/Weak Group) – are the detectives, unconfined by the boundary of their organisation and its rules, and as much at home, socialising and interacting with criminals and outside contacts, as with colleagues. These are the most competitive and achievement-oriented of the police and they have the highest status. It is they who provide the heroes of their organisation. Like entrepreneurs elsewhere, they are short-termist in outlook and actions and prepared to bend rules and procedures to gain a given end. As such they are a source of worry to their more rule-bound hierarchical superiors.

4) It might be surprising to some, to locate a category of policemen who satisfy the requirements of egalitarian Ideologists, (Weak Grid/Strong Group). These however, are to be found in the ranks of the crime prevention officers who see themselves in a parallel sense as social workers, rather than as police. They tend to dislike

wearing uniforms, and, like the generality of egalitarians, believe in the perfectibility of human nature. They see themselves under siege in the police force, unified in opposition to the insensitivity, and perceived opposition, of the hierarchy. They find it difficult to justify their role to other police constituencies since, like most Ideologues, they deal essentially in intangibles – and crime prevention is not as calculable as are crimes detected. Their status among colleagues is not high.

Standardised police operations are well set up to oppose, that is to contain rather than to eradicate, Organised Criminal Hierarchies and to a degree, Criminal Individualists. When, through media or political pressures, or both, they find it necessary to adapt quickly to changes in operational needs, they have tended to find normal policing structures inadequate. Their response has been to set up Regional Crime Squads. These primarily comprise individualists – detectives – who tend, through networking and unorthodox extra-organisational means, i.e. by rule bending, to by-pass normal police procedures. In their early days their successes are invariably high until they eventually have to be reined in. The problem for the police is that individualist detectives are likely to exceed the constraints required by hierarchists. This leads to a cycle of periodic scandals and the dissolution and rise of new crime squads under various names.

The police are prepared to live with and can readily understand and indeed relate to Organised Criminal Hierarchists because their own cultural bias is similar. The police can also deal with criminal individualists because they can readily categorise them: they are the over ambitious who, through greed, go too far. For a similar reason they have little difficulty in relating to the isolated fatalists who are also readily categorisable, in their case as system failures.

One intransigent problem facing the police lies in their dealings with Ideological Criminals. As one retired senior policeman explained: "We're terrified of ideology. Take the NCCL (the National Council for Civil Liberties). The police just don't understand how ideology can motivate them to do what they do. It's the same with the ALF (The Animal Liberation Front), but they're more easily dealt with". Not only do the police face difficulty in interpreting motives when these are morally derived, they also fail to understand Ideologists' 'irrational' criteria for allocating resources or their typical lack of interest in maximising returns.

Interesting distinctions and similarities are apparent in a comparison of the *modus operandi* and cultures of the two law enforcement agencies that operate against the IRA in Northern Ireland – the police, in this case the Royal Ulster Constabulary, and the Army: the one essentially hierarchic, the other also biased to hierarchy but with a stronger representation of Individualism.

The Army see themselves as group-based units, as a 'band of brothers' who will perish if need be in a 'glorious last stand'. Their heroic image is essentially collective, as epitomised, for instance, by the Charge of The Light Brigade. They view operations against the IRA as a war against another army and by definition, as leading essentially to a finite conclusion.

The police on the other hand see themselves as dealing with criminals, and their activities as an ongoing fight, spearheaded not by group based heroes but by their archetypal hero, 'the lone copper'. He tackles his foe bravely but knows this is a conflict that will go on perpetually. Whereas the Army were, until 1984 (when political dictat prevented it), accustomed to identify their opponents by their military ranks, the RUC (and the politicians) refer to the IRA in terms of 'gangs', 'terrorists and 'criminals'. This is indicative perhaps of why there are difficulties in collaboration between the two.

Both the Army and the RUC, however, find a similar problem in understanding and therefore, dealing with, the Ideologues among their opponents. Serving specialists who develop expertise in this area, (like the Crime Prevention Officers referred to earlier) have at best an ambiguous status: they are called 'The Funnies'. And the Army, from its stronger hierarchical standpoint, look with suspicion on the detective elements in their ranks, seeing them, as my informant put it: "as almost on the verge of trading with the enemy".

Conclusion

This chapter offers an alternative to the more usual ways of classifying crime and criminals that is based upon the way criminal activity is organised 'on the ground'. It began by identifying cultural archetypes but then emphasised that pure forms are rarely found. After identifying clusters of values and attitudes associated with each archetype it aimed to demonstrate that it is their interactions and inevitable conflicts that leads to their strengths – and also their vulnerability.

It should be emphasised that Cultural Theory deals in behaviours as operating within a total social field. The use of a 2 x 2 matrix and the resultant four archetypes that emerge from it: they are not, as they have sometimes been portrayed, distinct and insulated behavioural packages. In the messy world the distinction of upgraded petty Criminal Isolates and the more powerful bosses of Criminal Hierarchies is essentially a question of gradation. Similarly the distinction between competitive criminal entrepreneurial activity dependent on networks and the fully institutionalised controls of hierarchic organisation are also graduated. And of course these gradations can be sequential.

References

Coogan, T.P. (1993), *The IRA*, London: Harper Collins Publishers.
Cressy, D.R. (1972), *Criminal Organisation: its elementary forms*, London: Heinemann.
Douglas, M. (1978), 'Cultural Bias', Royal Anthropological Institute, Occasional Paper No. 35. Reprinted in M. Douglas (1982) *In the Active Voice*, London: Routledge & Kegan Paul, 183-254.
Gouldner, A. (1957-8), 'Cosmopolitans and Locals', *The Administrative Science Quarterly*, **2**, 281-306, 444-80.
Hobbs, D. (1988), *Doing the Business: entrepreneurship, the working class and detectives in the East End of London*, Oxford: Oxford University Press.
Kefauver, E. (1968), *Crime in America*, New York: Greenwood.
Maas, P. (1969), *The Valachi Papers*, New York: G. P. Putnam's Sons.
Mars, G. (1996) [1982], *Cheats at Work: an anthropology of workplace crime*, Aldershot: Dartmouth Publishers.
Mars, G. (1988), 'Hidden Hierarchies in Israeli Kubbutzim', ch. 5, in *Rules, Decisions and Inequality in Egalitarian Societies*, J.G. Flanagan and S. Rayner (eds), Aldershot: Avebury Press.
Mars, G. and Mars, V. (1993), 'Two Studies of Dining' in G. Mars and V. Mars (eds), *Food Culture & History*, London: The London Food Seminar.
Passas, N. and Nelken, D. (1993), 'The Thin Line Between Legitimate & Criminal Enterprises: subsidy frauds in the European Community', *Crime, Law & Social Change* **19 (3)**, 223-43.
Porter, M.E. (1983), *Cases in Competitive Strategy*, New York: Free Press.
Thompson, M. (1996), *Inherent Rationality: an Anti Dualist Approach to Institutions*, Bergen, Norway: Los Centre.

Thompson, M., Ellis, R. and Wildavsky, A. (1990), *Cultural Theory*, Boulder: Westview Press.

Young, M. (1991), *An Inside Job: policing and police culture in Britain*, Oxford: Clarendon Press.

Note

1 Mary Douglas (1978) made the breakthrough that established and extended Cultural Theory as universally applicable. She and Mike Thompson have been the most assiduous developers of this approach since then. My gratitude for insights and stimulus is due to both of them. See Thompson et al. for a fuller exposition of the theory as at 1990 and his further development in 1996. The appendix to Thompson et al. contains an extensive bibliography of all work on Cultural Theory to 1990. From 1990 to date there has been an explosion of applications in widely divergent areas.

3 The Structural Analysis of Criminal Networks

DUNCAN McANDREW

Crime is a social activity. This includes co-offending, where groups of offenders carry out specific criminal activities together, and the social interactions between criminals, through familial ties, friendship and shared locations, such as prisons. Identifying such relationships has been a major concern for police officers and crime analysts investigating areas ranging from highly organised enterprises, e.g. Triads, through to individual incidents such as armed robberies. Several methods have been used to aid such investigations by creating visual representations of relationships and connections. These representations are sociograms, one of a variety of measures used in a methodological approach called Social Network Analysis (SNA). SNA is used as part of a field in the social sciences termed Structural Analysis, which explicitly measures details of the structures of networks. A wide variety of research has been carried out that implicitly studies structure. Work on organised crime discusses concepts such as hierarchy and individual position. Descriptions of drug trafficking include differentiation of roles within the networks and how commodities are moved between different stages of the operations. There has been little research using SNA on criminal networks, in such areas as white-collar crime, juvenile delinquency and organised crime. A number of SNA measures have the potential to aid investigators - measures that identify how central individuals are and what subgroups are present, for example. These techniques need to be systematically tested to determine which ones will be of the most benefit in the analysis of criminal intelligence, with the aim of aiding in the development of operational and strategic action plans. A case study illustrates the application of SNA to a criminal network.

Duncan McAndrew has completed his PhD on the structure of criminal networks at the University of Liverpool. He completed a BSc (Hons) in Psychology/Social Anthropology at Dalhousie University in Canada before coming to the UK to complete the MSc in Investigative Psychology. His Masters dissertation was a study of serial murderer crime scene behaviour patterns. Current research interests include methods of intelligence gathering and analysis, crime analysis, proactive policing strategies, social network analysis and researching the organised sexual abuse of children. He is continuing his research at the University of Liverpool for a year, before returning to Canada to pursue a career in work related to his research interests.

3 The Structural Analysis of Criminal Networks
DUNCAN McANDREW

Criminal Networks

Few offenders operate in a vacuum, never interacting with other criminals. Some crimes, such as armed robbery and burglary, often involve teams which can be viewed as small networks of individuals interacting with each other (Walsh, 1986). In a broader sense, the solo burglar must dispose of property taken, and so connect into a larger network made up of those who steal and those who handle stolen goods. Even those offenders who commit "solitary" crimes, such as child sex abuse, usually have previous convictions for other crimes and so are part of these larger networks (Canter and Kirby, 1995). Offenders meet when serving time together. Friends and associates of offenders may also commit crimes though not with those offenders, also creating connections. These social connections can lead to sharing new methods of committing crime, identification of potential targets, information about police activities and opportunities to be part of specific criminal enterprises. Criminals, like all humans, are part of groups and these groups shape their behaviours. This does not detract from the study of the criminal as an individual. We can not, however, afford to ignore the social aspect of criminality, be it as explicit as professional armed robbers or the implicit groups of friendships and business associates. This is particularly true in the investigation of crime, and forms the basis of "intelligence-driven" policing, where intelligence on criminal activities and networks plays a key role in shaping police efforts.

Intelligence Analysis and Criminal Networks

Intelligence Objectives

Information management has always had an important role to play in policing, ranging from the effective handling of informants (ACPO 1994) through to complex data storage/management systems such as HOLMES. The use of intelligence in whatever form, e.g. records of financial transactions, has increasingly become a key part of police investigations, particularly when dealing with criminal networks of any form (Anderson and Peterson, 1990; Maguire and John, 1995; Schneider, 1997). At a proactive level, information is used to prevent crimes from taking place or to ensure a police presence when the crimes are carried out. Identification and targeting the core minority of criminals that commit the majority of crimes is another aspect of intelligence-driven policing. Pittman (1996), for example, found that the most crimes committed by gangs were actually carried out by a "core" of 15-20% of the members. Focusing on these individuals will increase the likelihood of their removal, albeit temporarily, from the system. When studying networks of any size, the investigators will try to draw out certain aspects of the structure to aid both investigation and prosecution (Humphreys 1996):

- Who is central and peripheral in the network?

- What are the different roles or jobs within the network?

- What subgroups exist in the network?

- What are the important communications and methods of communicating?

- Which individuals should be removed to disrupt the network?

- What individuals might be more likely to give information to the police?

- What is the overall structure of the network?

To achieve its goals, the intelligence process involves a series of stages, with the exact number depending on the author describing the process (e.g. Prunckun, 1996; Schneider, 1997). One version involves five stages - collection, evaluation, collation, analysis and dissemination (Humphreys, 1997). The structural analysis of criminal networks takes place in the fourth stage of the process.

Current Criminal Intelligence Analysis - To What Extent Does it Achieve Those Objectives?

A major part of current intelligence analysis involves the conversion of large amounts of information into an understandable and interpretable format. One of the main ways this is achieved is through the production of graphical representations of networks. The standard form of analyst-drawn visual representation, the link chart, is based on the ANACAPA system (Sparrow, 1991). Using this system, various categories, e.g. individual members of the networks, vehicles, addresses, are given specific symbols. Sparrow identified three guidelines that affect the layouts produced:

- The analyst will try to place individuals relative to each other - the stronger the association, the closer together they will be.

- For clarity, the analyst will move individuals around to avoid connecting lines crossing each other.

- The analyst will aim to place the individuals with the most connections (highest "degree" - see below) in the centre of the graph. The lower the individual's number of connections, the farther out that individual will be.

The end result is a two-dimensional representation of the network, showing the links between individuals, for example, living at the same address, the strength of association between members and a rough guideline to a member's importance, determined by how central they are on the plot.

Sparrow describes several potential problems with the approach of having the analyst do the graphical representation "by hand". The first of these is the limitations of two-dimensional representations. Often, the complexities of a network will prevent the analyst from accurately representing the relationships in only two dimensions. Sparrow admits on the other hand, that two-dimensional images are much easier to understand and interpret. Not having lines cross also makes for easier interpretation, but may make the diagram not accurately represent the network. In a two-dimensional layout, minimising crossed lines may be difficult without some significant alteration of the diagram. This limitation can prevent an accurate model being created of the connections between individuals relative to all the other connections, as individuals will be moved from one location to another. Finally, Sparrow points out the use of degree as a measure of centrality is arguable in crime analysis. Degree can represent how much information is known about an individual rather than the amount of contacts he or she has in reality. If an individual is seen as central to a network early in the intelligence-gathering phase, then he or she will be the focus of more intensive observation. Since a greater amount of information is being gathered, more connections are likely to be found, making that individual seem relatively more important. This cycle continues, whether the first assumption is accurate or not.

More recently, computer-aided analysis has come to the forefront. Software packages have made the production of such images faster and more effective. The software automatically generates links and the graph (or chart) can be presented in a variety of formats. These different layouts include circular diagrams, illustrating connections without placing one individual in the middle relative to the rest, or graphs with crossed lines. However, the assistance the computer gives can go beyond just creating diagrams. The limitation of the current level of analysis is that the information gathered is only being converted from one form, such as phone bills, into another, a generated graphic that is easier to understand. What is required are methods that can aid that decision-making process of the crime analyst, e.g. scientifically proven procedures that show what subgroups may exist in a network. The analyst can then take these results and compare them with what she or he knows about the network, leading to the identification of new ways of developing the investigation. Such decision-support methods change the process of analysis from just making intelligence out of information into using the information as data that can be scientifically analysed (Heritage, 1996). What is required is the identification of methods and research in the social sciences that have the most application to this particular aspect of intelligence analysis (Prunckun, 1996).

Implicit Structural Research

Extensive work has been carried out by social scientists on aspects of the structures of criminal networks, but without using methods to explicitly analyse the structure. Terms such as "structure", "network" and "roles" are used, but the work is mainly descriptive in nature, with no analyses carried out to give more exact meanings to such terms. Some of the research makes up the more general literature, covering a broad range of areas - smuggling, delinquency, fraud, handling stolen goods etc. (e.g. Passas & Nelken, 1993; Fijnaut, 1990; Walsh, 1986; Naylor, 1994/95; Wiegand, 1994; van Duyne, 1996, 1997; Kock, Kemp & Rix, 1996). The main area of implicit structural studies has been in drug trafficking; due to the various roles required for the market, its transnational nature and the variety of crimes carried out by criminal groups involved with it (Dorn & South, 1990; Dorn, Murji & South, 1992; Kleinman & Smith, 1990; Jenkins, 1992; Lewis, 1994; Reuter & Haaga, 1986; Ruggerio & South, 1995; Williams, 1993). Structural themes can be seen through the various research, whatever the form of criminal network under study. Aspects of the degree of hierarchy in the structure, how organised the networks are and what kind of roles individuals have within the network are identified throughout. Levels within the networks have been described along with differences and similarities. The importance of cohesiveness and the flexible nature of most networks are common themes. There is a general consensus in the research that organised criminal activities are more entrepreneurial in form than the rigid hierarchies of stereotypical "organised crime" (Smith, 1980; van Duyne, 1996).

While highlighting these themes and trying to develop models of criminal networks is beneficial, there is little in the way of actual analysis of data to develop such models. Conclusions are typically reached through case studies or reviews of the literature. While beneficial, what is required are large-scale studies based on what data can be obtained. The concept of a "hierarchy" is a good example. When a Triad is described as very hierarchical, what is it being compared to. How hierarchical does "very" mean? Explicit analysis of network structures and comparisons between the various types of networks would allow more precise definitions to be developed. One feature that has come out of the research is the possible identification of levels of networks.

Levels of Networks

When looking at the literature, a broad three level classification of crime networks can be identified, though no clear boundaries exist between the levels. Each can overlap with either of the other two. The distinction is more one of size and focus than of the three being separate entities. At one level, small groups of offenders frequently commit some crimes together. This is particularly true of juvenile crime, such as fire setting and other delinquent activities. Most young offenders who continue their criminal careers into adulthood move towards committing crimes alone (Reiss, 1986; Reiss & Farrington, 1991). However, the commission of such criminal activities as ram raids and armed robberies, and various forms of white-collar crime, involve teams of offenders (Walsh, 1986; Waring, 1993). These team networks are the smallest form of criminal networks, carrying out a series of a particular crime or of similar crimes. For investigation, these groups can be the focus of intense intelligence-gathering activities. The relative smaller size and limitation of activity relating to a particular range of crimes make investigation easier than the higher levels of networks.

Harder to investigative is the level termed as organised networks. While no clear definition exists of this kind of activity, it can be said that groups of individuals do gather to commit a variety of legal and illegal activities over an extended time (Home Affairs Committee, 1995). A typical form of organised network is drug trafficking. Individuals produce, transport, distribute and sell the drugs, while the profits are processed through such methods as money laundering (Ruggiero and South, 1995; Montagne, 1990). Other forms can involve fraud and related white-collar crime (Passas and Nelken, 1993) or racketeering, prostitution and so on (Arlacchi, 1986). Team networks can exist within organised networks as subgroups of the whole that carry out specific duties. Due to the more complex nature of the activities carried out and the larger numbers of individuals involved, investigation can be more problematic than for team networks. However, the police do regularly carry out intensive investigations of such groups.

At the most extensive level are the general networks. These encompass any population of offenders who interact, though not specifically to commit crimes together. The solo burglar, thief or robber often uses handlers to dispose of goods. Various members of families can be co-offenders (Foster, 1990). Criminals associate with each other and non-offenders outside the commission of actual crimes in such locations as pubs. General networks, then, are general populations of criminals within defined boundaries or areas, and can include organised and team networks. These areas can be geographic - areas within communities where many offenders can be found, towns or cities and so on. They can also be defined institutionally, such as in a prison. A variety of criminals constantly interact, both criminally and non-criminally, within a prison. Links outside the prison to other networks also exist. General networks are the hardest to examine, as gathering the vast amount of information about interactions in such large groups would be impossible. Only key events in the activities of the network will come out of information drawn from intelligence and informants. Prison networks have the advantage (in comparison) of a more controlled environment, so a better understanding of these networks may be possible.

Defining exact boundaries can be problematic. Is a very small group of offenders who commit a variety of widely different crimes a team network, or an organised one? For team networks, which individuals are included - is it just the team itself or should the network also include any individuals they associate with that in some way are involved in the offender's criminal lifestyle? Deciding which of the associates are important will depend on the exact circumstances of the case. When looking at larger networks, the researcher must develop some cut-off point for inclusion in a network. This could include specific geographic boundaries, e.g. individuals who operate in a particular area, or those individuals directly involved in a specific group of crimes, e.g. burglars, fences and associates. Previous research has used these levels as part of implicit descriptions of the structure of criminal networks.

The concept of network levels has a number of implications for intelligence analysis. Depending on the network size, different aspects of the structure will be emphasised. For any criminal networks larger than teams, it is often logistically impossible to arrest and successfully prosecute all individuals involved in the network. The police must attempt to disrupt the networks by concentrating on certain individuals within it. Subgroups would be less likely to occur in team networks than in organised ones and so identifying them would be of less importance. Identifying central and peripheral members will be important whatever the network size. Overall, the literature largely points out trends and concepts without being too specific. One collection of methods that can carry out more specific analyses of structure has been developed in the field of Social Network Analysis (SNA).

Social Network Analysis

Social Network Analysis (SNA) is a major approach in structural analysis. Its methods are designed to study interactions between entities, individuals, corporations etc.. It bridges the fields of anthropology, sociology and psychology, and encompasses a variety of methods and definitions. Researchers have used these techniques to examine the basic relationships within groups of individuals (Warner & Lunt, 1941), the links between corporations (Scott & Hughes, 1980) and in determining social support networks (Seed, 1987). Fundamental to the SNA approach is the idea that interactions within any group shape both its individual membership and development. As a result, examining the structure of the network, in terms of the consistent patterns of interactions, will give insight into:

- The significance and roles of its individual members.

- How the group behaves and what form it will take.

To address these two areas, research in SNA falls into two camps - relational and positional (Rogers, 1987; Mizruchi, 1994). Research in the former group focuses on the ties or connections between the actors in the network. Ideas such as individual centrality and subgroup identification are explored in this area, and so covers both individual significance and aspects of the group. Positional research is concerned with how similar actors are in the patterns of connections that they have. Identifying the roles of individuals within the network, determining types of roles and looking for roles that occur in different networks are all part of this approach. Both approaches have relevance for the study of criminal networks, as described below.

Studying Criminal Networks

Previous research in the area has identified many of the particular strengths of SNA (Davis, 1981; Sparrow, 1991; Prunckun, 1996). It has also identified a number of issues. Waring (1993) used models of network structures to generate a classification scheme for forms of co-offending white-collar crime. The author made four points about the appropriateness of applying network analysis to this form of crime:

- When crimes involving more than one offender occur, often some offenders never meet. As a result, classical definitions of a "group" would be inappropriate, as the members of the network may not see themselves as such.

- Any criminal activity that has a certain amount of specialisation and complexity, like some forms of white-collar crime, requires certain skills. More than one individual would be necessary to carry out the task, resulting in the development of a network.

- Networks, unlike static formal groups, can be adaptable, altered or cease to exist easily (Powell, 1990). This is particularly useful when carrying out illegal activities.

- The author describes networks as co-operative ventures, rather than competitive ventures, and so they are more appropriate for illegal activities that "requires some amount of trust between participants" (p. 10).

While trust has a large part to play in the functioning of criminal networks (Reuter & Haaga, 1989; Zhang & Gaylord, 1996), those involving bargains or other forms of negotiations (Marsden, 1982) may not be so co-operative. These points cover some of the major reasons for the structural analysis approach.

Issues in the Use of SNA

Sparrow (1991) provides a series of cautions about applying SNA to criminal networks (in italics):

- *Criminal networks are often much larger than those traditionally focused on by social network analysts.* However, not all criminal networks are so large, and size can also be dependent on at what level of criminal activity the researcher examines. In addition, network size can have little impact on the actual measures, and the power of computers today make computations of large data sets easy.

- *Criminal networks will often be incomplete, with missing points and connections.* Any network, with the possible exception of those in the most tightly controlled experimental context, will be incomplete. It is merely a question of to what extent. Any form of "real world" research (Robson, 1993) will suffer from this problem, though often researchers choose not to confront this issue. While recognising that the data is incomplete, the analyst can still analyse the network in terms of what is known.

- *Criminal networks involve the potential for extensive overlap, where members belong to multiple networks and/or networks have multiple connections to each other.* Again, this depends on the type of network being looked at. The key is carefully defining the networks being studied. Expanding the boundaries of the size of the network being examined as it becomes apparent that two separate networks are associated with each other, would be one example.

- *Criminal networks are dynamic, in that they are constantly changing over time.* Again, this is true of all networks. Analysis of networks is also not a static process. As more information comes in, reanalysis is required. In addition, major changes to a network require new intelligence collecting efforts and new analyses. A network that has had several key people removed will either disintegrate or try to reform in a different structure. If the latter takes place, a new network exists to be investigated.

Jackson and Herbrink (1996) have carried out some preliminary work, resulting in the identification of a number of additional points relating to the application of SNA to intelligence. To examine a case of a Dutch drug network, the authors drew on two sources of information. The first source was summaries of interviews between the suspects and investigating officers. The second source was interviews carried out with a senior officer in the case. It was intended that each identified interaction would be classed as one of three types, from which a network structure could be drawn out:

- Authoritarian - where one member would order another.

- Advice - where one member would give information to another.

- Social - where one member would initiate a purely social interaction.

Unfortunately, in this particular case, the authors found it extremely difficult to draw out network information and were unable to analyse the structure of the drug network. Interviews with offenders may contain some information about interactions, particularly in terms of who committed crimes together, yet they may not necessarily contain enough information to allow the analyst to look at the network structure. Interviews may not be as useful as surveillance and phone records, which explicitly record information about interactions. The authors produced several pointers for police interviews that would give more information about the structure of networks. These included:

- Finding out who each interviewee knows.

- What sort of relationships exists between the interviewee and other network members?

- Getting the interviewee's perspective on his or her role and other member's roles in the network.

The second source also supplied insufficient information. This is understandable as the officer was contacted two years after the case. As the authors point out, intelligence is rarely of sufficient detail outside actual recordings of interactions through phone taps and similar methods, to permit subtle divisions into types of interactions. At this stage of research, the presence and number of interactions are all that can readily be analysed, and so a less refined study of networks must be carried out.

There are additional issues that are worth noting:

- Different types of connections are used in intelligence, unlike most SNA research, which focuses on one specific form of connection or looks at each type of connection separately. Ideally, criminal intelligence involves collecting the maximal amount of relevant information possible, e.g. associations through surveillance, recorded business transactions and phone calls. A simple solution is to define connections at the broadest possible level - any form of interaction. However, examination of specific connections could reveal details lost in a more general form. Running SNA measures on just phone records may draw out different information than a combination of all interactions. This is already part of link analysis and should be part of the SNA approach to crime. An additional strength of SNA is the ability to run the same analyses on a group of different measures of association and have the appropriate software give overall as well as separate results.

- The quality of the contact, for example, how important the transmitted information is to the case being investigated, is often not part of SNA. A hypothetical example would be where one individual is on the fringe of the network, connected to only one or two other individuals, who are central to the network. In addition, the central pair usually contact this individual. In an SNA sense, this individual may seem very minor. Actual intelligence might show, however, that this individual is the head of the network, working through specific intermediaries. These lieutenants usually seek out the individual to bring information to and to elicit decisions about business matters. The SNA measures still show up the two subordinates as important, and their removal would separate the leader from the rest of the network, but the analyst must use the SNA measures with what he or she knows about the network.

All these concerns warrant consideration. They do not, however, prevent the effective use of SNA by the analyst who is aware that, like any other method, it is not a perfect solution. Extensive research in the SNA field has examined similar forms of data drawn from imperfect sources (Alexander and Danowski, 1990), and few networks match all of Sparrow's points. This research has found SNA to be an effective method of analysing and understanding incomplete and problematic networks despite such potential concerns. Criminal networks are no different than these.

What SNA Techniques Can Help Achieve Intelligence Objectives?

Certain concepts are fundamental to SNA, and so must be understood before the methods in the field can be used. While these terms are standardised, often researchers vary considerably in how they define and measure more complex concepts. Two researchers, for example, use the same word to describe entirely different measures. To maintain consistency, the terms in this chapter are from Scott (1991):

- *Point* - represents the individual, group or whatever unit of the network being examined.

- *Line* - a connection of whatever form between two points.

- Two points directly connected are *adjacent*.

- Any route that can be followed to go from one point to another, through any intervening points, is the *path*.

- The *length* of the path is the number of lines that must be followed along the path.

- The *geodesic* between A and B is the shortest path out of all possible alternatives.

Details of the contacts between offenders are also important. One aspect is what the individual "lines" connecting the members of the network are composed of. These lines can have a variety of details about them:

- The intensity of the connection, e.g. how often two offenders communicate. The amount of communication between offenders can be as important as who they connect with.

- Lines can have direction - lines between individuals can represent some flow or movement in a particular direction, e.g. individual A contacts individual B more often than B does A. Someone who is constantly initiating contacts is potentially more important than a passive recipient.

SNA Techniques

One area of SNA is already extensively used in crime analysis. The ANACAPA diagrams described above are variants of the sociogram, a method developed by Moreno (1934) in the earliest days of SNA. The formats are the same, with guidelines for the selection of icons to represent people, locations and types of relationships, and how to design the layouts of the charts. Moreno and associates used sociograms to develop a better understanding of the impact of interactions on social relationships. Over time, researchers in the field began to look for more scientific methods of exploring relationships. The problem with sociograms was that they were too individualistic, although they remain an effective method to examine subjective views of networks by members of those networks (McCluskey and Wardle, [8][1]). A researcher examining a network from the outside requires more rigorous methods, when possible. A wide range of the SNA measures that have come out of the development of such methods have implications for the analysis of intelligence. They are best grouped by referring to each of the intelligence objectives.

---

[1] Numbers in [ ] refer to chapters in the present volume.

Who is Central and Peripheral in the Network?

Centrality in SNA defines the relative position of individual members within a network, in terms of power and influence. Within any given network, there will be a continuum of levels of centrality, ranging from those individuals who are leaders or have a major impact on the network through to those individuals with little involvement with or influence on the network. Determining where an individual falls in such a continuum is very important for investigators who are trying to develop an understanding of how the network operates. Chains of command, leaders and subordinates must be identified to allow for prioritisation of targeting. The advantage of the SNA approach is that it can identify individuals who are not obviously central to the network (i.e. not leaders) but who hold central positions in other ways, such as controlling communications.

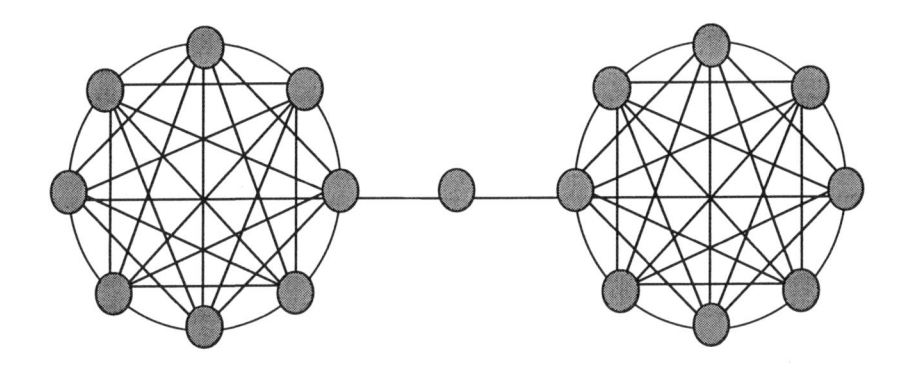

Figure 3.1 Betweenness Example

The one measure currently used in crime analysis is *degree* (for a mathematical description of this measure and the two following, see Freeman 1979) - the number of other points to which one point is adjacent. As mentioned previously, there is a danger that degree represents amount known about an individual, rather than how central that individual is. This does not necessarily mean that the measure is inaccurate, but analysts must use it with caution. A second measure that potentially avoids such problems is *betweenness*. This measure represents how much one point falls on the geodesic, or shortest path, of all possible pairs of the other points. By falling on the geodesic, that point has some control over the flow of information, goods etc. between the pair. The more geodesics a point falls on, the higher the betweenness score. Since the measure involves paths, the number of adjacent points has less of an impact on the score. The most extreme example of this is illustrated in figure 3.1. The point between the two tightly interconnected groups only has a degree of two, but acts as the only contact point between two groups. Anything that has to move between the two must pass through that point. As a result, its betweenness score will be high, relative to its degree score. Betweenness is a particularly useful measure for intelligence analysis as it will not just indicate individuals who have many connections, but also those who act as key channels for the flow of transactions.

A third measure of relative centrality is *closeness*. This is also dependent on examination of geodesics, but determines the length of the geodesic paths from each point to all other points. The shorter the total of the geodesic paths, the more close that point is to all the others in the network. Closeness, then, represents a different form of how "connected" a point is to the network. It is not the number of connections the point has, but how easily that point can contact all other points, with the least number of go-betweens. A final measure of centrality is Stephenson and Zelen's (1989) *information*. A development from betweenness, the measure adds two factors to be considered beyond just positioning on geodesics. The first factor is that when there is more than one geodesic to follow, the one that contains points with higher degrees will be used more. Effort is minimised by using those points who are more connected overall. The second is that, for any number of reasons, the geodesic may not be the preferred path between two points. Member A might be suspicious of B, believing him/her to be an informant, and so will go through C and D to contact E, instead. All paths a point is on between pairs of points are included, with the shorter the path, the more importance it is given. The information score, then, is a measure of how involved a point is in all possible connections in the network, not just the shortest ones. The applications of the information scores are the same as for betweenness. Using a variety of centrality measures will allow the analyst to identify two groups of individuals:

- Those individuals who are well connected.

- Those individuals who play a key role in the flow of contacts within the network, but who may not appear to be well connected.

Both groups of individuals, which will frequently overlap, could warrant targeting for further intelligence gathering or removal from the network.

What Subgroups Exist in the Network?

Scott (1991) defined a sub-graph as a "collection of points selected from the whole graph of a network, with the lines connecting those points" (p. 103). A researcher can carry out this selection in either of two ways, or a combination of the two. The selection of points can have some investigative purpose, e.g. looking at the connections between individuals involved in money laundering after drawing them out of larger population of a complete drug trafficking network. Alternatively, the basis for choosing the sub-graph can be based on some statistical measure, e.g. dividing the network into a core and periphery based on a specific SNA measure. The two can be combined when the statistical measure also represents some meaningful construct. The statistical core may represent the key members of some criminal group, thus having more connections to each other. This would make them more cohesive and lead them to perceive themselves as a particular "group".

Identification of sub-graphs has several uses in crime analysis:

- When examining general networks, sub-graphs may represent specific groups that operate as teams or groups that have developed into mutually supportive "communities" of offenders. For example, several solo burglars may have a common handler of stolen goods, and, thereby, meet each other. Over time, the burglars and handler develop into a sub-graph with frequent associations with each other, and less with others. The handler may put in requests for certain items that the burglars would then obtain. This is the creation of a form of crime network at a very basic level. Through identification of subgroups as they develop, the police can take steps to disrupt or destroy them.

- In organised networks, identification of subgroups can give insight into the structure of the group - whether it is organised into separate "cells" connected by key people or into a hierarchy of groups with, for example, a core of leaders at the top. An additional feature is the identification of team networks within the organised network. These teams may be devoted to particular activities, e.g. a team of individuals within a drug network who are primarily involved in financial matters. Targeting these individuals, using financial investigations, would be effective not just for investigating them, but for other network members who are connected to the subgroup.

- In both team and organised networks, sub-graphs may represent the core members of a group or different cells of offenders. Identification of such individuals would have a major impact on the emphasis of target selection within such networks.

Cliques and related measures are the most typical forms of sub-graphs used in the SNA literature (Wasserman and Faust, 1994). A perfect clique would be a subset of the graph where all points are connected to each other, and those connections are reciprocated. In figure 3.1, either of the two subgroups would qualify as perfect cliques as all of the members are connected to each other. In the real world, this ideal is rarely attained, so researchers need to reach some sort of compromise. Using a standard called the *n-clique* is better, where all points do not require direct connections, but can be separated by a path distance of n. A "perfect" clique would be a 1-clique (all directly connected), while a 2-clique would include all points connected through an intermediary. One problem with n-cliques is that they can be artificially created when two points in the clique are connected by a point that would not itself have enough connections to be part of that clique. This would falsely give the impression of there being an n-clique. Mokken (1979) suggests the n-clan as an alternative to the n-clique as a way of avoiding this problem. The *n-clan* method uses the value of n not only as the length of the path between points, but also as the *diameter* of the clique (the maximum distance between the two farthest apart points). This would eliminate the problem of artificial cliques, as points that merely connect other points but do not qualify for the clique would be excluded from the analysis. The n-clan would appear to represent the best clique variant for identification of criminal subgroups.

The *component* is the most basic form of sub-graph in the SNA literature. This is a sub-graph made up of any number of points connected through paths of any length. A graph can be made up of only one component if all the points are directly or indirectly connected to each other. For criminal groups, analysts can use components to identify wholly separate networks and individuals who are isolated from those networks. Those wholly separate networks may then be subjected to separate analyses. Additionally, lack of connections might suggest that there is insufficient information about the links between different sections of the graph. The analyst could request further investigation of these "empty zones". An additional approach that comes out of the component idea is the production of link diagrams or other visual representations using cut-off levels, e.g. only using links where individuals have been in phone contact with each other at least six times. A new link chart based on this criterion would highlight concentrations of communications by removing individuals not frequently involved in the network.

What are the Important Communications and Methods of Communicating?

Another approach to intelligence analysis is focusing on specific interactions between two individuals rather than on individual members. Key communication channels are those interactions that move highly relevant information from one part of the network to another or pass along new information that comes from outside the network itself. For communications within the network, several measures are relevant. Individuals with high betweenness or information scores would be involved in key communications. In addition, Hage and Harary (1983) used *cutpoints* and *knots* to determine the role of key points in the structure of components within the network. Cutpoints are those points whose removal would result in the component disintegrating into several smaller units. The cutpoint joins various sub-components. Knots are each of these sub-components along with their cutpoints. Cutpoints can play a pivotal role in the flow of resources or information through the components, and possibly through the network as a whole. Cutpoints function, in a sense, as 'gatekeepers' between the various sub-components. The obvious application of cutpoints for crime analysis is in the identification of individuals whose removal from the network will result in its break-up or disruption.

With regards to new information coming from outside the network, or between highly distinct parts of the network, Sparrow discusses the importance of the existence of *weak ties*. A concept developed by Granovetter (1973), weak ties are infrequently used key communication channels through which groups of individuals interact in order to access new information. These differ from the *strong ties* that exist between individuals who are in frequent contact with each other, and so have access to the same information. This idea lead Sparrow to two propositions:

- More important communications/interactions are likely to occur through weak ties.

- Targeting the weak ties for disruption will have a significant impact on the ability of the network as a whole to interact quickly and effectively.

There is no specific measure for identifying weak links per se. It is rather a concept for the analyst to be aware of.

What Individuals might be more likely to give Information to the Police?

Determining which individuals may be more likely to give information can be an important part of gathering sufficient evidence in order to prosecute offenders. SNA can facilitate this process in two ways. The first method is based on individual centrality. Peripheral network members may perceive themselves as less a part of the "group" than members more deeply involved. Peripheral individuals, then, may be more likely to give information to the police. Targeting these individuals is something of a trade-off, however. Being less involved in the network also means they are likely to have less relevant information about the activities of the network. Targeting of high level members would yield the best information, but they may be too loyal to the network to reveal useful information. Members who are in the middle-range may be the best compromise between willingness to give information and quality of information. The second method is a similar process, but involves a series of reanalyses of a network at different stages of its existence. As loyalties shift and individuals gain and lose influence, their positions in the structure of the network will also shift. Over the series of analyses, some individuals may be continually shifting into increasingly less central positions. These individuals may see themselves as rejected by the network and may begin to feel increasingly frustrated with their position. As a result, they may be more open to giving the police information when the opportunity arises. The advantage of the second approach is that the individuals being targeted were originally in positions of influence and would be more likely to have highly significant information.

What is the Overall Structure of the Group?

An understanding of the overall structure of the group can aid in interpreting the results obtained from the other methods. As mentioned before, a problem exists in presenting accurate visual representations of networks. Software packages have gone a long way towards alleviating this problem, by giving a variety of options for layouts, e.g. standard ANACAPA linking, circular patterns, link charts with lines that can cross. An alternative approach is to use one of several packages in the social sciences that carry out multidimensional scaling (MDS). The most established form of MDS in the SNA field is smallest space analysis (SSA) (Shye and Elizur, 1994). Technical information about SSA can be found in the introductory section of the book. The output of an SSA represents the relationships between the nodes by placing each entity as a point on the graph. The stronger the association between points, the closer they will appear on the graph. The weaker the association, the farther apart. In Investigative Psychology, this procedure is usually carried on crime scene behaviours to determine which behaviours are more strongly associated with each other (Canter and Alison [1]). In SNA research, the strength of association is not determined between behaviours, but between individuals within the network. Each point on the SSA plot, then, represents one person. The closer two individuals are, the stronger their association. Association can include presence of a link, frequency of interaction or whatever form of connection the individuals or groups have. An examination of the output can give the researcher some insight into the structure of the network and the roles the members play within it. Researchers have used this technique to examine such networks as the structure of the criminal justice system in Cook County, Illinois (Heinz and Manikas 1992). For actual examples of the application of SSA, see the case studies described below.

Examination of an SSA plot can reveal several features of a network.

- Strength of association is the most basic feature. Those points far apart have less relative association within the network. Groupings of individuals near each other can suggest subgroups, which can be supported through the various measures for identifying sub-graphs.

- A second feature is some indication of potential core and peripheral members. Individual points in the centre of the spread of points have a more central position in the network. Points out on the edges have a more peripheral position. Again, these results can be confirmed through measures of centrality and influence. The SSA allows the researcher to look at the overall layout of the network, e.g. highly decentralised and spread out versus tightly linked together.

- A final, as yet unexplored feature of the SSA is the indication of potential gaps in the intelligence information. Areas within the spread of the network may be void of points, a sort of "vacuum". This area may result from a lack of strong associations between different parts of the network, resulting in their moving away from each other on the graph. An alternative explanation is that associations may be present, but have not been picked up, for whatever reason, by the intelligence. The analyst may suggest further investigation into these areas of vacuum.

Baker and Faulkner (1993) examined the impact of network structure on cases of price-fixing in the American electrical equipment industry. They identified two factors affecting network structure - organisational objectives and information-processing requirements. Organisational objective refers to the main aim of the conspiracy, either to maintain secrecy or to co-ordinate activities. While both would exist in a conspiracy, whichever one was dominant would influence the structure of the group. Concealment, as they term secrecy, would lead towards a highly decentralised structure with minimal interaction. This would reduce the risk of the group's activity being recognised and of individual members being linked to the network. Co-ordination would lead towards the most efficient interactions. Information processing affects co-ordination, leading to a potential conflict with concealment. Groups best accomplish simple, clear tasks (low requirements) in highly centralised structures, while complex tasks (high requirements) fare better in decentralised structures. If the information-processing requirement is high, both the concealment and co-ordination elements push for decentralised structures. When information-processing demands are low, concealment needs still push for decentralisation, while co-ordination needs push for a centralised structure.

Using transcripts of a congressional committee on price-fixing, they identified seventy-eight individuals from the thirteen companies that made up the three conspiracies. Each was ranked as either upper, middle or lower management. Of the three conspiracies, the researchers identified one as having high information-processing requirements, while the remaining two had low information-processing requirements. While they expected that the former would be decentralised, they determined that the opposite was true - it was the most centralised and dense of the three. For the remaining two, both were decentralised, suggesting secrecy was more important than co-ordination of activities. Baker and Faulkner concluded that, unlike the situations examined in the literature on small-group structures and information processing, the need for secrecy in high requirement conspiracies results in centralisation. This is due to the need for extensive co-ordination to deal with the high level of information processing required, a process made even more complex by the fact that individuals in the group were unable to interact freely. It was the secrecy that led to the conflicting result.

76 The Social Psychology of Crime

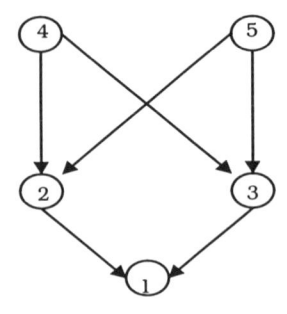

Figure 3.2 Equivalence Example from Wasserman and Faust (1994)

What are the Different Roles or Jobs within the Network?

The term "role" in SNA refers to the patterns of connections as opposed to a job definition. Two individuals have the same role within a network if they have connections with the same people. This is illustrated in figure 3.2, taken from Wasserman and Faust (1994). Points two and three have the same roles, in that they are both connected to points one, four and five. Likewise, points four and five are equivalent as they have the same pattern of connections - to two and three. Sparrow (1991) termed equivalence measures as including substitutability, stochastic equivalence and role equivalence. For substitutability, if an individual has a counterpart(s) who can maintain the same pattern of connections, then that individual is less important than someone without substitutes. Stochastic equivalence, which does not require exactly the same patterns, would fulfil the same purpose. It has the advantage of being adaptable to incomplete information about connections between points (though Sparrow does not state this). The main use of role identification is the targeting of individuals with relatively unique roles, rather than those who share the same role with others. The removal of one of the latter members would have little impact on the network, as others could replace him/her. Role equivalence is slightly different, in that it is a comparison of individual roles in separate networks. Role equivalence can be used to develop typologies of roles in similar criminal networks. This would allow investigators to develop the most effective strategies for dealing with general roles, rather than having to examine each individual separately.

Which Individuals Should be Removed to Disrupt the Network?

Disruption can be as important for policing of networks as actual arrests. Preventing a network from operating effectively will reduce its ability to carry out further criminal activities, while the investigation continues. Several of the measures already detailed can aid this aim. Most of the key measures mentioned so far have highlighted different ways to disrupt networks. Removal of central individuals, as identified through such measures as degree, will have an adverse effect on leadership or organisation. Removal of central subgroups would also have such an effect. The elimination of individuals with the most influence on the flow

of communications will prevent the network from interacting successfully. Measures such as betweenness and information would aid in identification of such individuals, as would determining weak ties within the network. If these network members who tie subgroups together, such as the cutpoints that link together knots, can be identified, such as the cutpoints that link together knots, then their removal will prevent these subgroups from interacting. Finally, the identification and elimination of individuals with unique roles within the network would also disrupt the network, as other individuals would not have the necessary connections to easily replace their contribution to the network.

Case Study

The case study will illustrate the application of several SNA measures, specifically measures of centrality, subgroups and cutpoints/knots, as well as the application of SSA to the study of criminal networks. Larger groups were not used in order to ensure clear examples of the results. UCINET (Borgatti, Everett and Freeman, 1992) was used to generate all of the measures apart from the SSAs, while the visual representations of the network structures were produced through a separate SSA package (Lingoes, 1973). In the case study, phone records were used from a network involved in a wide variety of criminal activities. The network consisted of twenty-two offenders, with phone billings used to determine associations between individuals. In this case, Degree represents total phone calls made or received.

The various measures of centrality, as shown in table 3.1, are generally consistent across the four measures used - Degree, Closeness, Betweenness and Information. The first column in table 3.1 is the ranking range, up to number 10. The following four columns are the offenders listed in rank order, from the most central to the tenth-most central offender, across the four measures, with the actual score for each measure in brackets. For example, in the column for Degree, the fifth offender is the most central figure in the network, in terms of phone communications between offenders, with a degree score of 107. Offender 4 comes second with a degree score of 83, with offenders 3, 2 and 17 following. Offenders 1, 10, 6 and 14 make up the sixth through ninth highest scores, while offenders 7,8 and 22 tie for the tenth position. Overall, the top five offenders remain fairly consistent, with offender 4 being marginally closer to the rest of the network than offender 5, and offender 5 having a slightly higher betweenness score, and both tying for first in information scores. Offenders 3, 2 and 17 remain in the same rank positions, while the remaining positions are filled by a variety of other network members.

The two offenders 4 and 5, along with offenders 3 and 2, make up what can be seen as a group of highly central members. Offender 17 is also quite central to the network, but has scores significantly lower than the core four, though higher than the remainder of the network. The analyses reveal a core to the network, in terms of both how connected individuals are and how much they control the flow of communications. One other member has a fairly important position in the network, with the rest being more peripheral. The analyses indicate that the five most central offenders dominate communications in terms of amounts and in acting as intermediaries.

Table 3.1 Centrality Measures

Ranking on measure	Degree	Closeness	Betweenness	Information
1	5 (107)	4 (64)	5 (45)	4/5 (2.13)
2	4 (83)	5 (60)	4 (44)	-
3	3 (61)	3 (58)	3 (23)	3 (2.11)
4	2 (46)	2 (55)	2 (21)	2 (2.07)
5	17 (15)	17 (47)	17 (11)	17 (1.87)
6	1 (9)	6 (45)	6 (6)	1 (1.75)
7	10 (8)	1/14/22 (42)	8 (3)	10 (1.72)
8	6 (7)	-	22 (0.75))	14 (1.62)
9	14 (6)	-	7 (0.36)	6 (1.61)
10	7/8/22 (3)	8 (41)	remainder (0)	22 (1.27)

The list of subgroups (see table 3.2) confirm the findings of the centrality measures. The first column of table 3.2 represents the type of subgroup being described - perfect clique or 2-clan. The second column indicates how many of each type of subgroup exists. The members of each subgroup are listed in column three of the table. The final column is made up of short comments about the nature of each subgroup, which are elaborated on below.

In terms of perfect cliques, the first clique consists of the four most central offenders (offenders 2 through 5), with all connected directly to each other. The remainder of the cliques are made up, in general, of either pairs of core members with the addition of a peripheral member who is in contact with both (e.g. the fifth clique is made up of offenders 3 and 5, plus offender 14), or a core member and offender 17, with a connecting peripheral member. Some example perfect cliques are shown in figure 3.3. The list of 2-clans extends this pattern to larger subgroups. All of these subgroups are made up of either the core with a number of peripheral members, or of offender 4 from the core, offender 17 and a number of peripherals. Examination of the connecting lines placed on the SSA of the network (see figure 3.3 below) reveals that for all of the 2-clans involving the core and peripheral members, those peripheral members are directly connected to only one core member. For example, all of the peripheral members in the first 2-clan are connected to offender

80 The Social Psychology of Crime

5 of the core. This confirms the idea that the network core has significant control over the network as a whole. The peripheral members are dependent on usually one, sometimes two of the core members and/or offender 17. Two examples of 2-clans are shown in figure 3.4.

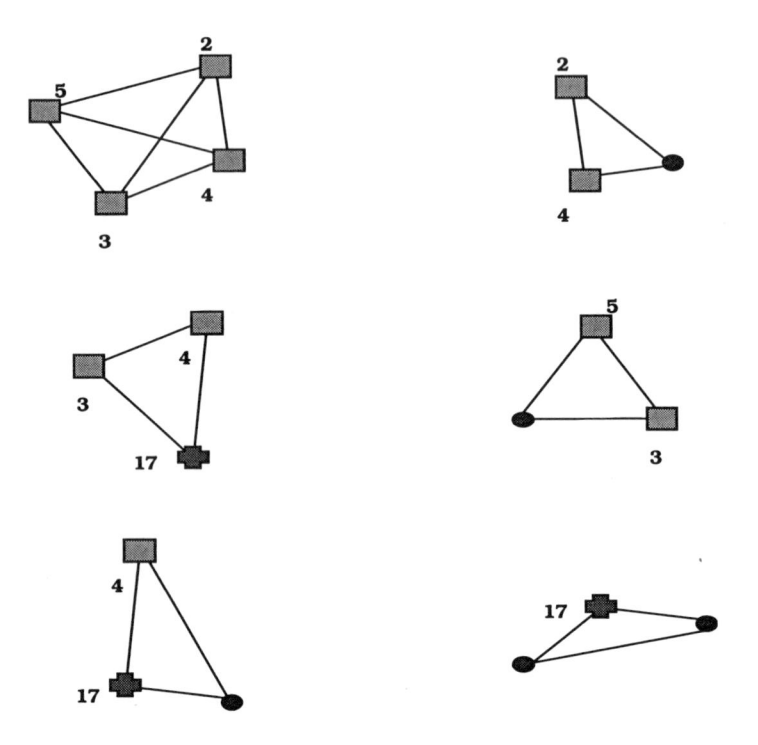

Figure 3.3 Examples of Perfect Cliques

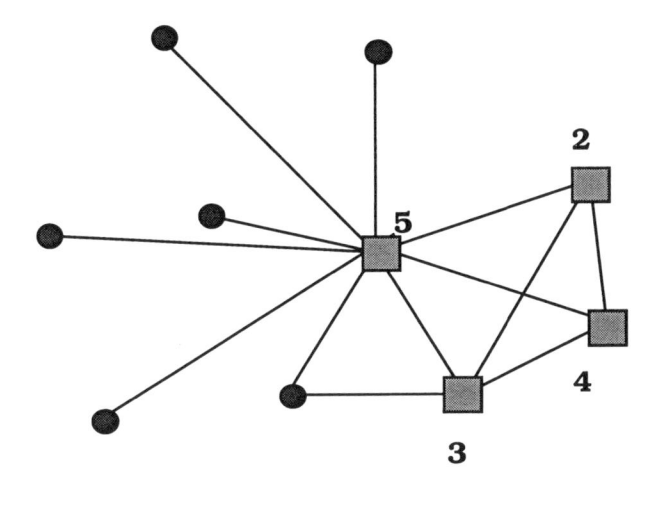

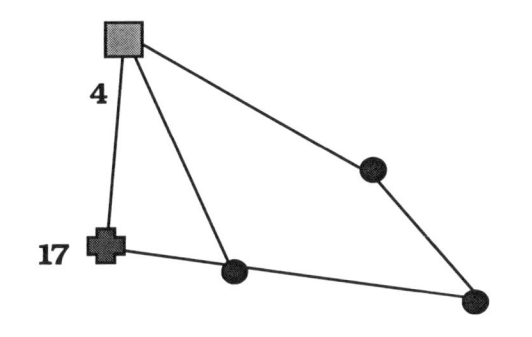

The Structural Analysis of Criminal Networks 81

Figure 3.4 Examples of 2-clans

Table 3.2 Subgroups

Subgroup Type	Subgroup #	Members	Comments
Clique	1	2-5	Core
	2	1,2,4	2 of core (2,4)+ connector
	3	4,6,17	1 of core (4) + 17 and connector
	4	3,4,17	2 of core (3,4)+ 17
	5	3,5,14	2 of core (3,5)+ connector
	6	6,17,22	17 plus connectors
	7	3,17,22	1 of core (3)+ 17 + connector
2-clan	1	2-5,10,12-16	core + group linked to offender 5
	2	2-5,14,17,21,22	core + 3 group
	3	1-6,8,9,11,17	core + 4 group
	4	2-6,17,22	core + start of 4/17 group
	5	1-5,19-20	core + 2 group
	6	3,4,6,17,18,22	4/17 group 1
	7	4,6-8,17	4/17 group 2
	8	4,6,7,17,22	4/17 group 3

The final analyses of cutpoints, as shown in table 3.3, do not reveal findings radically different from the results above. The first column indicates the cutpoint (which offender whose removal would separate sections of the network). The second column lists the number of knots the cutpoint brings together. The final column lists the members of each knot. As already indicated by the 2-clans, the core members are intermediaries between some peripheral members and the rest of the network. The removal of offender 5 would result in offenders 10, 12, 13, 15 and 16 becoming isolated from the rest of the network, should they not have the ability to contact or are not acquainted with the other core members.

The SSA (figure 3.5), based on number of phone calls made between network members, illustrates the overall structure of the network. The SSA plot does not include lines to show actual connections between individuals, so they were added to aid in interpretation. Unsurprisingly, the four core members are centrally located in the network and are close to each other. Those peripheral members who are connected to two core members (e.g. offender 1 is associated with offenders 2 and 4), are located off to a side, but between the two core members. Peripheral members with only one core connection are generally farther out and clustered near that core member. Offender 17 is located close to offender 4 and those peripheral members connected to both 4 and 17. Offender 7 is the only network member without at least one connection to a core member. The overall structure of the network is one that is highly dependent on the core members. All but one offender has direct contact to at least one core member, with 11 peripheral members having associations to the network through links to the individual core members or offender 17. With the exception of the subgroups associated with offender 17, the core maintain a tight control on the flow of communications between peripheral members.

84 The Social Psychology of Crime

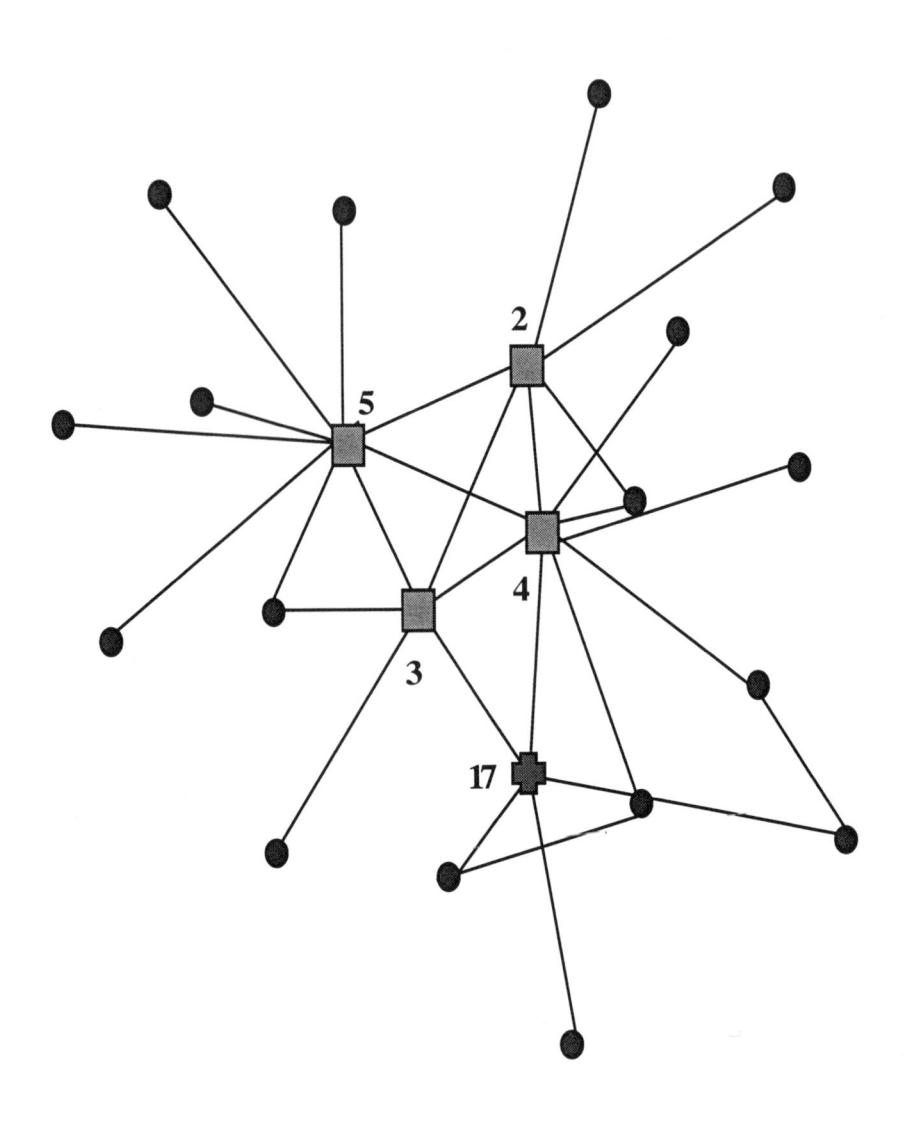

Coefficient of Alienation = 0.063

Figure 3.5 SSA of Case Study (Links Added)

Table 3.3 Cutpoints/Knots

Cutpoint (Offender)	# of Knots Cutpoint Joins	Block Members
5	6	1. 1-8,14,17,22 2. 10 3. 12 4. 13 5. 15 6. 16
4	3	1. 1-8,14,17,22 2. 9 3. 11
2	3	1. 1-8,14,17,22 2. 19 3. 20
3	2	1. 1-8,14,17,22 2. 21

The overall pattern of subgroups also indicates a core to the network, with a series of overlapping subgroups based on individual members of that core. This confirms the suggested strategies from the centrality measures. The individual members of the core act as gateways between subsections. An additional feature is the close relationship between offenders 4 and 17, as indicated by both being members of three 2-clans. If offender 17 does turn out to be the "weak link" in the network, then this close association may be of use, by using member 17 to reach member 4. The results from the cutpoint analysis also confirm the role of the core members, with these members making up all of the significant cutpoints. Finally, the SSA acts as an overall confirmation of the network structure. By adding the connections, and so mimicking a link chart, the core members control over the network is indicated again.

At least in terms of phone communications, peripheral members would only be able to give evidence as relates to those core members they are in contact with, protecting to some extent the other members of the core. In addition, peripheral members are unlikely to know what communications have gone on between core members and the rest of the network, unless the core member(s) they have contact with choose to tell them. In terms of investigative strategies, the four core members are obviously key to the network and should be targeted for surveillance/removal. In addition, member 17 has an influential position, which would become even more important if core members were removed, so this offender also warrants attention. In terms of potential targeting of members as informants, the three tiers of the network would allow selection based on relative involvement. The peripheral members may be willing to give information, not being heavily involved in the network, but may have correspondingly less information. Offender 17 may be too much a part of the central organisation of the network to give information, but would have more to offer. It might be the case that exclusion from the core group would make that offender more willing to co-operate. This assessment must be made based on additional information known to the analyst and investigating officers about the individual.

Conclusion

Many potential areas exist for the application of SNA to the structural analysis of intelligence on criminal networks. The first major area is the examination of criminal activities by groups ranging from teams through organised crime to general networks. This has been the main focus of the chapter. Other applications have been only touched upon. A second area is the control of prison populations. Using security information, networks of offenders can be analysed. A particular application is the identification of potential problem subgroups. As a prison network is analysed and reanalysed over time, a group of individuals may shift towards forming a subgroup as they increasingly interact with each other. Once a group has been identified as engaging in a criminal or disruptive activity, steps can be taken to break it up by moving prisoners to new locations or taking measures to prevent the members from meeting. A final area for analysis is the examination of links between criminal networks outside and within prisons. This could involve continued involvement in the "management" of criminal networks by incarcerated offenders, as well as criminal activity within the prison with links to the outside. The supply of drugs to prisoners is an example of the latter. The networks involved in moving drugs into prison, distributing them and paying the suppliers outside may then be investigated in order to disrupt their activities.

Identification and cultivation of potential informants for information-gathering purposes is a major part of a proactive strategy. Network position can be used to identify potential sources. The emphasis is on assessment of the individual's position - measures of centrality may highlight individuals who may be targeted as potential sources. Those individuals on the periphery of the network, like those with low levels of cohesion to a group, may feel excluded or have little loyalty to the network. These individuals may be willing sources. Individuals in the middle-range, or those who hold key positions, in terms of controlling the flows through networks, but are not part of the core are a second level of sources. They also may feel excluded, though from the benefits of membership in the top levels of the network. This exclusion, relative to their actual positions in the network could engender a willingness to act as a source. Those in the core of a network would be the most useful sources, but would be the hardest to acquire. This points out a key aspect of the process of identification of sources through group or network membership. There is a trade-off between amount of involvement in a group/network and amount of information known. While low-level members may make more willing sources, they are also likely to have the least amount of useful information. Those with the most information would be the hardest to acquire. This highlights how knowledge of position relative to power must be a major part of source targeting. Those individuals with high responsibilities and influence, but who have little power are likely to be the best sources.

An additional approach is through assessment of individual change of position over time. Repeated analyses of a network at various stages in its existence should be carried out. Individuals who move from positions of power to more peripheral locations in the network may be optimal sources for information as:

- They would be more likely to have high quality information than those members that have always been peripheral.

- They may feel rejected or betrayed by the network as a result of their loss of position, and so may be more willing to give information.

Ultimately, research into a variety of forms of networks will allow for the generation of systems of classification based on structural components. Networks will differ in amount of hierarchical structure, what limitations are placed on general interactions, how varied or focused their activities are, how subdivided they are and in their size. These factors will be influenced by the goals of the network, what kinds of time scales and geographical areas they are operating within and such elements as ethnic or familial ties. Consistent patterns of types of networks should emerge - networks with similar goals and operating conditions should form broadly similar network structures. Once consistent types have been identified, a system of classification can be created.

This system could be described as a series of templates, to which new networks could be matched. Once this matching has been carried out, flexible action plans suggesting optimal courses of action can then be implemented. These action plans would be developed based on two sets of information:

- Guidelines based on what was determined to be the best plans of action used against the networks that make up that particular template.

- Details from the particular case on hand.

The guidelines would give the analyst and the investigating officers direction as to what were effective or counter-productive actions against similar networks in the past. These guidelines are not intended to be accepted as the only option. No case will exactly match a template, so the analyst must be aware of specific details that may make some of the guidelines ineffective or make some more important than others. Once the action plan is fully developed, implementation can take place. The action plan must remain flexible, as further information, particularly in terms of how successful the actions have been up to any point in time, may require changes to be made by the analysts and decision-makers. Further details on the network could also require changes in the plan.

Examples of actions can include: targeting individuals for removal, for feeding disruptive information, or for possible recruitment, collecting further information on particular individuals or subgroups of the network and focusing on the communication activities of individuals identified as having key positions as gatekeepers in the flow of information.

A second general application is disrupting and/or destroying the network. In ideal circumstances, the removal of key figures and subgroups along with other non-SNA related actions would destroy a network. There are a number of reasons why in reality this is unlikely to occur. The first is the limitation placed on actions by financial and time constraints. With the optimal set of actions and enough money and time, any network can, in theory, be destroyed. Time and resource allocations are usually such that the most practical actions must be carried out rather than the optimal ones. The second factor is that networks can resist disruption and can reform themselves, albeit with different aspects to their structures, for example, new leaders. Attempts to destroy organised crime groups and drug trafficking networks by the removal of the leaders have not always been successful. While some disruption takes place, new leaders often emerge as restructuring takes place. Networks that operate against society are flexible entities that adjust to the pressures operating against them, as they have to be able to survive opposition not just from competitors, but from the state itself.

This is not to say that networks are untouchable. In the short-term, the main aim may have to be disruption of network activities, rather than actual network destruction. Disruption is beneficial in that the inability of the network to function properly, even for short periods of time, will limit its ability to operate and allow other operations to be carried out against it. A network that has lost a number of its "gatekeepers" and is trying to restructure its patterns of communications may be more susceptible to being fed false information, as there are no longer any regular sources of information. Enough of this form of cumulative disruption can lead to the collapse of the network or to its effectiveness being reduced to such a level that its existence has little actual impact. Another aspect of the use of short-term disruption rather than a sustained effort to destroy a network is that it allows for simultaneous operations against a number of networks. Networks themselves must be prioritised in importance, thus affecting resource allocations. Resources will primarily be designated by decision makers to those networks determined to have the highest threat potential.

Minor actions can still be carried out against other networks to keep them "off balance" and, at least, partially disrupt their functioning until such a time as more involved actions are decided upon.

Research into the application of SNA to crime analysis is still very much in its early days. Work still needs to be done to determine the value of the various sources of data, e.g. phone records versus surveillance logs. The issue of the quality of the data being received must also be dealt with. A number of other questions must also be addressed. For example, to what extent does the information the analyst receives reflect the emphases of the investigation and to what extent does missing data skew the results generated? At what point does it actually contribute to investigations - is it the case that SNA only comes into its own when an analyst is trying to disentangle the complex web of associations in networks involving large numbers of offenders? SNA still holds great potential for application in crime analysis. It remains to be seen which techniques researchers will identify as being effective. In addition, it must be kept in mind that the techniques are not meant to act as anything more than tools to aid in analyst decision making. For effective crime analysis, a triangulation process must take place. Computer results, the analyst's experience and interpretation of the results, and the experience and "in-field" knowledge of the officers involved must be brought together. SNA techniques are intended to assist decision-making, not replace it. The analyst must carefully examine results from analyses compared with what additional intelligence he or she knows. These results can then be presented to the officers involved. The team as a whole can then generate the best possible action plan based on the best possible criminal intelligence analysis.

References

ACPO Crime Committee (1994), *Guidelines on the Use and Management of Informants,* London: Association of Chief Police Officers.

Alexander, M.C. and Danowski, J.A. (1990), 'Analysis of an Ancient Network: Personal communication and the study of social structure in a past society', *Social Networks,* **12**, 313-35.

Anderson, Jr., P.P. and Peterson, M.P. (1990), *Criminal Intelligence Analysis,* Orangevale, CA: Palmer Press.

Arlacchi, P. (1986), *Mafia Business: The Mafia ethic and the spirit of capitalism,* Oxford: Oxford University Press.

Baker, W.E. and Faulkner, R.R. (1993), 'The Social Organisation of Conspiracy: Illegal networks in the heavy electrical equipment industry.' *American Sociological Review*, **58**, 837-60.

Blumstein, A. (ed.) (1986), *Criminal Careers and Career Criminals*, Washington, D.C.: National Academy Press.

Borgatti, S.P., Everett, M.G. and Freeman, L.C. (1992), UCINET IV *Version 1.62*, Columbia: Analytic Technologies.

Canter, D.V. and Kirby, S. (1995), 'Prior Convictions of Child Molesters', *Science and Justice*, **35 (1)**, 73-78.

Davis, R.H. (1981), 'Social Network Analysis - an Aid in Conspiracy Investigations', *FBI Law Enforcement Bulletin*, **50 (12)**, 11-19.

Dorn, N., Murji, K. and South, N. (1992), *Traffickers: Drug markets and law enforcement*, London: Routledge.

Dorn, N. and South, N. (1990), 'Drug Markets and Law Enforcement', *British Journal of Criminology*, **30 (2)** 171-188.

van Duyne, P. (1996), 'The Phantom and threat of Organised Crime', *Crime, Law and Social Change*, **24**, 341-77.

van Duyne, P. (1997), 'Mobsters are People Too', in D.V. Canter and L.J. Alison (eds), *Investigative Psychology Volume III: Criminal Networks*, Aldershot: Dartmouth.

Fijnaut, C. (1990), 'Organised Crime: A comparison between the United States of America and western Europe', *British Journal of Criminology*, **30 (3)**, 321-40.

Foster, J. (1990), *Villains: Crime and Community in the Inner City*, London: Routledge.

Freeman, L.C. (1979), 'Centrality in Social Networks: Conceptual clarifications', *Social Networks*, **1**, 215-39.

Granovetter, M.S. (1973), 'The Strength of Weak Ties', *American Journal of Sociology*, **8**, 1360-80.

Hage, P. and Harary, F. (1983), *Structural Models in Anthropology*, Cambridge: Cambridge University Press.

Heinz, J.P. and Manikas, P.M. (1992), 'Networks among Elites in a Local Criminal Justice System', *Law and Society Review* **26 (4)**, 831-61.

Heritage, R. (1996), *Personal Communication*.

Home Affairs Committee (1995), *Organised Crime*, Third report, London: HMSO.

Humphreys, R.J. (1996), 'An Examination of Social Network Analysis as a Decision Support Model for Investigating Organised Crime', *Unpublished MSc Dissertation*, University of Liverpool.

Humphreys, R.J. (1997), Personal Communication, drawn from Course Notes, Northumbria Police Intelligence Operative Course 1994.

Jackson, J.L. and Herbrink, J.C.M. (1996), 'Profiling Organised Crime: The current state of the art', *Report NSCR WD 96-01 -* **June**, Leiden, Netherlands: Netherlands Institute for the Study of Criminality and Law Enforcement.

Jenkins, P. 'Speed Capital of the World: Organising the Methamphetamine Industry in Philadelphia 1970-1990', *Criminal Justice Policy Review,* **6 (1)**, 18-39.

Kleinman, M.A.R. and Smith, K.D. (1990), 'State and Legal Drug Enforcement: In search of a strategy,' In Tonry and Wilson (eds), *Drugs and Crime. Crime and Justice: A review of the research,* **13**, Chicago: University of Chicago Press.

Kock, E., Kemp, T. and Rix, B. (1996), *Disrupting the Distribution of Stolen Electrical Goods. Crime Detection and Prevention Series paper 69,* London: Home Office Police Research Group.

Lewis, R. (1994), 'Flexible Hierarchies and Dynamic Disorder', In Strang and Gossop (eds), *Heroin Addiction and Drug Policy: The British system,* Oxford: Oxford University Press.

Lingoes, J.C. (1973), SSA1, *Guttman-Lingoes Nonmetric Program Series,* Ann Arbor, Michigan: Mathesis Press.

Maguire, M. and John, T. (1995), 'Intelligence, Surveillance and Informants: Integrated approaches', *Police Research Group Crime Detection and Prevention Series,* **64**, London: HO.

Marsden, P.V. (1982), 'Power and Politics in Organisations: The social psychology of conflict, coalitions and bargaining', *Social Forces,* **60 (3)**, 932-935.

McCluskey, K. and Wardle, S. (1997), 'Networks of Robbery,' in D.V. Canter and L.J. Alison (eds), *Investigative Psychology Volume III: Criminal Networks,* Aldershot: Dartmouth.

Mizruchi, M.S. (1994), 'Social Network Analysis: Recent achievements and current controversies,' *Acta Sociologica,* **37**, 329-43.

Mokken, R.J. (1979), 'Cliques, Clubs and Clans', *Quality and Quantity,* **13**, 161-173.

Montagne, M. (1990), 'The Social Epidemiology of International Drug Trafficking: Comparison of source of supply and distribution networks', *The International Journal of the Addictions,* **25 (5)**, 557-77.

Moreno, J.L. (1934), *Who Shall Survive?,* Washington, D.C.: Nervous and Mental Disease Publishing Company.

Naylor, R.T. (1994/95), 'Loose Cannons: Covert commerce and underground finance in the modern arms black market', *Crime, Law and Social Change,* **22**, 1-57.

Passas, N. and Nelken, D. (1993), 'The Thin Line between legitimate and criminal enterprises: Subsidy fraud in the European Community', *Crime, Law and Social Change* **19 (3)**, 223-43.

Pittman, A. (1996), *Gangs*. Presentation to Community-Based Police Response: Third Research and Development Conference, Staffordshire University.

Powell, W. (1990), 'Neither Hierarchies nor Markets', in B. Shaw and L.L. Cummings (eds), *Research in Organisational Behaviour,* **12**, Greenwich: JIA Press.

Prunckun Jr., H.W. (1996), 'The Intelligence Analyst as Social Scientist: A comparison of research methods', *Police Studies* **19 (3)**, 67-80.

Reiss, A.J. (1986), 'Co-offending Influences on Criminal Careers', in A. Blumstein (ed.), *Criminal Careers and Career Criminals,* Washington, D.C.: National Academy Press.

Reiss, A.J. and Farrington, D.P. (1991), 'Advancing Knowledge about Co-offending: Results from a prospective longitudinal survey of London males', *Journal of Criminal Law and Criminology,* **82**, 360-95.

Reuter, P. and Haaga, J. (1986), *The Organisation of High-Level Drug Markets: An Exploratory Study,* Santa Monica: RAND.

Robson, C. (1993), *Real World Research: A resource for social scientists and practitioner-researchers,* Oxford: Blackwell Publishers.

Rogers, E.M. (1987), 'Progress, Problems and Prospects for Network Research: Investigating Relationships in the Age of Electronic Communication Technologies', *Social Networks,* **9**, 285-310.

Ruggiero, V. and South, N. (1995), *Eurodrugs: Drug use, markets and trafficking in Europe,* London: UCL Press.

Schneider, S.R. (1997), 'The Criminal Intelligence Function: Toward a comprehensive and normative model', *IALEIA Journal,* **9 (2)**, 1-34.

Scott, J.P. (1991), *Social Network Analysis: A handbook,* London: Sage.

Scott, J. and Hughes, M. (1980), 'Capital and Communication in Scottish Business', *Sociology,* **14 (1)**, 29-47.

Seed, P. (1987), *Applied Social Network Analysis: A set of tools for social services research and practice,* Tunbridge Wells, UK: Costello.

Shaw, B. and Cummings, L.L. (eds) (1990), *Research in Organisational Behaviour,* **12**, Greenwich: JIA Press.

Shye, S. and Elizur, D. (1994), *An Introduction to Facet Theory,* Newbury Park, CA: Sage.

Smith Jr., D.C. (1980), 'Paragons, Pariahs and Pirates: A spectrum-based theory of enterprise', *Crime and Delinquency,* **26 (3)**, 358-86.

Sparrow, M.K. (1991), 'The Application of Network Analysis to Criminal Intelligence: An assessment of the prospects', *Social Networks,* **13**, 251-74.

Stephenson, K. and Zelen, M. (1989), 'Rethinking Centrality: Methods and applications', *Social Networks,* **11**, 1-37.

Strang, J. and Gossop, M. (eds) (1994), *Heroin Addiction and Drug Policy: The British system,* Oxford: Oxford University Press.

Tonry, M. and Wilson, J.Q. (eds) (1990), *Drugs and Crime. Crime and Justice: A review of the research,* **13**, Chicago: University of Chicago Press.

Walsh, D. (1986), *Heavy Business: Commercial burglary and robbery,* London: Routledge and Kegan.

Waring, E.J. (1993), 'Co-offending in White Collar Crime: A network approach', *PhD Dissertation.* Ann Arbor, MI: UMI.

Warner, W.L. and Lunt, P.S. (1941), *The Social Life of a Modern Community,* New Haven, CN: Yale University Press. Referenced in Scott (1991).

Wasserman, S. and Faust, K. (1994), *Social Network Analysis: Methods and applications,* Cambridge: Cambridge University Press.

Wiegand, B. (1994), 'Black Money in Belize: The ethnicity and social structure of black-market crime', *Social Forces,* **73 (1),** 135-54.

Williams, P. (1993), 'The International Drug Trade: An industry analysis', *Low Intensity Conflict and Law Enforcement,* **2 (3),** 397-423.

Zhang, S.X. and Gaylord, M.S. (1996), 'Bound for the Golden Mountain: The social organisation of Chinese Alien Smuggling', *Crime, Law and Social Change,* **25 (1),** 1-16.

4 Investigating Fraud
ALAN DOIG

Fraud has increased dramatically in the past decade, as has the concern at its pervasiveness in the public and private sectors. Whether for cultural or other reasons, fraud now is a crime that is as associated with millionaires as it is with those on benefit. In value terms it represents a significant part of the cost of crime today. This chapter takes an overview of the growth of fraud, and the circumstances in which fraud may be committed. Changing attitudes to honesty, different types of fraud in the public and private sectors and who investigates it, are explored. What are the legal and other problems involved, and what have been the institutional and other means dedicated to its prevention, investigation, detection and prosecution?

Alan Doig is Professor of Public Services Management, Liverpool Business School, John Moores University where he also runs the Unit for the Study of White Collar Crime. He is author of *Corruption and Misconduct in Contemporary British Politics,* and a number of articles on corruption, fraud, conflict of interest and investigative agencies.

4 Investigating Fraud
ALAN DOIG

Introduction

Until the 1980s fraud was of little significant interest to investigators or academics. While there were cases of corruption in local government, fraud in the secondary banking sector or benefit fiddles in the public sector, they were not seen as financially or numerically significant. By 1991, however, private sector fraud was headline news (The Sunday Times, 29 December 1991). With cases such as that of Polly Peck where it was alleged that its founder, Asil Nadir, had perpetrated 'the biggest fraud in English commercial history', with some £450 million reportedly having been redirected out of the company and into a byzantine network of offshore companies. The Bank of England then closing down the Bank of Credit and Commerce International, one of whose employees said that, "this bank would bribe God"; and Robert Maxwell falling off his luxury motor cruiser to leave in his wake debts of £3 billion, looted from his pension funds to sustain his business activities. The Serious Fraud Office announced that "the sum lost through management fraud in 1991 was double that lost in household burglaries; the main victims have often been small investors and pensioners" (Independent, 26 January 1994).

In relation to the public sector, the House of Commons Committee of Public Accounts issued a damning report in 1994 on what it reported to be 'a number of serious failures in administrative and financial systems and controls within departments and other public bodies, which have led to money being wasted or otherwise improperly spent'. These failings represent "a departure from the standards of conduct, which have mainly been established during the past 140 years". (Committee of Public Accounts, Eighth Report, HC 154, 1993-94, p.v) Some months before the Committee of Public Account's report, and some months after, the Audit Commission – the public body that appoints external auditors for local government and the National Health Service – published two reports into probity in local government (Audit Commission, Protecting the Public Purse: Combating Fraud and Corruption in Local Government, HMSO, 1993) and the National Health Service (Audit Commission, Protecting the Public Purse 2: Ensuring Probity in the NHS, HMSO, 1994). Its recommendations talked of the importance of ethical environments and anti-fraud cultures in which staff awareness, procedural controls and shared information and expertise could be effective. It argued that providing the ethical environment has been "rendered more demanding and complex by numerous recent changes to the nature and operation of local government services. Many of the changes, such as the delegation of financial and management responsibilities, while contributing to improved quality of service, have increased the risks of fraud and corruption occurring..."(Audit Commission, op.cit., 1993). Fraud has now become a significant issue in terms of who perpetrates it, who investigates it, how much it costs and how it will be dealt with in the future.

Administrative, Economic and Cultural Change in the 1980s

In his 1988 Hibbert Lecture on BBC Radio 4, a City solicitor warned that, "With licensed greed creeps in the dry rot of corruption. For the value-system which tolerates the one will not be likely to resist the other, if that is necessary to achieve 'success'" (The Listener, 25 February 1988). Mrs Thatcher's tenure as Conservative Prime Minister was noticeable for the fundamental changes her governments' policies brought to the administrative, economic and cultural fabric of the country. Many commentators gave due credit for her enthusiasm for economic realism, self-discipline and the promotion of the enterprise culture. There was also concern over her failure to consolidate her successes, to accept a degree of consensus on the nature and speed of change or to balance the promotion of material gain and personal ambition with ensuring the adaptation of the means of accountability and integrity.

The economic climate engendered by the Conservative Government from 1979 on was that of promoting entrepreneurial activity, removing controls from commercial, economic and financial sectors, promoting financial gain as a reward for and an indicator of worth and hard work. The private sector cultural revolution managed to integrate corporate and individual aspirations by combining company profit margins with management commissions, bonuses, performance-related pay, and share options. The accumulation of wealth, display of material success, and the promotion of personal ambition also left a downside of management greed, acquisitiveness and pursuit of individual ambition that has sometimes been perpetrated, or colluded in, by senior management. Business scandals have regularly made the headlines, including, among others, Guinness, Lloyds of London, the Stock Exchange, Polly Peck, Barlow Clowes, Maxwell, BCCI, and Barings, reflecting the presence of a culture capable of moral ambivalence and the primacy of financial gain.

That culture is increasingly evident among private sector companies and individuals working in the public sector and very evident when private sector practices are encouraged for use in the public sector. At the same time, successive Conservative governments in local government, the NHS, the world of non-departmental public bodies and central government, have promoted the political enthusiasms for initiative, efficiency and cost control. As the impact of Rayner, FMI, Next Steps, Compulsory Competitive Tendering and market-testing continue to send ripples of the permanent administrative revolution throughout the public service, the promotion of private sector practices within organisational devolution and managerial autonomy have overridden the strong sense of public service. It is reflected in the variety of recent cases of mismanagement, misconduct, inefficiency and conflict of interest that include those involving the Wessex and West Midlands Regional Health Authorities, the Ministry of Defence, Forward Catering, Welsh Development Agency, and Lambeth, Westminster and West Wiltshire councils (Doig, 1995).

Such examples from both sectors may not all be directly concerned with fraud, but they reveal the potential for fraud. Waste, mismanagement, conflict of interest and so on; they invariably involve circumstances where the rules, procedures, checks and supervision that govern commercial or administrative behaviour are not complied with, have changed or are absent. Individuals or groups have power to make decisions, give approval, and authorise work or payments without effective monitoring or accountability. There is little risk of being caught and held responsible for one's actions, and the organisational culture or ethical environment may be conducive to the pursuit of personal financial gain, whether legally or illegally.

That such activities now attract attention, however, also owes as much to changes in attitudes in the media and in public opinion where terms such as 'fat cats' and 'sleaze' provide a focus (Mortimore, 1996). This attention is drawn to a range of stories that reflect an increasingly critical view of excessive personal financial gain by management in both public and private sectors whether those gains are achieved through acceptable, unacceptable or illegal means. Such criticism is seen in itself as significant and has been recognised by the establishment; the Nolan Committee on standards in public life and the Cadbury Committee on corporate governance (Nolan Committee, 1992; Cadbury, 1992).

What is Fraud?

Fraud does not exist as a specific criminal offence. Fraud encompasses deception - the using of 'false representations to obtain an unjust advantage or to injure the rights and interests of another'. It also includes loss, where deceiving causes the state of mind to which defrauding adds the course of action. This usually means obtaining benefit by the deception and causing another financial loss; the loss is usually treated as theft. Fraud may therefore include obtaining (and using false accounting, forged or counterfeit documents or statements to obtain) money, access to money, information, assets, evading paying taxes of various types, acting, reporting or indicating untrue state of financial affairs, and the use of false identity or statements. Financial theft or theft of assets has a long provenance, with numerous pieces of legislation covering offences. The major pieces of legislation are the Theft Acts.

To facilitate fraud there may be a 'degree of co-operation from those in the employment of the victim, as such co-operation will normally be procured by dint of bribery or other forms of corruption'. This is often referred to as 'collusive fraud' because both parties, the donor of the bribe and its recipient, will work to conceal the influence of the bribe on whatever advantage the donor was seeking. That advantage will invariably involve fraud in terms of deception and of financial loss. Bribery, or corruption, is defined within the context of two laws; a third, unusually, transfers the presumption of guilt to defendants charged under the other two Acts in relation to public sector contracts. The legislation relates to the giving or receiving of rewards, fees, advantages and so on to a person to do - or not do - something in relation to their employment that has benefited or may benefit the donor (Arlidge and Parry, 1985).

Who Studies Fraud?

What has made fraud a particular area of academic and professional study is its increasing prevalence, as well as the nature of the crime involved. The inclusion of bribery and deception implies a relationship between the parties involved. The prevalence of such offences implies at least one of those involved is an employee, owner, client or customer of the organisation. The offence is also normally part of, or related to, routine or expected procedures in which at least one or more of those involved has a legitimate (or apparently legitimate) relationship with or in the organisation. Furthermore they have the power or authority to make appropriate decisions that may benefit, legally or otherwise, consciously or not, the other party or parties.

Fraud is thus sometimes termed 'white collar' crime or economic crime to reflect the occupational or work-place-based context, or the class status of those involved. These offences may reflect the non-violent, undramatic and lack of immediate or direct personal loss with which the offences are sometimes (erroneously) linked. Accordingly, although contemporary political science and public administration literature is remarkably sparse on the issue of public sector fraud and corruption. Invariably they comprise of case studies or manuals (Jones, Chapman and Hall, 1993 and Doig, 1984), however there has been a growing literature from investigative and financial journalists (Hodgson, 1986; Jennings, Lashmar and Simson, 1991; Mantle, 1992; Lever, 1992; Gunn, 1992). Research undertaken by sociologists and criminologists who have a disciplinary framework within which to focus, includes the following examples; organisational culture and workplace crime (Mars, 1982 and Ditton, 1977) patterns of private sector fraud (Leigh, 1982; Clarke, 1986; Levi, 1987; Clarke, 1990; Croall, 1992) benefit and tax fraud (Cook, 1989) specific types of industry fraud (Levi, 1981; Ashe and Counsell, 1990; Levi, Bissell, Richardson, 1991; Clarke, Hall 1991).

How Long Has Fraud Existed?

Fraud is not new; theft of property, or obtaining by deception or forgery, by whatever means has been the subject of the criminal law for centuries while business fraud has been a noteworthy feature of the development of the industrial state (Robb, 1992). Corruption has been a significant issue in the past and it is noteworthy that the legislation to deal with it coincided with concerns over business or public morality at the turn of this century (Searle, 1987). Most cases in this century, however, have been treated as atypical of both private and public sector practices. Where concerns did exist, for example, were cases involving public figures. Figures such as Jeremy Thorpe, Liberal Party Leader, who was a non-executive director of a secondary bank, Labour MP John Stonehouse's spectacular failed banking venture, or significant mismanagement (as with the Crown Agents) or extensive, longstanding misconduct (the Poulson case, and the Property Services Agency). Invariably these attracted major public or parliamentary inquiries. On the surface, the use and outcome of such inquiries has been seen as evidence of official willingness to react positively to allegations of fraud or corruption and condemning the particular behaviour under investigation. Meanwhile it is seen as reaffirming the general integrity of the sectors. General sector-wide or legislative reform has not usually been an implemented outcome of official inquiries (Doig, 1996).

There was evidence of fraud as high-volume, low-cost activity in both sectors; activities such as 'fiddling' the benefit, paying in cash, 'adding' to personal insurance claims or working in the 'hidden economy' (Ditton, 1977; Henry, 1978: Henry, (ed.), 1981; and Mars, 1983). The lack of major political or financial significance, allied to cultural traditions and definitions that belied such activity as criminal, meant there was little attempt to quantify the problem and little official concern evinced at its presence. Consequently little work, apart from research into the black economy and evasion of tax (Pyle, 1989; Smith, 1986) has been done on the total value of fraud.

What is the Cost of Fraud?

The 1980s have been notable for the perception that not only has the value of fraud risen rapidly, but also that what was once an activity defined by class and culture was becoming pervasive throughout society and found regularly at all levels in both public and private sectors. According to the British Retail Consortium who surveyed 54,000 shops and stores in January 1994, fraud by employees and customers comprised some £21.7 million. In 1994 accountants KPMG were reporting frauds and investment frauds involving £254 million (running at twice the 1991 levels). In 1994 the Serious Fraud Office was dealing with 48 cases with a total value of over £5 billion. In 1995 the Association of British Insurers suggested that insurance companies were dealing with over £250 million in fraudulent claims annually (most in relation to motor and household insurance). In the same year, the Credit Industry Fraud Avoidance System which co-ordinates organisations with financial services, from banks to fleet car insurers, was reporting a 46% increase in notified cases, saving its members some £23 million in attempted frauds. In 1995 the National Criminal Intelligence Service, the intelligence-gathering and collating arm of the police, was reporting fraud levels of £10 billion, of which £2.5 billion related to money laundering, and £250 million to frauds against banks. In 1996 the Department of Social Security was reporting over £2 billion in benefit fraud (internally reassessed later to some £4 billion).

Neither the increase in fraud over the past decades, nor the true value of fraud can be accurately determined. What is known is that the financial value of fraud is greater than that relating to other crimes. In 1990, the police forces in England and Wales reported 123 robberies, 419 burglaries and 819 thefts over £50,000, very few of which would have been significantly over that amount. The 168 current investigations by the West Yorkshire Fraud Squad in 1991 involved an average loss of £509,174 per case (Levi, 1993). What is of more importance are the priorities for policing crime. While not being as great a financial significance, crime against the person or personal property is seen as more important. For example, auto crime costs £775 million but involves some 3.8 million offences, while the average loss from domestic burglaries is over £1000 but involves over half a million households (Doig, 1995).

What Types of Fraud Are Committed And Who Commits Them?

The 1985 British Social Attitudes report makes it clear that the public makes distinctions between the legality and the acceptability of certain types of behaviour; 'fiddling' is still very much generally accepted. Such behaviour is predicated on perceptions of right and wrong of fairness and acceptability. Such perceptions are influenced by custom, practice, class, colleagues, who does what with whom, and why. Variations of perceptions noted by the survey 'appeared greatest where the situations were complicated by questions of motive and where the circumstances were fairly distant from most people's experiences'. In those cases, people seemed to fall back on the norms of their social group, generation, or personal philosophy. Class, age and religion, for instance, came into play most powerfully. On the other hand, where laws or rules are known to be at odds with common practice, as in the case of tipping dustmen or evading VAT, people in all subgroups tended to come down in favour of practice. They did not judge breaches of the rules very harshly (Johnston and Wood, 1995). A 1994 survey by Research Surveys of Great Britain found from its 1,022 interviews that 'fiddling' social security payments was acceptable because need rather than greed appeared to be the cause (The Sunday Times, 10 April 1994). Meanwhile, 'fiddling' income tax is determined by what individuals determine is 'fair' and helps wrap up the justification in terms of personal contacts. A self-employed plumber explained,

> People tell their friends about us. There has to be a personal connection so we can trust people to pay up, cash in hand. I mean proper cash, money, and notes - not a cheque or credit card or anything, nothing that goes near a bank...Who am I cheating? No one. The taxman, what's he ever done for me? I pay enough on the jobs I declare. I pay the rates, the tax on the car, all that stuff. My kids never have free school meals or anything. Because I do this and make that extra cut I can pay my way.

> (Independent on Sunday, 27 March 1994)

It is interesting that a similar survey in 1995 by Moneywise Magazine reported that the younger the person, the lower the ethical standards, with one commentator warning of "a worsening trend with fewer and fewer sources of guidance and standards for young people to follow" (Moneywise, April 1995.)

Above the 'fiddling', and what is seen as a shift in attitudes among the professional and middle classes, comes the larger and more sophisticated fraud. In April 1994, nearly a score of company directors, lawyers, bank and building society officials and others were arrested in a £1 billion mortgage fraud that involved multiple loans, inflated valuations and bogus sales. It was estimated that banks and building societies might have lost up to £100 million. Amounts defrauded in the public sector are as equally large. This is illustrated by the senior Ministry of Defence official convicted of receiving millions of pounds in bribes from contractors, while a senior Metropolitan police accountant used the millions of pounds he defrauded from the informant's fund to set himself up as a laird in Scotland.

These, however, are not isolated incidences. In 1994 the Audit Commission's report on probity in the National Health Service noted that the total population of three London boroughs was 25% less than the number registered on the relevant GP practice lists. It was suggested, this may have created a 'smokescreen for fraudulent activity' (Audit Commission, op cit., 1994). Meanwhile, its 1996 report noted that prescription fraud by GPs and pharmacists, as well as the public, had risen an estimated £45 million (Audit Commission, 1996). In 1995, a MORI survey suggested that 34% of employee fraud within Britain's top 1,000 companies was carried out by middle management (Guardian, 5 June 1995).

Such people may become involved with fraud because of the recession, fear of job loss, company reorganisation that removes supervisory controls, and change in organisational culture. This adds to those who are the 'straightforward, opportunist crooks'.

> Among this group are collectors for bogus charities, who strike like burglars when they think they can get away with it; or those in business who delude themselves as well as their victims...who rob because their own, usually ludicrous, sense of self-importance has convinced them that the rules need not fetter their genius. Often they genuinely believe they are doing the best for their shareholders or employees. Often too, they receive fawning praise from politicians, newspapers, bankers and lawyers who hail them as visionary entrepreneurs.
>
> (CQ, November 1992).

One interesting feature of analysing fraud cases is that there is no standard profile of a fraudster; indeed, it is as much as the circumstances and the motivation that leads to the fraud as much as the type of person, who commits fraud. Examples include:

(1986)
The power station supervisor who received over £300,000 in bribes and gifts during a rebuilding programme took the money in the first instance to set up a factory to ensure income for his handicapped son but later used it to fund a lavish lifestyle.

(1989)
Two junior cashiers in a High Street bank were sentenced to 12 months detention in a young offenders institution for transferring nearly £1 million through the bank's computer; the judge noted that 'the general chat within the bank seems to be how easy it is to defraud that bank'. The bank's personnel head later noted that 'increasing numbers of young bank staff were being caught 'with their fingers in the till', including taking cash from the till, suppressing cheques and making unauthorised transfers for personal gain; some 150 had been dismissed. A spokeswoman for the British Bankers Association suggested that "The problem seems to be that young people have higher material expectations nowadays".

(1991)
The son of a former chaplain to the Queen used his 'impeccable social contacts' and 'considerable charm' to persuade family, friends and acquaintances to give him over £3 million ("he made it all sound so wonderful I couldn't wait to take part in it" said one). He assured up to 100% return on an offshore investment fund, which he then spent on horse betting and an extravagant lifestyle before receiving a four-year jail sentence.

(1993)
A businessman was sentenced to 4 years' imprisonment after pleading guilty to 8 charges of fraudulently trading and evading VAT and import duty. His company bought and sold expensive toys - winning for its owner a Queen's Award for Industry and TV appearances. It collapsed in 1991 with debts of £15 million after loans were raised from banks on the basis of false documents and non-existent sales. These loans were intended as advances to cover the 'period' between sales and payments. They were spent on luxury cars, a Madison Avenue gallery and a jet-set lifestyle because, said his counsel, his "Primary motive was not financial gain. It was to be at the centre of the antique toy market. It gave him great respectability and a persona".

(1996)
A vicar who stole £81,000 from a national charity by asking for funding for youth projects but 'frittered' it away on conspicuous expenditure, including personal debts.

(1996)
A junior Inland Revenue official who defrauded the Inland Revenue of £3,000 by falsifying friends' tax returns in a pub where he was paid in free drinks.

Motivation also takes many forms. The owner of an Old Peoples' home which went bankrupt but who was allowed to remain as its manager went to prison for a £60,000 PAYE fraud after she was found to be paying cash-in-hand over a certain rate to qualified nurses working part-time. She argued she had not benefited personally (her sentence was halved by the Court of Appeal as "an act of mercy"). A petition was well-subscribed to in her town because it was, said media reports at the time, a place which could not "understand how one of its own, doing the sort of things considered commonplace, could have been mistaken for a criminal". In another case, a young woman who resented the lack of rewards in her life for caring for her younger siblings while both parents worked, turned to shoplifting. Her other activities included credit card fraud, and using a false identity. With her "comfortable appearance and homely charm" she could lie with credibility and skill. Fraud was "some sort of kick where prison held no more threat than terminal boredom". At the other end of the scale, the Chief Executive of an investment trust found himself trapped in the middle of a take-over by the late 1980s stock market crash. He was able to siphon off, conceal, and lose some £13 million of the trust fund's money. He was able to falsely maintain its share price to continue the take-over because he 'had immense responsibility and absolute power...the normal executive functions had started to break down and the company was run more and more as an autocracy'.

Another type of fraud, arson fraud, exists as a response to circumstances, but from two very different perspectives. Financial records may show that arson could be a response to imminent financial collapse. On the other hand, they may not because, while the company was still financially sound, the owner may have been aware of the 'loss of a crucial trader or the withdrawal of a trading partner which, at the time of the fire, had not yet impacted on the business'. The owner may thus be taking a commercial decision on the future, less because of 'imminent or actual financial decline', than because:

The insured may reach a judgement that the business has gone as far as it can and wish to cash it in. He may know that there is no ready market for it, or may recognise that further progress is dependent upon new premises, modern equipment, or capital. He may be intent on a quantum fraud on stock and substitute low-grade stock in the premises for premium grade before setting the fire. Overall he may be motivated by a simple calculation of financial gain, rather than financial distress.

(Clarke, 1996)

Similarly, the circumstances and the permutation of frauds are endless. Any activity where some benefit is available, where the opportunity and incentive is present and the risk of discovery perceived as low, then the potential for a fraud exists. Examples of types of fraud include:

- *Benefit Fraud*: most frauds involve the deliberate misrepresentation by claimants of their financial position on claiming, or any subsequent change to that position. This is usually related to undeclared capital, to working over a specific number of hours, to failing to declare a partner or spouse working and to concealed cohabitation, including where the spouse or partner is claiming benefit from another address.

- *Mortgage fraud*: may involve the use of collusive solicitors, surveyors and estate agents. These are used to arrange multiple mortgages on properties, mortgages on non-existent properties, and to overvalue properties. The likely returns are much greater on commercial properties and were much greater during the late 1980s property boom (when the quick turnaround and repayment of the mortgage concealed signs of fraud).

- *Common agricultural policy fraud*: may include several tactics such as: d*iversion of goods* to secure refunds from specific countries; *misleading descriptions* of a product to gain a higher refund; *evasion* of customs and smuggling; *ghosting* (fake documents, non-existent goods); and the *substitution* of goods (importing cheap goods to store or claim as other goods).

- *Long firm fraud*: may include the obtaining of rent-free or cheap premises, ordering high-value, quick-disposal goods (such as wines, spirits or cigarettes), paying promptly and steadily increasing the volume of goods to be ordered. The selling of goods via pubs, clubs or car boot sales or street markets, securing a 28-day credit period from suppliers and then defaulting on payment for the last and most valuable orders after sale.

- *Asset stripping*: In 1994, three men were sent to prison for a wine store theft. They purchased an established firm where customers paid for upmarket wine to be stored until it was ready to use. It was stored in bonded warehouses to postpone the payment of duty, which was likely to happen for numbers of years. They then looted the stock - valued at around £2 million, and set up a dummy company to which the subsidiary firm that dealt with storage would be sold. The new but fictitious owner of this company could then be blamed for the losses.

- *Sting*: In 1990, an African barrister persuaded two businessmen to part with $150,000 to charter the tanker to transport a cargo of oil, a gift by a President to a loyal army officer, using apparently genuine documents and sending a telex from the oil tanker, to Rotterdam. On their behalf the barrister was also making arrangements to sell the oil in advance of arrival, with the three agreeing splitting the profits. Investigated by the International Maritime Bureau - the tanker and cargo were genuine but both belonged to an oil company not party to the fraud - the deal was shown to be bogus. This sort of offer was not unusual and driven, as IMB's director put it, by the desire to make money, 'about three or four people phone us every week asking whether the African crude oil they have been offered is genuine. Even when we have told them it is a con; many are very reluctant to pull out'.

Who Investigates Fraud?

There are approximately 125,000 police officers in 43 forces in England and Wales; of these some 800 are members of dedicated fraud squads which carry out inquiries into allegations of fraud and, occasionally, corruption, in the public and private sectors. The police are only one organisation (and not in any case a national organisation) in a landscape with:

> A mixture of police forces, regulatory bodies, governmental and quasi-governmental agencies, involved in policing and law enforcement duties of one sort or another. Such bodies may operate in the public sphere, in the private sphere, or across both ... rigorous classification is probably an impossible task since the functions, practices, jurisdictions, and legal powers of the various bodies overlap in potentially complex ways.

(Johnston, 1992).

Within the UK public sector there are a number of organisations, or dedicated units within organisations, with preventative, detection, investigation and prosecution functions. These organisations are in whole or part, related to fraud or corruption in relation to both public and private sectors, and sometimes with dedicated powers. They include the Benefits Agency; Charity Commissioners; Customs and Excise; Department of Trade and Industry Investigation Division - Companies Investigation Branch and Investigation Section; Export Credit Guarantee Department; Inland Revenue; Intervention Board; Ministry of Agriculture, Food and Fisheries Investigation Branch; and the Post Office Investigation Department.

In relation to the private sector, the investigation of fraud either falls within the remit of designated public sector agencies such as the Department of Trade, or on in-house investigative units which are part of private sector companies. Additionally, the financial services revolution of the 1980s introduced a number of regulatory agencies (SRO), established by the 1986 Financial Services Act, and intended to reduce the risk of fraud by controlling entry to the market. The Act was a consequence of the Gower report, a review of investor protection designed to protect the public from fraudulent or incompetent investment advice. In its reform of the City Conservative Governments from 1979 wanted on the one hand a less scandal-ridden Stock Exchange to attract wider financial participation. On the other hand they wanted an end to the cosy restrictive practices which were also seen, in part, as a cause of the scandals. Rather than follow the US model of a specific regulatory agency with criminal and prosecution powers, the Government accepted an approach of regulation and self-policing. This was intended to maintain the traditional approach by being neither intrusive nor instrumental. The 1986 Financial Services Act was to take responsibility away from the public sector and hand it to SROs under the responsibility of the Savings and Investment Board (SIB). In the hand over period, where the DTI retained a residual regulatory interest, one interesting case was that of Barlow Clowes. Slowness to fall into line with regulatory procedures contrasted sharply with the speed the company transferred money abroad, causing one official to comment: "I have no concrete reason to worry, although one naturally tends to look askance at business controlled from Gibraltar and harbour unworthy thoughts about the real motives in moving there".

In 1987, Clowes' application to join the Stock Exchange and with it some financial irregularities, had attracted the attention of the Greater Manchester Police. This triggered investigations into his activities - "We find all this rather worrying", wrote the Bank of England to the DTI. Months of haranguing was spent by officials from DTI, SIB, the Treasury and other regulators on what to do (and who was to do it). When SIB agreed to petition for winding-up Clowes' operations, Clowes' collapse attracted the attention of journalists who discovered with embarrassing ease the use of the overseas funds for a lavish lifestyle and to pay the (unachievable) premium rates for existing investors and for attracting new investors.

SROs have the ability to charge membership fees, revoke licences and consider claims for compensation but are not police forces; as Fimbra's Chief Executive said in 1990. "We are supposed to vet people to see that they are, in basic terms, honest, solvent, and competent." Approval that a firm has passed through 'stringent vetting checks' is no guarantee that they may later turn to fraud. Dunsdale Securities collapsed in 1990 after being suspended by Fimbra, who had given its highest category of approval in 1988. This followed legal action by investors who had experienced problems getting their money out, an unsuccessful gamble in Reuter's shares and the calling-in of a large debt by the Swiss Bank Corporation. Some £17 million (later revised to £8.1 million) was owed to over 200 clients; many of these were friends and acquaintances of owner Robert Miller. At his 1991 trial, he admitted to 19 charges of deception, forgery, publishing false information and failing to keep accounting records. Much of the money went to fund his extravagant lifestyle. Dunsdale accounts turned out to be "neat but meaningless" and by its own admission, Fimbra claimed that "It is very difficult to see how any regulator can discover information that is being hidden from it".

Where criminal offences are considered, most organisations in both sectors use the police. The size of fraud squads varies from a complement of four up to 150; and with size comes functional specialisation. In larger forces, there are specific teams who may deal with credit card fraud, mortgage fraud or public sector corruption. Most police forces employ civilian staff and rely heavily for IT on document control case management and prosecution preparation. Training for fraud squads is usually through one of three programmes working to a national standard and, until the recent policy on tenure, a substantial number of years on-the-job learning. In the wake of reorganisation, there has been an emphasis on devolved budgets and point-of-delivery policing. The value and relevance of fraud squads to core policing objectives have either seen some fraud squads diminish in size or become amalgamated into larger squads. For example, drugs and serious crime squads have merged with fraud squads as major crime squads, with the former two keen to take over Financial Investigations Units in order to pursue confiscation of the proceeds of crime. Other fraud squads have developed a higher profile with business plans, case strategies and service level agreements with other parts of their force on the types of cases, in terms of seriousness and value, that each will handle. Most of the larger squads have funds for and access to accountants, and usually work closely with lawyers from the Crown Prosecution Service's Central Casework with fraud experience. On particular cases they may also be asked to undertake fraud investigations by the Serious Fraud Office (SFO).

The SFO was set up to pursue more effectively and quickly large, complex fraud. There were inherent problems before the SFO, including; the delay in lengthy police investigations, lengthy reports and further delays in assessing the possibility of conviction, followed by further inquiries required by the lawyers. This was before a case for the prosecution was even ready. Allied to the cost of hiring accountants (whose use was thus usually left as late as possible), this meant fraud investigation was expensive, slow and inefficient. The first development was a Fraud Investigation Group (FIG) - which included police, DPP lawyers and seconded DTI accountants. Their purpose was to focus solely on fraud cases and to ensure constant interaction between the three groups. Its success, primarily in terms of the agreement to co-operate, was less than perfect because the police were still not returning the statements and evidence on a fast enough basis to allow for a full overall ongoing review. It was on this review that the lawyers could decide whether or not to prosecute.

The Roskill Committee (Roskill, 1986) approved the development, but proposed: (i) that the concept of FIG should be superseded by a physical grouping and (ii) that grouping should have specific powers. This would be similar to those of the DTI under the Companies Act, including the power to require statements and the handing-over of documents in relation to fraud investigations. The Conservative Government quickly endorsed the proposals, incorporating them into the 1987 Criminal Justice Act to establish the Serious Fraud Office (SFO) to introduce a novel, integrated approach to the handling of complex issues using several different disciplines. Purposes of the SFO would include economic benefit of its operations to generate greater confidence in the City of London, a reduction in crime to the extent that the SFO deters fraud, and an increased efficiency in the criminal justice system. Lawyers and accountants staffed by the SFO would be recruited from major city firms and other government agencies. The SFO works on lawyer-led teams working with police forces to carry out investigations. It picks its cases on three core criteria:

- The facts and/or the law are of great complexity.

- The money lost or in serious danger of being lost exceeds £5 million.

- Great public interest and concern.

The SFO has specific powers under the 1987 Act, particularly the extensive Section 2 powers by which it can require a person to answer questions and provide information believed relevant to an investigation. Such a power is particularly useful in obtaining confidential financial information, but often attracts strong criticism from those who feel the right to silence has been abolished. Other powers include the criminal offence of 'failing' to comply with an SFO requirement, to mislead or deceive SFO, and to conceal or destroy documents relevant to an inquiry. FIG remained until recently as a group within the Crown Prosecution Service; lawyers with fraud experience now work within Central Casework (Fraud). The average prosecution success rate between 1990 and 1995 was 64% for the

SFO and 73% for the CPS on fraud cases. Current case load is, for the SFO, about 75 at over £1 million but usually over £5 million lost or at risk; for the CPS Central Casework the caseload is about 350 at a minimum of £750,000 a case.

The police however, are not the only investigators of fraud. Fraud has never been seen as one of the major police priorities. These are determined by the political agenda where public order and crimes against the person and their property predominate. It is, in part, because many organisational victims of fraud do not publicise the incidence of fraud. This may be to protect their public reputation, protect the public's confidence in their activities, and in part because of a concern that a rigorous prosecution approach may damage customer service and may threaten market-share (Les Johnston, op.cit.). Additionally, police intervention may be seen as disruptive to staff relationships and ongoing organisational functions as well as potentially embarrassing in terms of publicity and commercial credibility. At the same time fraud is not high on the politicians' and public's agenda because:

> Public order is not violated in business offences as it is in conventional crime. There is normally no violence to persons or property, and the conduct in question takes place in private not public places. It occurs between people with a pre-existing and usually continuing relationship. The privacy and complexity of fraud makes it difficult to investigate the pre-existing relationships between victim and offender. The likelihood of claim and counter-claim as to who occupies which role, and in many cases the police may take the view that their victims have only themselves to blame for their lack of caution. It may also be necessary to have the resources to remedy the situation by civil action.
> (Clarke, 1990)

With fraud not high on the agenda, resources haven't always been forthcoming:

> The cuts in resources that the Metropolitan Police Company Fraud Department experienced in the 1980s forced them to prioritise cases more sharply on the basis of their estimated likelihood to yield a result. This may not have affected the numbers of recorded frauds or the clear-up rate but, what the policy *has* done is to shift the economic burden of crime investigation onto victims, in particular corporate victims, and has thus transferred public law back into the sphere of private law.
> (Levi, 1987)

Furthermore, reduced resources devoted to fraud investigation reduce the cost of taking cases to court for complex and costly trials. In the 1990 trial of those involved in the collapse of a Derbyshire theme park, the inquiry involved 402 witnesses, 531 statements, and two courtrooms knocked into one. Each juror was equipped with a computer screen for the 14,000 pages of exhibits. There were six defendants, 27 charges of fraud, theft and obtaining money by deception. There were five convictions (with sentences from four years to a fine) and a cost to the Derbyshire police of £1.8 million (Observer, 9 February 1992).

Such considerations have long had important implications for encouraging public sector agencies to take responsibility for investigating fraud. Research for the 1980 Royal Commission on Criminal Procedure, for example, reported that the Department of Social Security (DSS) encountered difficulties in obtaining the 'co-operation and assistance' of the police. It was reported that they gave other areas higher priority and, in one particular case, informed the DSS and other agencies of its wish to 'limit its activities to the maintenance of law and order, and crime against private individuals' (Lidstone, Hogg, Sutcliffe, 1980). This not only affects who investigates fraud, but also how they investigate fraud, and to what end.

Public sector agencies, which adopt the criminal and prosecutions approach to fraud and corruption, tend to reflect the police in their methods. Indeed, such organisations tend to recruit former police officers because they are fully trained in investigative techniques and the gathering and collation of evidence, both of which require a methodological approach to paperwork, interviewing and analysis to demonstrate both the likely offence and the intention. Similarly, where law and where compliance or enforcement is necessary so this pattern of recruitment also occurs. The Gaming Board has an inspectorate staffed largely by former police officers with CID experience who receive a two month intensive course on the law relevant to gaming, casino games, casino and bingo accountancy practices and basic gaming machine technology. They then undertake detailed enquiries to satisfy the background of owners and employees and the conduct of gaming by visits, interviews, checking of references, enquiries through Companies House and other official sources, both at home and abroad. A MAFF Investigation Branch officer will:

> Study the legislation involved and the points needed to prove an offence to a Court of Law. She or he will then try to identify and locate witnesses, and obtain

statements and documentary evidence where possible, Finally he will interview the suspect within the strict conditions of the Police and Criminal Evidence Act. This may not be as simple as it sounds. Some witnesses do not wish to be seen. Some go missing or may be in another country. They may not even speak English. Documentary evidence could be either concealed or destroyed, or is so vast that it requires a three-ton van to remove it to headquarters. Then it may take three officers 12 months to sift in order to sort the false documents from the truthful ones. Finally, when interviewed, the suspect may choose to exercise their rights by remaining silent. The facts of the case on their own may be clear-cut, but other considerations such as the age, infirmity, incompetence or ignorance of the culprit, the matters of 'public interest' will be taken into account and can affect the outcome.

(MAFF Bulletin, March 1992)

Other organisations have developed their roles in the detection and investigation of fraud in terms of their primary functions, traditions, and resources. These have in turn influenced the nature and extent of their emphasis on prevention, detection and prosecution. All of which are influenced contemporaneously by the availability of alternative sanctions, resources to investigate offences, difficulty of proof, political pressure, staff attitudes, perception of criminality of the offence and relations with the police. The Department of Social Security, for example, was aware of the conflict between, 'on the one hand, the need to deter benefit fraud through conscientious investigation and prosecution of offences and, on the other, the maintenance of the public's confidence in it as a welfare agency'. Thus the Benefits Agency - the Department's Next Steps Agency, which actually pays the benefits - has significant anti-fraud staffing levels of nearly 4000 officials. These were focused on client (sector) fraud or on organised or trans-sector fraud. Reasons for the level of staffing concerned the longstanding recognition of the existence of benefit fraud. The volume of cases and the detail of the benefits system have made the police reluctant to take on claimant-fraud investigations. There is the awareness that prosecution is only cost-effective for persistent offenders or is used as a deterrent. Most cases of fraud are likely to be dealt with in terms of sign-offs or procedures for recovery of overpayments.

Other organisations also view prosecution as only one core defence against fraud given the prime function of the organisation concerned. The Inland Revenue, as a revenue-raising agency, seeks to maximise the returns to the Treasury. It uses the 'Hansard' policy to offer organisations under enquiry a chance to make full disclosure of their true financial affairs followed by financial restitution, including financial penalties (which can also be imposed for negligent or fraudulent activity). Occasionally the Inland Revenue will have recourse to the courts but usually only in circumstances where there are those involved in serious cases of fraudulent behaviour, of false invoicing, or involving professionals (such as accountants) and where there may be a deterrence effect through prosecution and subsequent publicity. Another area where protection of assets and the interests of those involved may influence the structure and focus of investigation is in relation to charities. The Charity Commissioners are responsible for about 170,000 charities that turn over some £17 billion a year with a staff of 170,000 involved in everything from high-profile Telethons to flag-days. Since most charities are established to do good and invariably rely on part-time or volunteer help to operate, their tax status and their resources are particularly attractive to misuse or misappropriation. This has led to the establishment of three Charity Commissioners Monitoring and Investigation Offices to monitor charities and identify risk areas, using legal and financial 'trigger' lists to assess both. Given the public interest nature of charities, the impact of publicity and the effect on beneficiaries, the investigation - and its outcome - must be thoroughly thought-out. When a potential case is uncovered, whether from monitoring or by public allegation, the case would be vetted by an investigator. It is then authorised by a line manager (in terms of cost-effectiveness) for investigation (or not), followed by an internal review (legal and financial). Then a fact-finding process (internal and external) is initiated from those with a reasonable knowledge of case, and resubmitted to the line manager (within an average of six months) for reassessment. It is then decided whether to close the inquiry or, if abuse is found, to determine any further course of action. The typical types of abuse, and action, are:

- Lack of management control (leakage of cash often coming from the lack of experience and judgement of those involved) which might result in guidance from the Commission to trustees, and the possible replacement of trustees.

- Misapplication of funds (a 'controlled' charity to benefit an individual) which restitution and replacement of trustees or possible prosecution would follow.

- Criminal acts (largely street fundraising by bogus collectors which is low cost but high volume) which requires close co-operation with councils and police for possible prosecution.

Conclusion: The Future for Fraud Investigation

The balance between regulation, prosecution and alternative sanctions have raised a number of issues about investigating fraud today. The private sector combination of regulation with SROs and the taskforce-approach of the SFO to deal with financial service fraud have come in for much criticism. SROs have been described as having very unique characteristics. They have limited powers of inquiry and control, no prosecution authority, and complex rules that sought not only to prevent abuse but also to encourage 'best practice'. They have also been described as having low salaried regulators; the presence of those overly predisposed to the activities of those they were supposed to regulate, and the low level of frequency in the detection of frauds. At the same time, the robust taskforce approach adopted by the SFO had won convictions but it appeared to some that it was part of the 'effective framework' failure in terms of failing to tackle rising private sector fraud, particularly in the financial services.

> It is only the success of the regulatory machinery as a whole, of which criminal prosecution only forms a small element in the case of fraud, that keeps offences down to a level that can be processed with a degree of efficiency. If wrongdoings ... mount beyond a certain level, many within the fields affected will become cynical, encouraged to sharp practice themselves to compete, and unwilling to give evidence against wrongdoers, still less blow the whistle. Only in an environment where high standards prevail will practitioners feel the sense of indignation and personal security essential to denounce the wrongdoer promptly and accurately. In time, high ethical standards cannot be encouraged except by measures to ensure competence, disclosure of dealings, and inspections to enforce compliance with public standards and procedures.

(Clarke, p169)

Of particular note has been the lack of judicial condemnation at the end of the criminal route, especially in terms of high-profile trials and sentencing. The collapse of the Guinness II and III trials (involving secondary players in the purchase of Guinness and Distillers shares) raised several issues. Strong judicial comments on the length and complexity of major fraud trials and concern over the SFO's capabilities as well as the suitability of the criminal route to justice were mentioned. There were also wider questions of both value for money and a perceived equality of punishment. In particular, two high profile cases focused attention on the latter. In 1993 Terry Ramsden, owner of Glen International, was awarded a two-year suspended sentence after pleading guilty to four charges of fraud, involving £90 million. He persuaded four finance houses to invest in his firm, knowing that he would not be able to repay them. He had built up his business into a major international trading house doing business worth over £3 billion but took the loans (out of criminal financial recklessness not dishonesty, said SFO) as gambling and company debts mounted and company finances fell into chaos. The judge told Ramsden that he had built up "an honest, impressive and phenomenally successful business and that is something of which you can justifiably be very proud. Your previous good character stands you in good stead now. Normally offences of this sort warrant a sentence of immediate imprisonment but justice can be done in this case with a period of imprisonment suspended". Roger Levitt was once a Marks and Spencers trainee manager who turned to insurance selling with such success that, by 1987, he ran the largest independent company in the financial services field in the UK, managing investments, and selling mortgages and life insurance, with an equally lavish lifestyle. The group of companies was valued at £150 million by the end of the 1980s. By 1990, the company had collapsed with debts of £34 million as a result of overexpansion, poor management and high costs. These were first covered up by faking results and accounts and by the secret injections of funds of investors' money. The SFO conducted the investigation at a cost of £1.4 million. Originally intending to bring 42 charges, the SFO focused on one charge of fraudulent trading with further charges scheduled for a subsequent trial. Levitt denied fraudulently injecting funds into the company and producing false accounts but unexpectedly soon after what had been expected to be a long case admitted a charge of fraudulently misleading Fimbra that had uncovered the company's indebtedness. The SFO accepted the admission and the trial ended. Levitt's sentence was 180 hours' community service and banned from acting as a company director for seven years. The judge said that Levitt had not been the originator of the deception, but had the support of 'very distinguished businessmen' who had also been 'a very substantial benefactor to a whole series of institutions'.

Limited police resources, and the concern over the prosecution route has raised questions about the best way to deal with fraud. From 1988, when computer terminals were first used to allow jurors to examine evidence, judges including Judge Rant warned, "If documents accumulate and evidence piles up, a trial judge may have to say that the case must come to the end simply because the task of deciding it is beyond the grasp of any jury however intelligent and conscientious they may be". One proposal considered by Roskill was the use of judge advised by expert lay members rather than juries, a proposal rejected by government partly because they then felt that cases were not excessively complicated and that there may be a perception that civil liberties were being infringed.

There are, however, a number of developments relating to the prevention, detection, investigation and prosecution of fraud which seek to address the current limitations against what is seen as a major area of criminal activity at all levels. The first is an emphasis on prevention. Unless there are significant prosecutions or savings to be made from investigations, then reactive policing is giving way to proactive measures designed to prevent fraud taking place. However, to minimise cost (since by its nature prevention is difficult to quantify), such measures are being integrated into standard operating procedures or material. Organisations are paying close attention to their 'instruments of payments' (IOP) - cheque books, credit cards, giro cheques and order books - to discourage forgery and counterfciting as well as the misuse of stolen genuine items. Special paper and inks, ultra-violet-active inks, photos, watermarks, barcodes, and so on, as well as physical checks - such as signature patterns, fingerprints and other forms of biotechnology - are being considered to attempt to make the task more difficult, both to copy and to use.

Verification systems are being introduced to check the trustworthiness of the applicant or the veracity of the information on the application form. In relation to high-volume, low profile fraud such as household insurance, benefits, mortgages and credit cards, much more effort is focused on the exploitation of the latest technology. It is seen as an aid to dissuade fraud from taking place. Data matching and new information are used either to prevent fraud or to refine potentially fraudulent cases for investigation. On credit cards, for example, banks have computerised intelligence systems that look for sudden changes in patterns of expenditure. High-volume, standardised activity is especially attractive to the growth in data matching and data mining. This technology uses software and hardware to conduct high-speed checks on creditworthiness against existing public domain information. It may also compare and contrast application information against other applications, using a series of indicators that test the likely veracity of the application. This information provided may show, for example, how many housing benefits applications could come from one address, or why does a loan applicant have a telephone number that does not relate geographically to the postcode. Data matching and data mining become even more effective when done on an industry basis. Mortgage applications are run by most lenders through software packages which screen applications according to a series of risk indicators determined by previous patterns of fraud (and updated with new cases) to allow lenders to identify those that may require further checking. Such industry co-operation is increasing, with suspicious information now held on registers - including the motor insurance anti-fraud and theft register which logs stolen and written-off vehicles - that record information on attempted frauds which are shared among industry organisations.

If fraud has been committed then there is now an increasing recourse to civil law for the restitution of property and assets where the burden of proof is less demanding. There are legal powers available to non-police organisations to assist in the collection of evidence and prevent the disappearance of the funds or assets. These include Mareva injunctions - which allow plaintiffs unilaterally to freeze a potential defendant's assets - and Anton Pillar orders, which allow plaintiffs to enter a defendant's premise and search for assets and evidence. This type of work invariably involves the larger firms of solicitors and accountants who either have staff with specialist backgrounds such as police or customs experience, or call on firms of private investigators again who often have staff with similar backgrounds. The focus is on identifying assets, or evidence of criminal activity to allow their principals to initiate proceedings to reclaim assets or negotiate settlements that could avoid costly trials. Where criminal investigations are still an option, then the development of the private sector's capabilities in investigations, as well as the number of public sector organisations working on fraud and corruption, has led steadily to closer working relationships. There are those who still believe that there should be stronger demarcation boundaries in terms of criminal investigations. An unpublished, late 1980s efficiency scrutiny into one government department argued that most organisations in the private sector did not get involved in surveillance and other methods to track down those involved in defrauding their systems. They saw this as the responsibility of the police. It was considered difficult to draw up rules that were sufficiently flexible to meet the needs of each case. There were concerns that the correct interface with the police had not been achieved. The more resources that were devoted by organisations to this activity, the more likely the police were to commit less. Redrawing boundaries between what was and was not police work, appeared to be moving incorrectly away from the police to the organisations itself.

The answer is that such boundaries are being eroded for three reasons. First, fraud is still not a major police priority and resources will continue to be limited, irrespective of who else may conduct investigations, and at what level. Furthermore, the more effective organisations are in dealing with fraud so the focus on deliberate and criminally motivated fraud becomes a more attractive proposition for police criminal investigations. The promotion of industry-wide co-operation came with the 1991 Home Office Report on the Prevention of Cheque and Credit Card Fraud, led by Mike Levi. It was later noted that there was a "sufficiently large reduction in the number of preventable frauds for the police *now* to feel that time spent on investigating the remaining cases is not wasted on the undeserving".

Finally, the fact that boundaries are shifting reflects the fragmented landscape for fraud prevention, detection, investigation and prosecution by both private and public sector organisations. The lack of any permanent or central organisational framework also raises cross-organisation fraud where individuals or groups are defrauding several organisations at the same time or working across organisational or geographic boundaries. On the other hand, while there is considerable inter-agency co-operation on a case basis, moves toward unified or inter-organisational structures, as well as the matching and analysis of inter-organisational information as a more effective means to prevent or investigate fraud, are still fraught with important organisational and political issues. The current structures and arrangements may reflect an imperfect but pragmatic and incremental approach to dealing with fraud which, in the short-term, is acceptable to most organisations. External factors may, however, promote wider changes to policing crime that will have implications for this approach. There are developments toward a unified approach on crimes such as money laundering, and wider European discussions on a cross border approach to crime investigation. This would suggest that, if not a unified structure, then some more permanent or integrated means for analysis and investigation of crime, including fraud, is necessary for dealing with fraud in the next decade.

References

Arlidge, A. J. and Parry J. (1985), *Fraud*, London: Waterlow Publishers Ltd.
Ashe, M. and Counsell, L. (1990), *Insider Trading*, London: Fourmal Publishing.
Audit Commission (1993), *Protecting the Public Purse: Combating Fraud*, London: HMSO.
Audit Commission (1994), *Protecting the Public Purse 2: Ensuring Probity in the NHS*, London: HMSO.
Audit Commission (1996), *Protecting the Public Purse: Ensuring probity on the NHS - 1996* Update, London: HMSO.
Cadbury (1992), *Report of the Committee on the Financial Aspects of Corporate Governance*, London: Gee and Co.
Clarke, M. (1996), 'Fraudulent Arson: A War of Position', *Crime, Law and Social Change*, **25 (2)**, 126.
Clarke, M. (1990), *Business Crime*, Oxford: Polity Press.
Clarke, M. (1981), *Fallen Idols: Elites and the Search for the Acceptable Face of Capitalism*, London: Junction Books.
Clarke, M. (1986), *Regulating The City*, Milton Keynes: Open University Press.
Clarke, M. (1991), *Mortgage Fraud*, London: Chapman Hall.
Committee of Public Accounts, *Eighth Report, HC 154, 1993-94, pv*, London.
Cook, D. (1989), *Rich Law, Poor Law*, Milton Keynes: Open University Press.
Corruption in Local Government, (1993) London: HMSO.
CQ, November 1992.
Croall, H. (1992), *White Collar Crime*, Milton Keynes: Open University Press.
Department of Environment, (1983), *Wardale Report*, London.
Ditton, J. (1977), *Part-Time Crime: An Ethnology of Fiddling and Pilferage*, London: MacMillan.
Doig, A. (1985), 'Corruption in the Public Service; the case of the Property Services Agency', *Public Money*, **4 (4)**.
Doig, A. (1995), 'Changing Public Sector Approaches to Fraud', *Public Money and Management*, **15 (1)**.
Doig, A. (1996), 'From Salmon to Nolan: Corruption Panics in British Politics', *Journal of Law and Society*, **23 (1)**.

Doig A. (1995), 'Mixed Signals? Public Sector Change and the Proper Conduct of Public Business', *Public Administration*, 73 (Summer).

Doig, A. (1995), 'No Reason For Complacency? Organisational Change and Probity in Local Government', *Local Government Studies*, **21 (1)**.

Doig, A. (1984), *Corruption and Misconduct in Contemporary British Politics*, London: Penguin.

Fitzwalter, R. and Taylor, D. (1981), *Web of Corruption*, London: Granada.

Gillard, M. (1974), 'A Little Pot of Money', *Private Eye and Andre Deutsch*

Guardian, 5 June 1995.

Gunn, C. (1992), *Nightmare on Lime Street: Whatever Happened to Lloyd's of London*, London: Smith Gryphon Publishers.

Henry, S. (1978), *The Hidden Economy: The Context and Control of Borderline Crime*, London: Martin Robertson.

Henry, S. (1981), (ed.), *Can I Have It In Cash? A Study of Informal Institutions and Unorthodox ways of Doing Things*, Oxford: Astragal Books.

Hodgson, G. (1986), *Lloyd's of London*, London: Penguin.

Independent on Sunday, 27 March 1994.

Independent, 26 January 1994.

Jennings, A., Lashmar, P. and Simson, V. (1991), *Scotland Yard's Cocaine Connection*, London: Arrow.

Johnston, L. (1992), *The Rebirth of Private Policing*, London: Routledge. In addition to what is normally understood to be police forces there are a number of designated forces including: the Royal Parks Constabulary, Royal Botanic Gardens Constabulary, Royal Naval Regulating Branch, Royal Marines Police, Military Police, RAF Police, UK Atomic Energy Authority Constabulary, British Transport Police, various Port, Waterways, Tunnel and Airport police forces.

Johnston, M. and Wood, D. (1985), 'Right and Wrong in Public and Private Life', in Roger Jowell and Sharon Witherspoon (eds), *British Social Attitudes: The 1985 Report*, Aldershot: Gower.

Jones, P. (1993), *Combating Fraud and Corruption in the Public Sector*, London: Chapman and Hall.

Leigh, L. H. (1982), *The Control of Commercial Fraud*, London: Heinemann.

Lever, L. (1992), *The Barlow Clowes Affair*, London: Mcmillan/Channel Four.

Levi, M. (1993), The Investigation, Prosecution and Trial of Serious Fraud, *The Royal Commission on Criminal Justice Research Study No. 14*, London: HMSO.

Levi, M., Bissell, P. and Richardson, T. (1991), *The Prevention of Cheque and Credit Card Fraud*, London: Home Office.

Levi, M. (1987), *Regulating Fraud: White-Collar Crime and the Criminal Process*, London: Routledge.

Levi, M. (1981), *The Phantom Capitalist*, Aldershot: Gower.

Lidstone, K., Hogg, R. and Sutcliffe, F. (1980), 'Prosecutions by Private Individuals and non-Police Agencies', *Royal Commission on Criminal Procedure, Research Study 10*, London: HMSO.
MAFF Bulletin, March 1992.
Mantle, J. (1992), *For Whom The Bell Tolls*, London: Mandarin.
Mars, G. (1982), *Cheats at Work*, London: Counterpoint,Unwin paperbacks.
Moneywise, April 1995.
Mortimore, R. (1996). 'Politics and Public Perception', in F. F. Ridley and A. Doig, *Sleaze*, Oxford: OUP.
Nolan Committee, (1995), *Standards in Public Life*, Cm 2850, HMSO.
Observer, 9 February 1992.
Pyle, D. J. (1989), *Tax Evasion and the Black Economy*, London: Macmillan.
Report Of The Tribunal Appointed To Inquire Into Certain Issues Arising Out Of the Operations Of The Crown Agents As Financiers On Own Account In The Years 1967-74, HMSO, 1982, HCP 364.
Robb, G. (1992), *White-Collar Crime in Modern Britain: Financial Fraud and Business Morality 1845-1929*, Cambridge: University Press.
Roskill Report: *Fraud Trials Committee*, HMSO, 1986.
Searle, G. R. (1987), *Corruption in British Politics, 1895-1930*, OUP.
Smith, S. (1986), *Britain's Shadow Economy*, Oxford: Clarendon Press.
The Listener, 25 February 1988.
The Sunday Times, 10 April 1994.
The Sunday Times, 29 December 1991.
Tomkinson, M. and Gillard, M. (1980), *Nothing to Declare*, London: John Calder.

5 Rules and Roles in Terrorist Hostage Taking

MARGARET WILSON AND ALASTER SMITH

This chapter examines what happens during terrorist hostage taking incidents and explores the way that behaviour can be used as an indication of underlying psychological concepts. It is argued that people's behaviour in hostage taking incidents appears to be guided by certain predictable patterns. Hostage taking is therefore viewed as a social interaction based on a set of mutually understood rules with associated role structures. The roles and rules of hostage taking are explored and considered in the context of what happens when the rules break down. In particular, it is proposed that hostage taking can be understood in terms of the interaction between two sets of behavioural 'rules'; one which guides the 'normal' behaviour expected during hostage taking incidents, and a 'fall back' set of rules which underlie people's everyday interactions with one another.

Margaret Wilson is a lecturer in the Department of Psychology at the University of Kent at Canterbury. She has worked in a number of areas of Applied Social Psychology, and has a range of interests in Investigative and Environmental Psychology. She is well known for her work on hostage taking, particularly in the U.S. where she has lectured on the topic extensively.

Alaster Smith completed his first degree in Psychology at Aston University, after which he gained a Masters degree in Environmental Psychology at the University of Surrey. He worked as a research officer in the Safety Research Unit for two years, participating on various projects addressing the attitudes to safety in various heavy process industries. Following this he was appointed principle researcher on a project looking at behavioural variation in Trans-national terrorist hostage taking. This work was continued following relocation of the research unit to the University of Liverpool and the work on kidnapping became the topic of his forthcoming PhD thesis. Alaster now works for the Home Office Police Research Group and is principally involved in research on matters relating to traffic policing and vehicle crime.

5 Rules and Roles in Terrorist Hostage Taking

MARGARET WILSON and ALASTER SMITH

Introduction

The aim of this chapter is to examine the nature of terrorist hostage taking incidents and to describe the underlying psychological dimensions that characterise such events. Much has been written on terrorism in general and many different perspectives on the causes and processes have been outlined. Some authors see terrorism as a rational strategy chosen to further aims that cannot be achieved through other means (e.g. Crenshaw, 1990). Similarly, Ferracuti (1990) and Sprinzak (1990) discuss terrorism as an extreme form of political and ideological belief. Whilst most authors confine their views to political and sociological rhetoric there are also a small number of researchers who have tested their ideas against empirical data. Most notable amongst these are those coming from an economic and game theoretical perspective (e.g. Sandler and Scott, 1987; Lapan and Sandler, 1988; Overgaard, 1994; Atkinson et al., 1987). These authors have tested models of the transaction between the parties involved in hostage negotiations in an attempt to categorise the typical patterns of bargaining found in hostage taking incidents. Their work focuses on the demands issued and the concessions received in order to understand the likely outcomes of these negotiations.

On the other hand, there are a substantial number of authors who seek to understand terrorism in terms of the psychopathology of its participants. The work takes as its starting point the perspective that those involved in terrorist activity are likely to be different in some way to those who are not. This may be in terms of their social background (e.g. Strentz, 1988), formative experiences (e.g. Post, 1984), personality (e.g. Rothman and Lichter, 1980; Johnson and Feldman, 1992), psychodynamics (e.g. Brunet and Casoni, 1991) and general psychiatric status (e.g. Oots and Wiegele, 1985; Turco, 1987). The majority of these theorists approach the issue from a clinical perspective that draws on the implicit assumption that terrorism is an irrational act to be understood in terms of abnormal psychological processes.

This chapter takes a different approach to understanding terrorist hostage taking. Through a detailed examination of what actually happens during hostage taking incidents it aims to elaborate the relationship between tangible, readily identifiable actions and the psychological concepts that may help understand the underlying processes of terrorist hostage taking. By studying groups of specific behaviours taking place in such incidents relating to the choices made by their participants it is possible to reveal more about concepts such as motivation, planning, use of resources and negotiation processes.

The model that emerges from this analysis is based on the principle that hostage taking is a social interaction based on a set of mutually understood rules with associated role structures. Donald and Canter (1990; 1992), Donald (1993; 1995), Canter (1990) and Canter et al. (1990) have all shown that even under life threatening circumstances people follow the social rules prescribed by their role in that particular setting. People's behaviour in hostage taking incidents appears also to be guided by certain predictable patterns. Taking a social psychological framework to examining the way that hostage taking incidents operate requires a consideration of those behaviours which will contribute to an understanding of the goals and expectations of the people involved.

In summary, the current chapter examines behaviour during hostage taking incidents as an indication of underlying psychological concepts. The chapter goes on to examine the roles and rules of hostage taking and what happens when the rules break down. In particular, it proposes that hostage taking can be understood in terms of the interaction between two sets of behavioural 'rules'; one which guides the 'normal' behaviour expected during hostage taking incidents, and a 'fall back' set of rules which underlie people's everyday interactions with one another. The themes and ideas developed in this chapter are derived from the authors' own empirical work in the area having conducted detailed study of the behaviour of hostage takers in three types of incident; kidnapping, siege and hijacking incidents (Wilson et al., 1995). The information drawn upon in the examples provided comes from a compilation of descriptions of hostage taking incidents put together from a variety of published sources. Central to these were the descriptive works of Mickolus and his colleagues (Mickolus, 1980, 1993; Mickolus et al., 1989).

Behind the Scenes

Motivation

The motivations that lie behind a hostage taking incident are important in understanding a number of other aspects of the incident. For example, a clearer understanding of why the incident is taking place can be of great benefit at the negotiation stage. It can provide some insight into how committed the hostage takers are to the cause, and what actions on the part of the authorities may meet enough of their aims to result in a peaceful resolution.

It is very difficult to ascertain the precise nature of the motives behind any hostage taking incident. Terrorists may have many and complex reasons for carrying it out. However, it is possible to gain a degree of information from the actions displayed during an event. For example, the nature and extent of the demands made, the target chosen and the use of the media may all give an idea of motives. A group demanding money alone is more likely to be personally motivated than a group demanding the release of prisoners or social reforms. Clearly such demands suggest that they are more likely to be politically oriented.

There has been some debate in the academic literature about the nature of the demands made by terrorist organisations that take hostages. The majority of this work has considered the nature of demands made as part of the process of negotiation and have been based on economic bargaining and decision making models (e.g. Sandler and Scott, 1987). However, as Mickolus (1987) warns, the demands made may not accurately reflect the actual aims of the terrorists in terms of their overall strategy. One might lose the battle in as much as not receiving the explicit demands, but win the war, with the resultant publicity. Indeed, some authors assert that the primary aim of hostage taking acts such as hijack and barricade siege are based on the publicity they attract, bringing 'real life soap operas' into the home through television coverage (Rubin and Friedland, 1986; Martin,

1985). A common response to the problem of not knowing the strategic aims of the terrorists is to suggest that terrorists be interviewed about their real goals in carrying out such an attack. When dealing with other types of 'criminal' activity this approach has been criticised as lacking validity.

However, the actual demands made by terrorists during the incident should not be dismissed so quickly. Whilst it is not possible to know what the terrorists hope to achieve in the long term, there may be something to learn from what they actually say. If the terrorists are so controlled and controlling in terms of their relationship with the media, then it stands to reason that there will be a structure in what they say and do to present the image of their actions. It can thus be hypothesised that far from being random, the types of demands made in hostage taking incidents reveal a lot about the organisation and its aims. For example, requests for the release of specific prisoners can be characterised as strategic demands. Frequently the demand is for the release of colleagues who have been captured on previous missions. Whilst one might consider this to be loyalty, it would make more sense to consider that the aim is to bring experienced and valued operators back into the organisation. This is therefore considered to be a specific and strategic move on the part of the terrorist. On the other hand, the demand for the release of a broad category of prisoners is more of a global statement of injustice rather than a strategic move. Since it is unlikely that large numbers of unspecified prisoners will be released, this demand is better characterised as a global statement, rather than an actual possibility for improving the personnel of the organisation. Empirical work has shown that the relationship between the demands issued is highly structured and may hold great potential for predicting the likely outcome of hostage taking incidents (Wilson et al., 1995).

The nature of the target may also give an indication of the motives. The selection of a company director or banker implies extortion rather than political gain whereas the taking of a government official or a foreign national implies a more politically directed emphasis of the attack. Another potential indicator is the use of the media. Groups making direct use of the media, either as a communication channel or to get a manifesto or statement published are likely to be more politically motivated than a group who pay no special interest in their message being transmitted to others. The involvement of the media is not an indicator *per se*, as any hostage taking is likely to invoke media coverage as a direct result of the impact of the event. What is of importance is any action on the terrorists' part to manipulate their media coverage for their own ends. In some cases the action is entirely devoted to some kind of 'publicity stunt'. For example, in Venezuela in 1963 six hijackers took over a small plane and circled a city in order to drop leaflets telling people not to vote in the forthcoming elections.

Planning

Planning is a very important aspect as far as the psychological make-up of an event is concerned. The extent of the planning which went into an incident may indicate how determined the terrorists are in completing the mission. An incident that has been well thought out and prepared for may be less vulnerable to mistakes or interventions. In a well planned mission, the authorities may have a better understanding of what the terrorists are likely to do, that is, it may be more predictable than a spontaneous incident which appears to have had little previous consideration of the way it will unfold. Planning could have implications for negotiation, as it could be related to the level of determination to see plans through to a conclusion. It also has intelligence implications through revealing something about the background of the terrorist organisation in terms of its size, commitment and training.

Planning can be related to a variety of tangible aspects of an event, such as the provision and use of materials, the selection of a location and/or target, use of information, allocation of manpower, and the provision of contingency plans should events not turn out as expected. The level and sophistication of planning will reflect the nature of the terrorists involved; well planned events being more likely to be carried out by large established organisations, less well planned ones being carried out by small and/or new groups and 'one-off' terrorists.

Planning is likely to be most central in pre-event stages of an incident. However, this is the stage in which little or no behavioural data is available. While specific details of planning are not likely to be available, an idea of the extent of the planning and sophistication of a group can often be inferred from the event details. An event which runs smoothly and appears to be well orchestrated can be considered to have had better planning than an event which appears to be disorganised and spontaneous.

The extent of planning can sometimes be gauged when things do not work out as expected for the terrorists. Under these circumstances it is of great interest to see what the terrorists do. For example, in many incidents it is the case that a specific hostage or hostages are targeted. If these individuals are not captured, the terrorists have two options; to abandon the plan, or to take the available hostages anyway. In the case of siege the latter strategy is most often employed. By the time they are able to identify who is amongst the hostages seized, they have usually gone too far to turn back. For example, in the 1973 siege of the Saudi Arabian embassy in Khartoum, eight Black September terrorists took over the building during a diplomatic reception. They had apparently hoped to find the West German and the British ambassadors at the reception but they had left earlier. Nonetheless, since they did have several other important diplomats as hostages they continued with the siege. Their original demands had included the release of prisoners in West Germany, but this demand had to be dropped in view of the nationality of hostages acquired. The type of hostage taking strategy employed is clearly an important factor in this decision. In barricade-siege it would be more difficult for the terrorists to escape, and holding some hostages may still be worthwhile. However, in a kidnap attempt it would seem more logical to abandon the plan rather than take a random hostage rather than the intended target.

Defining what is 'successful' in hostage taking is somewhat problematic. As Sandler and Scott (1987) point out, there are many levels of success at which the mission may be evaluated. Logistic success refers to the ability to actually conduct the incident in the way in which it was planned. Strategic success, whether they achieve their aims, is rather more difficult to define and will be considered in a later section.

However, there are numerous examples of logistic failure in hostage taking incidents and it is of real value to consider what the terrorists do when plans go wrong. For example, on the 19th January 1975 terrorists at Orly Airport in France were disturbed whilst putting their plan to attack an El Al aircraft into action. Following an exchange of fire between the terrorists and the security forces, the terrorists seized a number of hostages and held them in the toilets. The hostages were freed in return for a plane to take them out of the country. A similar incident occurred when a Palestinian gunman attempted to take control of the El Al offices in Athens in 1973. After being thwarted in his attempt, he took seventeen hostages in a nearby hotel. He was able to use this negotiating position to get a flight to Kuwait where he escaped arrest. These examples show how in cases of logistic failure the taking of hostages may be used to 'bargain' for escape. However, this strategy is not always effective. A similar scene ensued in Tel Aviv in 1975 when plans to capture the intended target misfired. Eight terrorists took ten hostages, again in a nearby hotel. However, in this case the building was stormed and seven out of eight of the terrorists were killed along with eight of the ten hostages and three Israeli soldiers.

Certain types of failure reveal information about the dynamics of the terrorist group in terms of leadership and distribution of information. For example, in the 1973 hijacking of a JAL flight, one of the terrorists accidentally set off a grenade and was killed. In the absence of this leader, the rest of the group did not have the information they needed to continue the mission. Similarly, in the 1970 hijacking of an El Al flight two of the four-man team failed to board the flight, and grenades used by the terrorists were found to be faulty. This type of incident tells us a lot about the organisation and training of the terrorists involved, as well as the preparedness of the other terrorists to undertake the mission. So, whilst the motives and planning of the incident remain unseen, there are a variety of tangible, identifiable actions conducted during an event which may be considered to point towards these more abstract psychological concepts. The results of a breakdown in plans can be very revealing in terms of the training and group dynamics.

Resources

In a similar way to planning, the resources available to the hostage takers indicate how well prepared they are for the incident and the level of background support that the organisation has. In the same way that planning may indicate determination and negotiation potential, knowledge of the resources associated with the mission may also be of direct relevance to understanding the way the incident may unfold.

Typically, resources are taken to be the physical things that the terrorists have available to them in terms of equipment and weaponry. The level of weaponry is certainly an indication of the amount of background resources the group has and the amount of planning that went into the incident. However, very many hostage taking incidents are carried out with minimal resources of this type and surprisingly often with nothing at all and a good deal of bluffing. In one of the early hijackings of planes to Cuba, the hijacker claimed to have a hand grenade wrapped in cloth. It was later found to be a bottle of Old Spice. Likewise, in the hijacking of a domestic flight in Poland in 1969 two hijackers were able to take over the plane armed with fake bomb, fake pistols, 'hunting knives, a pair of brass knuckles and a rubber hose' (Mickolus, 1980 p.149).

Other physical supplies are often identifiable as resources and can be taken to suggest a certain degree of planning. For example, hostage takers may take additional supplies with them such as provisions, indicating awareness that the incident may last some time. Others simply add them to the list of demands. Terrorists may be prepared with the resources required for the physical control of the hostages, e.g. rope to tie the hostages with, whilst others will improvise at the scene. For example, in one of the three sieges carried out by a group of Hanafi Muslims in Washington D.C. in March 1977, the hostages were bound using a variety of resources to hand in the City Council offices, including the phone wires and cords from the venetian blinds. Such resources are tangible and can be said to have been present or not in any hostage taking incident. However, resources should also be viewed in other terms. The number of people in the terrorist group and their level of training are also resources.

Well-established terrorist groups are likely to have ready access to a wide range of resources. They will have large pools of available manpower, well-accounted organisational funds, a number of safe houses and 'organisational buildings' as well as having access to sophisticated military and civil technology. In addition, they will have within their ranks a great deal of experience, a wide range of skills and access to a relatively large information network. In contrast, an 'amateur' group, or non-affiliated terrorists will be relatively under-resourced. They are less likely to have organisational funds and will have less access to weapons and information. This is likely to have further effect in the level of planning and the degree of sophistication displayed during an event.

The 'manpower' involved in an incident, that is the number of people taking part in the hostage-taking mission, is an interesting aspect of resources. Whilst a large group of terrorists indicates greater manpower, and by implication more support for the action, the relationship is not so straightforward. Clearly, the number of people required is related to the type of mission carried out. No more than a small group of terrorists could successfully board a plane. The number of hostages taken should also be considered in terms of the need for manpower. In a kidnapping incident of one or possibly two individuals, fewer terrorists would be needed to control the hostages than in an embassy siege where large numbers of people are to be held captive. Nevertheless, they are unusual examples where a large number of hostages are controlled by only a few terrorists, or many are employed to capture only a few.

The information which the terrorists have access to can be assessed in terms of the success of their targeting. For example, if a specific individual is targeted in a kidnap or in an embassy siege, the knowledge of where they will be and when is crucial. Information about procedures can be vital to successful take-over, for example, in those cases where tricks are employed, or when buildings are taken through part of an established procedure. The way that information may be used to gain access to hostages is well illustrated in the 1972 siege of the Israeli embassy in Bangkok. During a party at the embassy, two terrorists gained access to the building by walking into the grounds wearing white tie and tails. They were admitted by security guards who mistook them for guests. Whilst targeting specific individuals is frequent in incidents of siege, it is central to the strategy of kidnapping. Information is a crucial resource to hostage takers who adopt kidnap. In order to capture a specific individual, information is necessary regarding their usual movements. It is for this reason that potential targets of hostage taking vary their daily routines.

In summary, the resources available to, and utilised by, a terrorist group are very important in the consideration of their intent and potential. Resources need not necessarily be material assets such as weapons, vehicles, safe houses and other equipment, but in addition it is also valuable to consider features such as information, skills, experience, available finance and manpower as resources.

The Nature of Control

The study of behaviour in a number of different crimes has suggested a universal underlying distinction between crimes that are spontaneous and emotional, and crimes that are planned and well organised (Canter, 1994). Hostage taking is no exception, and empirical work has already identified this distinction in hijackings (Wilson et al., 1995). Whilst this distinction can most obviously be seen in the degree of planning required to undertake the particular incident, and the amount of resources upon which the terrorists draw, it is also interesting to consider the terrorists' behaviour with respect to the other players in the incident. For example, when a building is taken over, the terrorists must assert their control over the hostages. It is possible to do this through three different strategies. First it is possible to do actual physical harm, for example by shooting people such as the guards. The act of injuring or killing people in the initial take over indicates the terrorists' preparedness to kill and creates the fear they need for control. However, this type of action may also label them as dangerous and un-negotiable. This may not only have an adverse effect on the sympathy of the public for their cause, but also on the subsequent actions of the authorities. Rubin and Friedland (1986) hold that a 'successful' incident will not involve casualties of any kind. A similar display of serious intent can be achieved without casualties, through firing guns but away from people. Finally, some hostage takers are able to assert their control over the hostages without actually using their weapons at all. The strategies adopted will be influenced by the situation itself, for example, the number of people in the terrorist force, the number of hostages being controlled and the nature of the target taken. It is for this reason that all behaviour in terrorist incidents must be studied multivariately.

Whilst it is interesting to consider the terrorists' response to the intervention of the authorities, it is important to distinguish between the response at different stages of the hostage taking incident. Attempts may be made to intervene in the mission at three distinct stages; during the initial take over, during the holding phase and at the conclusion of the incident. The people involved in these roles also vary at each stage. Attempts to thwart the initial take-over may be the responsibility of guards or security officers. The hostages themselves may be involved in an attempt to subvert the holding phase, whilst the external authorities are almost always responsible for any action taken which results in a violent tending to the incident. At each of these stages the response of the terrorist is likely to be different, and analysis of behaviour must account for the influence of different temporal stages of the incident.

While the type of initial take-over and the response of the terrorists to intervention are an important index of the nature of their control, it is also important to consider the way in which the hostages are manipulated. Hostage treatment can have a great impact on the way the authorities and the public perceive the terrorists and their cause. It is therefore important from the terrorists' point of view to maintain control without ill treatment of the hostages. It can be hypothesised that mental and physical abuse of the hostages is likely to be associated with poorly organised groups, and the more spontaneous or emotional incidents. The way in which hostages are actually controlled, whether physically tied, or restrained through threat alone is important. Again the context of the incident must be considered since the number of hostages taken, while in the control of the hostage takers themselves, will have an impact on the way they need to control their subsequent behaviour.

Control is one of the most accessible aspects of terrorist behaviour. It can be seen to relate to three central areas; personal control, internal event control and external control. Personal control can be identified directly through reports of the terrorists' behaviour. Their apparent 'coolness' and their reactions to the actions of others are good indicators of personal control. Greater personal control may be expressed in terms of confidence, unhurriedness, consideration before reaction, where less personal control is more likely to be characterised by nervousness, hurried actions or violence in response to others' actions. It would be expected that the more sophisticated, better-planned, more experienced and more committed groups would exhibit more self/personal control. Despite their apparent determination this may result in them being easier to deal with than a nervous and uncertain group.

Internal control refers to the terrorists' handling of the hostage taking and holding itself. It is clearly interrelated with personal control but is distinct. Internal control covers aspects such as the manner in which the hostages are treated, initially in the take over, but also throughout their captivity. There are a wide range of hostage control strategies, from the killing of selected hostages to instil fear in the remainder, through to genial, almost 'house guest'-like treatment. External control refers to the way in which the terrorists relate to the authorities and other external parties. It is principally exhibited in the setting of deadlines, the nature of threats made and their role and actions during negotiations.

Negotiations

Give and Take: Negotiation Rules

Negotiation has been characterised in two ways. Economists and probability theorists have cast the interaction within a bargaining framework (e.g. Sandler and Scott, 1987; Corsi 1981). On the other hand authors such as Friedland and Merari (1992) have suggested that far from being amenable to bargaining rules, hostage taking is better viewed as a game of brinkmanship, where concessions are rarely granted by either party and the 'winner takes all'. Nevertheless, the evidence suggests that quite often at least some of the terrorists' demands will be met, or partially met in an attempt to resolve the incident. In other cases the terrorists will have none of their demands met, and will be overpowered in a violent ending. A successful outcome for the authorities relies on the terrorists surrendering to the authorities. The extent of the concessions granted by the authorities is very often related to where the incident takes place and the stated policies of the governments involved.

However, rather than focusing on the eventual outcomes it is interesting to consider the process itself. Contrary to Friedland and Merari's (1992) assertion that 'winner takes all', it seems that quite often concessions are granted by both parties. The unspoken rules of hostage taking can be characterised by both parties showing a willingness to enter into the negotiation process. Cases where this does not happen to some extent are quite rare. Occasionally governments make an explicit statement that they will not negotiate at all with the terrorists. This is a dangerous strategy from the government's point of view because they may risk losing the public's support by appearing not to care about the hostages.

In most situations, it is the actions of the hostage takers that directly shape the event, outside parties having a more reactive role. Usually the hostage takers attempt to reduce the role of external parties to giving concessions, granting demands, and no more. The authorities are largely limited to damage limitation. It is clear, however, that the actions of the external parties, particularly the authorities, are of great significance. External parties can choose whether to enter negotiations at all. If they choose not to enter a dialogue, the control of the event is put back into the hands of the terrorists. If negotiations are entered into it may be possible to move the situation to one in which the potential impact of the terrorists is minimised.

If the location of the hostages and hostage takers is known, authorities can opt to end an event forcefully. The location is always known in hijacks and sieges, although in certain cases hostages may be kept at locations away from the original scene. Location may be known in the case of kidnappings if security searches are successful. Forceful conclusions are typically only used as a last resort as it can result in death for all parties; terrorist, hostage and storming force. One way in which the government can make concessions to the hostages without actually giving in to their demands is through offering the 'Bangkok Solution'. The Bangkok Solution was so coined following an incident where the release of the hostages was secured through the promise of 'safe passage' for the terrorists. This can be a successful solution to hostage taking incidents as the government is seen not to have surrendered to the terrorists' demands, but not to have endangered the lives of the hostages.

On the part of the hostage takers there are certain concessions which are usual within the 'rules' of bargaining. The hostage takers are required to show 'negotiability'. One of the ways to do this is to extend the deadlines; another is to lessen the demands. Increasing demands and shortening deadlines are unusual and do not follow the rules of bargaining. Nonetheless it does happen. For example in March 1970 kidnappers in the Dominican Republic initially demanded the release of 12 prisoners. During the course of the negotiations they increased their demands to 24 prisoners. Eventually the authorities released 20 of those named and the hostage was freed. In an incident occurring the same month, the West German ambassador was kidnapped from outside the embassy. The initial demand was for seventeen political prisoners to be released. However, when the Guatemalan government refused to negotiate, the hostage takers increased the demand to 25 prisoners and $700,000. Five days later, when negotiations had progressed no further, the hostage was killed. However, whilst decreasing the demands and increasing the deadlines play an important role in showing willing to negotiate, the selection and timing of hostages to release is central.

Hostage Taking Currency

The taking of hostages provides terrorists a currency with which to bargain. In kidnapping incidents this currency is the hostages themselves who are almost always kept at an unknown location. However in siege and hijack incidents two forms of currency are involved, people and property. Whilst most attention is focused on the hostages, in many cases property is also used in the bargaining process. For example, in the 1970s the PFLP used hijacked aircraft as additional currency, removing hostages from the scene and destroying the planes themselves, causing many millions of dollars damage. Deliberate or threatened damage to the aircraft shows a different strategy from the currency focus on the passengers themselves. Similarly in barricade-siege incidents, the building itself may be wired with explosives. Sometimes this is done as part of the threat to kill the hostages, but part of the threat involves the building itself.

When the hostages are the currency there appear to be a number of expectations of the terrorists. First, it is expected that some hostages will be kept. Empirical work has shown that badly organised, personally motivated hijackings often result in the release of all the hostages on arrival at the desired destination (Wilson et al., 1995). Whilst keeping the plane alone may be considered as 'property as currency', it most often is not. These hijackers rarely have the means to destroy the plane. Sometimes personal hijacks are designed simply to facilitate the terrorists' travel to a certain destination, and so on arrival the hostages may be perceived as redundant. However, in terms of securing escape or acceptance in the country, they are still valuable negotiating currency. The release of all the hostages therefore shows the least sophistication, giving up the primary currency immediately.

On the other hand, keeping all the hostages is also a 'poor' strategy. The 'rules of exchange' require that certain hostages are released, and that more hostages will be released at different stages of the negotiation process. Rubin and Friedland (1986) have emphasised that hostage taking incidents are played out on the stage of mass media and that in a sophisticated operation every move is co-ordinated for the best publicity possible. 'Good publicity' requires that some hostages be released immediately. For example, experienced political hijackers will usually release women and children, elderly passengers, the sick, and in some cases nationalities with whom they have no grievance. Similarly in well-planned barricade-siege incidents, although target people (e.g. high ranking officials, ambassadors) will be amongst the hostages taken, so too will non targets. Although women, children and local support staff may be released shortly after take over, some non-targets may be kept for gradual release as part of the give and take of negotiation. Release on compassionate grounds may be viewed as a humanitarian gesture and allowing medical attention to the injured would also suggest terrorists with an interest in 'good publicity'. Sometimes it may seems surprising that the terrorists are willing to behave in this way, but shows the underlying rules of the 'game'. In the siege of the OPEC meeting in Vienna in 1975, the female support staff were 'allowed to leave to do their Christmas Shopping' (Mickolus, 1980 p.572).

Explaining the 'Irrational'

Quite frequently the people involved in hostage taking incidents do things which are difficult to explain. These actions may seem illogical, counter productive, or simply not what one might expect in the circumstances. It is therefore tempting to call these actions 'irrational'. This section will consider the idea of rationality at a number of levels and develop a new perspective on hostage taking behaviour that accounts for the anomalies of behaviour so often encountered in descriptions of these incidents.

On the one hand it is possible to consider irrationality within the hostage-taking arena as relating to the terrorists' 'grasp on reality' within a particular situation and can be identified through a number of actions. Totally 'irrational' acts are often not normally classed as terrorism. For example, it has been known for someone to attempt to hijack a plane to its intended destination. The scale of the demands issued may be more or less realistic in terms of their likelihood of success. A group of terrorists holding a government official and demanding the publication of a manifesto would appear to be more rational in their demands than a similar group demanding the release of all political prisoners, $60 million and food and clothing to all the homeless in a district. Similarly, the total changing of the demands or the unprovoked increase in the scale of the demands may indicate irrationality, as may a determination not to talk with certain negotiators or the setting of unattainable deadlines. What actions such as these indicate is a lack of awareness of the 'rules' of negotiation.

The second set of behaviours that may be described as 'irrational' are those that appear to be clearly at odds with the success of the mission. For example, when hijacking a plane, the safety of the pilot should be a primary concern. In the late 1950s and through the 1960s the hijacking of planes to Cuba was almost a daily occurrence. In many of these cases, if attempts were made to thwart the plan, members of the crew would get injured. However, the injury or death of the pilot is clearly counter-productive. In the 1958 hijacking of a plane out of Miami the pilot was hit over the head when he refused to change the direction of the plane. During negotiations on the tarmac in Nairobi in 1982, hijackers threatened to kill the co-pilot first. The Kenyan foreign minister's response summed up the lack of logic in this situation; 'Don't do that. You are going to need him.' (Mickolus et al., 1989 p.258). Other actions are so difficult to understand that it is questionable as to whether any planning went into the terrorist's actions at all. In 1970, one hijacker took over a plane from Washington D.C. with no specific destination in mind. When the plane began to run out of fuel the pilot pointed out that they would have to land somewhere. However, when he attempted to land the plane the hijacker got angry and started shooting at the pilot and co-pilot.

Actions such as these add weight to the arguments put forward by those who seek to explain hostage taking in terms of the psychological problems of those who resort to it. Whilst there are undoubtedly some people who take hostages who are indeed suffering from some form of mental illness, this does not adequately explain the full range of 'irrational behaviour' shown during hostage taking. Further, consider the distinction between 'irrational' acts which rather than being antisocial are actually pro-social. In the 1961 hijacking of a plane to Cuba, two hijackers released a number of passengers who were distressed by the ordeal on the request of the stewardess. In another incident occurring in 1970, the stewardess also showed some influence over the situation when she persuaded the hijacker to hide his gun so that the other passengers wouldn't be frightened. When U.S. Ambassador to Brazil Charles Elbrick was kidnapped in 1969, he was allowed to write letters to his wife and upon his release was given a book inscribed 'to our first political prisoner, with the expression of our respect for his calm behaviour in action' (Mickolus, 1980 p.136).

Next, consider the unusual behaviours that are sometimes displayed by the hostages themselves. These are people who, up until the point at which they were captured, can be assumed to have been functioning quite 'normally' and would therefore be predicted to adopt rational behaviour. Nonetheless, unusual responses on the part of the hostages abound. In the 1961 hijacking of a plane to Cuba, two hijackers agreed to release all but four of the hostages. Around half of the passengers volunteered to stay. In the 1973 siege of the Saudi Arabian embassy in Khartoum, three hostages were allowed to thank the Saudi ambassador for the party before they were killed. They were reported to have said 'I'm very sorry it has turned out this way, but I want you to know it is not your fault' (Mickolus, 1980 p.377).

These types of pro-social actions on the part of the hostages and hostage takers towards one another are often explained in terms of Hostage Identification Syndrome (HIS), otherwise known as the Stockholm Syndrome. The syndrome was coined following a hostage taking incident in 1973 that ensued following a bungled bank robbery. The authorities were surprised to find that that the hostages identified with their captor and were more afraid of external parties than the events unfolding inside the building (see, for example, Turner, 1985).

There are numerous examples of events that could be explained in terms of HIS. In the 1985 hijacking of a Jordanian plane by terrorists from the 12th June Movement, relations between the hijackers and crew were said to be good. It was reported that at the end of the incident one of the hijackers said to the captain, 'I hope next time I hijack a plane that it will be the same crew'. The captain replied, 'the next time I see you on a flight, I hope you have a ticket' (Mickolus et al., 1989 p.217). Such is the presumed power of HIS that all parties in hostage taking incidents may attempt to manipulate its occurrence. Those at risk of kidnap are trained in ways to 'humanise' themselves in the hope that a bond between themselves and their captors may save their lives. Authorities stand to benefit from HIS if it means that the hostage takers are less likely to kill the hostages. For the hostage takers themselves there are both positive and negative consequences of HIS. On the one hand, it may be harder for them to kill the hostages should the need arise, but on the other the hostages are more controllable and more likely to provide good publicity for them on their release (Turner, 1985). For example, in the late 1960s and early 1970s hijackers associated with the PFLP were often reported to have been very polite to the passengers. In the August 1969 hijacking, they broadcast a message to the passengers saying that there was only one person on board who was of interest to them. On arrival in Syria the rest would be free to go as they please as 'honoured guests in a hospitable and friendly country' (Mickolus, 1980 p.132). The passengers were wished a 'happy journey'. The Japanese Red Army has a reputation for successful manipulation of the passengers. In one very unusual incident, passengers leaving the plane were asked to fill in questionnaires about their experience of the hijacking, which they duly did (Strentz, 1988).

Hostage Identification Syndrome explains the positive actions that occur between hostage and captor. However, it still assumes that this is a function of abnormal psychological processes; it is in fact seen as a 'syndrome'. And this 'syndrome' is only invoked to explain unusual pro-social actions. How are we to explain unusual antisocial actions? The fact is that antisocial actions are not seen as unusual, because that is precisely what is expected from hostage taking incidents. The behaviour of hostages and captors is only questioned when it deviates from what is assumed to be normal hostage taking behaviour. Thus, there appears to be a set of roles and rules which people are expected to conform to within a hostage taking incident, just as there are for every other form of social interaction.

It follows then, that if an action is labelled 'irrational', it is only possible to make that judgement on the basis of the way it appears from the 'rules' that we understand as observers. The actions of those involved in the incident may make perfect sense to them in the circumstances in which they find themselves. The rules of hostage taking, which are seen as being broken, are based on our own 'social representations' of how a hostage taking incident should take place. This is precisely the argument put forward by Sime (1990) with regard to the sometimes seemingly irrational behaviour displayed by victims of major fires. When people behave in what appears to be a non-adaptive way in the face of emergency the media call it 'panic'. When people do not behave in the way we expect of hostages or hostage takers we call it irrational, and suppose that the participants are suffering from some sort of psychological malfunction. When this 'irrationality' involves some kind of positive interaction between the hostages and hostage takers it is called Hostage Identification Syndrome.

Explanations of the way in which people behave in fires have drawn on the notion of 'scripts'. Following earlier theorists (eg. Abelson, 1981), Donald and Canter (1992) assert that people act out their roles according to the scripts that guide appropriate behaviour in a particular setting.

However, they go on to use this concept to explain what happens when people find themselves in an unusual and potentially life-threatening situation. Donald and Canter (1992) point out that most people do not have 'fire scripts', that is an understanding of the appropriate roles and rules to adopt when caught in this unusual and dangerous setting. Further, people's notions of what fires are like are drawn from media portrayals that are far from accurate (Sime, 1990). In the same way then, it can be suggested that people are highly unlikely to have 'hostage taking scripts' in order to deal with the unfolding events. If people do have hostage taking scripts, they are likely to be based on their expectations of what is likely to happen on the basis of representations from the media, whether news based or fictional. It is these same expectations which allow outside observers to classify some behaviours as rational whilst others are not.

If there are 'hostage taking scripts' with roles and rules, then there are certainly examples of the breaking of these rules. On the part of the terrorists, 'bluffing' is one type of rule breaking. Examples include hostage takers' claims to have specific hostages when they do not, or to have wired the building with explosives when they have not. A faked show of strength by hijackers in Tehran in 1984 may well have been the factor that led to the plane being stormed. After actually killing an American and dumping his body onto the tarmac they pretended to kill two Kuwaitis. After taking them back inside the plane and pouring 'catsup' on them, they invited journalists to photograph the evidence. In the following rescue mission by Iranian security forces the authorities bluffed back. One security officer posing as a doctor came on board in response to the request to attend to a passenger. Two other came on as cleaning men and disarmed the hijackers.

Tricks on the behalf of the authorities are quite rare, but are most frequently employed as a means to bring an incident to an end. In some hijackings, disguised security forces may be introduced onto the plane. Terrorists have also been led to believe that they are landing at a different airport. In the Soviet Union in 1964, a pilot pretended to change course, but actually made a slow turn with the intention of returning to the airport. Although the landing was successful, upon discovering they were being tricked the hijackers both shot and stabbed the pilot and co-pilot. In a similar incident, a Cuban pilot headed back to the island whilst pretending to communicate in English with the American flight control of the desired destination. On arrival the hijackers realised the trick and when the pilot

148 The Social Psychology of Crime

refused to comply with their demands he was shot. A more complex attempt at this bluff is illustrated in the 1970 hijacking by the Japanese United Red Army. It was hoped that the terrorists would be fooled by an attempt to disguise a South Korean airport as North Korean. The hijackers had requested to land at North Korea's Pyongyang airport. On landing, the South Koreans had dressed up Kimpo Airport in Seoul to give the impression that it was the correct destination. They were met with 'soldiers and policemen in communist uniforms, girls singing greetings and a bullhorn calling for them to enter North Korea' (Mickolus, 1980 p.169). However, the trick was detected by the presence of 'an American car parked nearby, as well as a U.S. Northwest Airlines plane and a U.S. Airforce DC3 parked on the runways. The officials were unable to produce a photograph of Kim Il Sung, and were tripped up on several points of communist dogma' (Mickolus, 1980 p.169). Rule breaking by all parties has potentially serious results. When either party identifies rule breaking it is likely to result in the breakdown of the whole negotiation process. This strategy should certainly be viewed with caution by the authorities. Hostage takers who break the rules may be deemed 'unnegotiable' and may be stormed, and authorities whose plans backfire may result in deaths of hostages. Interestingly, the hostages also have clear social roles in the incident. They are expected to be passive victims and hostages who put up resistance to the terrorists may be injured, if not killed. The hostages themselves will expect other hostages to play their role. It has been suggested that an individual who attempts to subvert the terrorists plans will be alienated from the other hostages. It has been known for any retaliatory action towards unruly hostages to be described as justified by the other hostages.

Summary and Conclusion

This chapter has put forward the notion that there are predictable patterns to hostage taking incidents and that broadly speaking all the participants follow a set of rules prescribed by their role in the incident based on their expectations of what is appropriate in a particular situation. However, it has also shown that there are frequent actions on the part of all parties that do not fit with our 'social representations' of what hostage taking involves. It has been suggested that these anomalies arise from poorly rehearsed 'hostage taking scripts'.

It is possible then, that the 'strange' behaviours that often occur in hostage taking incidents can be explained in terms of non-adherence to the hostage taking script. Most importantly, it can be suggested that when the roles and rules of hostage taking break down, there may be a reliance on the principles of ordinary social interaction with which everyone is rather more familiar. This has certainly been found to be the case in other life threatening situations. Donald and Canter (1990; 1992) Canter (1990), and Canter et al. (1990) all found a tendency for those caught in major fires to continue to behave in ways compatible with their original roles and intentions before the fire broke out. It is therefore suggested that when the 'hostage taking script' breaks down, it is likely that behaviours linked to ordinary social interaction will be shown.

Finally, it is necessary to reconsider Hostage Identification Syndrome. It is possible that HIS is the positive side of the failure of hostage taking scripts, resulting in normal social interaction. Research has suggested that there are only certain conditions under which HIS can develop; situations where there is face to face contact, shared language, no pre-existing cultural prejudices and no unnecessary violence (Turner, 1985). Conditions, it may be argued, necessary for normal positive interactions. On the other hand, it is possible that Hostage Identification Syndrome is *itself* the precursor to the breakdown of hostage taking scripts. That is when HIS is present, that is when people revert to their more ordinary roles of social interaction.

Acknowledgements

The authors would like to acknowledge the support of the U.S. Army Research Institute through its European Research Office.

References

Abelson, R.P. (1981), 'Psychological status of the script concept', *American Psychologist,* **36**, 715-729.

Atkinson, S.E., Sandler, T. and Tschirhart, J. (1987), 'Terrorism in a Bargaining Framework', *Journal of Law and Economics,* **30**, 1-21.

Brunet, L. and Casoni, D. (1991), 'Terrorism: Attack on Internal Objects', *Melanie Klein and Object Relations,* **9 (1)**, 1-15.

Canter, D.V. (1990), 'An Overview of Human Behaviour in Fires', in D.V. Canter, (ed.), *Fires and Human Behaviour,* 2nd edn, London: David Fulton Publishers.

Canter, D.V. (1994), *Criminal Shadows,* London: Harper Collins.

Canter, D.V., Breaux, J. and Sime, J. (1990), 'Domestic, Multiple Occupancy and Hospital Fires', in D.V. Canter (ed.), *Fires and Human Behaviour,* 2nd edn, London: David Fulton Publishers.

Corsi, J.R. (1981), 'Terrorism as a Desperate Game: Fear, Bargaining and Communication in the Terrorist Event', *Journal of Conflict Resolution,* **25 (1)**, 47-85.

Crenshaw, M. (1990), 'The Logic of Terrorism: Terrorist Behaviour as a Product of Strategic Choice', in W. Reich (ed.), *Origins of Terrorism: Psychologies, Ideologies, Theologies, States of Mind,* New York: Cambridge University Press.

Donald, I.J. (1993), 'Behaviour in Fires: Preventing Disasters', *Health, Safety and Environment Bulletin,* **216**, 5-8.

Donald, I.J. (1995), 'Psychological Insights into Managerial Responsibility for Public and Employee Safety', in R. Bull and D. Carson (eds), *Handbook of Psychology in Legal Contexts,* Chichester: Wiley.

Donald, I.J. and Canter, D.V. (1990), 'Behavioural Aspects of the King's Cross Disaster', in D.V. Canter, (ed.), *Fires and Human Behaviour* 2nd edn, London: David Fulton Publishers.

Donald, I.J. and Canter, D.V. (1992), 'Intentionality and Fatality During the King's Cross Underground Fire', *European Journal of Social Psychology,* **22 (3)**, 203-218.

Ferracuti, F. (1990), 'Ideology and Repentance: Terrorism in Italy', in W. Reich (ed.), *Origins of Terrorism: Psychologies, Ideologies, Theologies, States of Mind,* New York: Cambridge University Press.

Friedland, N. and Merari, A. (1992), 'Hostage Events: Descriptive Profile and Analysis of Outcomes', *Journal of Applied Social Psychology,* **22 (2)**, 134-156.

Johnson, P.W. and Feldman, T.B. (1992), 'Personality Types and Terrorism: Self-Psychology Perspectives', *Forensic Reports,* **5**, 293-303.

Lapan, H.E. and Sandler, T. (1988), 'The Political Economy of Terrorism: To Bargain or Not to Bargain: That is the Question', *AEA Papers and Proceedings,* **78 (2)**, 16-21.

Martin, L.J. (1985), 'The Media's Role in International Terrorism', *Terrorism: An International Journal,* **8 (2)**, 127-146.

Mickolus, E.F. (1980), *Transnational Terrorism: A Chronology of Events. 1968-1979,* London: Greenwood Press.

Mickolus, E.F. (1993), *Terrorism 1988-1991: A Chronology of Events and a Selectively Annotated Bibliography,* London: Greenwood Press.

Mickolus, E.F. (1987), 'Comment-Terrorists, Governments, and Numbers: Counting Things versus Things that Count', *Journal of Conflict Resolution,* **31** (1), 54-62.

Mickolus, E.F., Sandler, T. and Murdock, J.M. (1989), *International Terrorism in the 1980's: A Chronology of Events,* 1 - 2, Iowa: Iowa State University Press.

Oots, K.L. and Wiegele, T.C. (1985), 'Terrorist and Victim: Psychiatric and Physiological Approaches from a Social Science perspective', *Terrorism: An International Journal,* **8 (1),** 1-32.

Overgaard, P.B. (1994), 'The Scale of Terrorist Attacks as a Signal of Resources', *Journal of Conflict Resolution,* **38(3),** 452-478.

Post, G. (1984), 'Notes on a Psychodynamic Theory of Terrorism Behaviour', *Terrorism: An International Journal,* **7,** 241-256.

Rothman, S. and Lichter, S.R. (1980), 'Personality Development and Political Dissent: A Reassessment of the New Left', *Journal of Political and Military Sociology,* **8,** 191-204.

Rubin, J.Z. and Friedland, N. (1986), 'Theater of Terror', *Psychology Today,* **20** (3), 18-28.

Sandler, T. and Scott, J.L. (1987), 'Terrorist Success in Hostage Taking Incidents: An Empirical Study', *Journal of Conflict Resolution,* **31 (1),** 35-53.

Sime, J. (1990), 'The Concept of Panic', in D.V. Canter, (ed.), *Fires and Human Behaviour,* 2nd edn, London: David Fulton Publishers.

Sprinzak, E. (1990), 'The Psychopolitical Formation of the Extreme Left Terrorism in a Democracy: The Case of the Weathermen', in W. Reich (ed.), *Origins of Terrorism: Psychologies, Ideologies, Theologies, States of Mind,* New York: Cambridge University Press.

Strentz (1988), 'A Terrorist Psychosocial Profile: Past and Present', *FBI Law Enforcement Bulletin,* **57 (4),** 13-18.

Turco, R.M. (1987), 'Psychiatric Contributions to the Understanding of International Terrorism', *International Journal of Offender Therapy and Comparative Criminology,* **31 (2),** 153-161.

Turner, J.T. (1985), Factors Influencing the Development of Hostage Identification Syndrome', *Political Psychology,* **6 (4),** 705-711.

Wilson, M.A., Canter, D.V. and Smith, A. (1995*), Modelling Terrorist Behaviour,* Final Report to the U.S. Army Research Institute, ARI, Alexandria, V.A.

6 Riot by Appointment: An Examination of the Nature and Structure of Seven Hard-Core Football Hooligan Groups

LYNNE JOHNSTON

An understanding of the nature and structure of seven 'hard-core' hooligan groups was gained using data from criminal records, and police intelligence reports of actual sightings between individuals in each group. Smallest Space Analysis (SSA), was explored as an appropriate methodology for examining the structure of relationships in each group. Results of these SSAs provided preliminary support for the hypothesis that there is a hierarchical structure to football hooliganism. The addition of frequency contours onto each of the SSA plots, enabled the allocation of individuals in each club to one of three structural groups. Results of the analysis comparing individuals in each structural group showed that known leaders and those with a predominantly violent background, including first convictions for violent offences, were more likely to be centrally located within the SSA structure groups

Lynne Johnston is a Research Fellow in the Department of Leisure Management at Cheltenham and Gloucester College of Higher Education. Her current research interests include sexual abuse within sport, and psychological factors in sports injury and rehabilitation. She holds a BA(Hons) in Psychology and Sport Science from Chester College, an MSc in Investigative Psychology from the University of Surrey, and a PhD in Sport Psychology from the University of Birmingham.

6 Riot by Appointment: An Examination of the Nature and Structure of Seven Hard-Core Football Hooligan Groups

LYNNE JOHNSTON

The Football Hooliganism Phenomenon

The word hooliganism is today synonymous with football, yet when one looks for a precise definition of 'football hooliganism' difficulties arise.

There is a tendency for the term to be used indiscriminately to cover any misbehaviour at or around football grounds, or when in transit to a match. Trivizas (1980) suggests that hooliganism is a "label covering a wide range of heterogeneous offences and other forms of misbehaviour" (p.278). Part of the problem with defining football hooliganism stems from the fact that there is no statutory offence by that name (Melnick, 1986). Trivizas (1980) attempted to overcome this problem by identifying the type of offences for which arrests were made in football crowds. The 10 offences that he identified were mainly public order and violence related offences, with a smaller number of dishonesty offences. This supports the popular perception of football hooliganism and provides a useful means of conceptualising the term, albeit from a legal standpoint.

Prior to World War One, attacks on referees and players were the most prevalent forms of misbehaviour at football matches, whilst today inter-group fighting is the most frequent occurrence, (Dunning, Murphy, & Williams, 1988). Thus, although the problem has always existed, it appears that today the individuals involved tend to be associated with established hooligan groups who fight against rival groups, the violence being premeditated and organised in nature. Preliminary discussions with police intelligence officers substantiated this trend. All references to police intelligence officers refer to a centralised UK police intelligence group tasked with examining this type of organised crime. Football hooligan groups are organised for one primary purpose, to fight each other. The leaders are known to communicate regularly amongst themselves to organise venues for the battles. One point of interest is the common joining of the groups, particularly when the national team is playing. This highlights the bizarre nature of such people who will fight each other one day only to join forces the next. The rules of combat specify that violence is preferred against another hooligan group first, any opposing fans second, and the police as a last resort. An examination of the actual number of arrests and ejections from football matches in recent years (1987-1993), compared with the total attendance figures for the same period, revealed that troublemakers comprised less than 0.05% of those ejected and or arrested from football grounds each season, (personal communication police intelligence, 1994). However this does not include arrests involving 'hooligans' travelling to and from the ground. Preliminary discussions with intelligence officers confirmed that planned violence will not be at or near the venue of the match, rather it tends to be at a distant public house or railway station. In addition, Canter, Comber and Uzzell, (1989), present graphical evidence which shows a steady increase in arrests outside football grounds, and a decrease in arrests within grounds, between the years 1975 to 1985. The move away from violence within football grounds is seen as a direct result of increased surveillance within grounds.

Intelligence officers confirmed that there is a tendency for the same group of individuals to be involved in the trouble, and that they may be arrested several times throughout the season. Thus although the extent of the problem may not be as grave as the media would suggest, there are a small proportion of persistent offenders.

Who is the Persistent Football Hooligan?

Empirical research that examines the demographic and criminal backgrounds of football hooligans is rare. The main barrier is the lack of any comprehensive and accurate statistics. Partial data is available from five studies: Harrington (1968); Trivizas (1980); Centre for Leisure

Research (1984); Dunning, Murphy and Williams (1988); and Van Limbergen, Colaers and Walgrave (1989). Thus the information pertaining to criminal background, and more general demographic details presented in this chapter add significantly to the existing literature.

Following a discussion with police intelligence officers, a group of 140 football hooligans were identified as being the prominent members of 7 hooligan groups. Of the hooligans examined 93% had an existing criminal record, and 130 criminal records were obtained. Information relating to demographic background, arrests and convictions was recorded. As all information was strictly confidential the coding of information was conducted by a police officer, ensuring the anonymity of the football clubs and hooligans involved. Details of the way in which the sample was selected cannot be disclosed for security reasons.

In the present study all 140 subjects were male. In Harrington's (1968) sample only one female was encountered out of the 497 subjects examined. Similarly in Trivizas's sample 99.2% of offences were committed by males. Discussions with intelligence officers confirmed this trend. Ages ranged from 19-44 years, (M=27.4; SD=4.8). Ninety five percent of offenders were aged between 21 and 40; 35.7% were aged between 26 and 30, 34.3% were aged between 21 and 25. More offenders were aged between 26 and 30 in hooligan groups 1, 2, 4 and 6, compared with groups 3 and 5. In group 7, more than half the members were aged over 30.

Over 80% of Trivizas and 60% of Harrington's subjects were under 25, however in the present study only 39% were under 25. Thus although the persistent football hooligans observed in this study were older than those examined in previous research this may simply be a reflection of the nature of the sample selected. They were all *known* by the police to be central members, which the police referred to as the 'hard-core'. An alternative perspective is that the results may reflect a general trend of increasingly older individuals becoming involved; or in fact that those involved are tending to remain associated with hooligan groups for a longer period than they tended to do in the past. This finding is supported by research examining delinquent American gangs where there is an increasing trend for older individuals to be and to remain involved in such groups (Short, 1990).

Table 6.1 Social Class of 140 Football Hooligans based on Occupations

CLASSIFICATION	NUMBER	%
Professional	0	0
Managerial	4	2.9
Skilled Non Manual	15	10.7
Skilled Manual	40	28.6
Partly Skilled	35	25
Unskilled	19	13.6
Unemployed	27	19.3

As table 6.1 shows most of the individuals in the present sample were involved in skilled manual or partly skilled occupations, this finding strongly supports the work of Trivizas (1980); Harrington (1968) and Dunning et al. (1988). However one of the problems with the collation of information pertaining to employment is that the occupation noted for the purpose of this study was obtained from each hooligan's criminal record. It was noted that many of the individuals reported different occupations following separate arrests. It is not known whether these individuals are currently involved in the same occupation, or if employed at all.

Sixty four percent of the total sample was known to travel abroad in support of their club or national side. It seems likely that those who travel abroad comprise the most committed hooligans. Fifty two percent were known to attend matches involving the national side (England or Wales). This may provide indirect evidence of the proportion of the hooligans examined who may be actively involved in a national hooligan group.

There is a theory surrounding football hooliganism, that a conspiracy by far right political groups is responsible for the more serious or violent side of hooliganism. Members of the National Front were reported to have been associated with the Heysel tragedy; however Poppelwell (1986) concluded that: "There is little to connect such groups with organised violence ... it is right that too much importance should not be attached to their activities". (p.7). Dunning, et al. (1988) suggest that the link between hooligans and the National Front or British National Party (BNP), is due to the fact that the kind of life experiences of those most frequently involved in football disorder "makes them susceptible to the ideologies of the racist right" (p.182). Thus the terraces hold an up-and-coming source of new recruits. Research at the Centre for Contemporary Studies (CCS) in 1981/2 suggested that "infiltration of the terraces by the far right has been a nation-wide phenomenon" (p.8), particularly in the larger industrial cities. However Canter, et al., (1989) noted that although some supporters believed political groups were involved in hooliganism, this belief tended to be based on hearsay and media reports rather than first hand observations.

In the present study, 29.3% of the sample were known to be associated with the BNP. Examining each of the seven clubs in detail, only three contained members of the BNP. In one club, 84% of hooligans examined were known members of the BNP. It is interesting to note that contrary to the research by the CCS, there are definite regional differences within this sample. The three clubs containing members of the BNP were all situated in the London area.

To date no published research provides a detailed analysis of the marital status of football hooligans. It is often quoted in the criminological literature that individuals may tend to move away from crime when they get married and /or have children. It was thus hypothesised that only a small proportion of this sample would be married. Overall the results support this with only 12.1% being married.

Criminal Background of the Persistent Football Hooligan

It should be pointed out that one of the problems with extracting information from criminal records is that it is not always made explicitly clear exactly what the circumstances of the offence were. It is therefore not possible to know for sure whether or not the offence was in fact related to football. Ninety three percent of the sample had an existing criminal record. This figure is higher than was found by Trivizas (36%) and Harrington

(63%). This difference may reflect the way in which police intelligence officers identified this sample. The total number of convictions for this sample were 1,597, (M=11.5; SD=12.5), this ranged from 10 individuals with no convictions to one individual with 81 convictions. Table 6.2.1 shows the average number of convictions within each hooligan group.

Table 6.2.1 Average Number Of Criminal Convictions For Each Hooligan Group

HOOLIGAN GROUP	M	SD	RANGE
1 (N=17)	6.8	5.5	0-14
2 (N=32)	12.1	9.9	1-54
3 (N=22)	7.4	9.0	0-30
4 (N=9)	15.6	10.6	2-36
5 (N=27)	13.3	16.7	0-73
6 (N=13)	12.5	8.4	4-31
7 (N=20)	14.3	18.4	1-81
TOTAL (N=140)	11.5	12.5	0-81

Table 6.2.2 shows this information in more detail. As can be seen the most common offence was for threatening behaviour. The majority of offences may be classified as being public order and/or violence related. This strongly supports the findings of Trivizas (1980). Unfortunately, Harrington (1968) only provided details of numbers of convictions, and did not specify their nature. The centre for leisure research (1984), noted that the majority of arrests in their sample were for "forms of vocal aggression

and possibly provocative behaviour" (p.4). However as they did not provide details of criminal backgrounds a direct comparison is impossible.

Table 6.2.2 Total Number of Convictions for Hooligans in Each Hooligan Group

OFFENCE	HOOLIGAN GROUP							
	1 N=17	2 N=32	3 N=22	4 N=9	5 N=27	6 N=13	7 N=20	Total N=140
Threatening Beh	36	68	30	30	74	24	32	294
Theft	14	34	31	13	91	25	70	278
Damage	7	43	10	13	24	16	16	129
B.O.P.	1	30	4	7	4	3	11	60
A.B.H.	16	28	16	10	7	11	13	101
Affray	4	22	13	6	9	10	6	70
Violent Beh	4	17	6	7	20	5	4	63
Weapon	6	32	5	2	16	8	7	76
Con Affray	0	16	0	0	0	0	0	16
G.B.H	4	9	6	0	3	6	3	31
Drugs	0	8	2	4	4	1	3	22
Con Assault	0	8	0	0	0	0	0	8
T.D.A.	1	7	0	4	4	5	4	25
Assault	4	6	3	13	6	5	9	46
Forgery	0	6	3	0	0	2	3	14

OFFENCE	HOOLIGAN GROUP							
Ass Police	4	6	1	2	5	2	2	22
Burglary	11	6	3	5	8	8	15	56
Disorder	0	6	0	1	0	0	0	7
Handling	2	6	3	3	7	6	18	46
Driving Offences	1	5	1	6	20	5	7	45
Drunk	2	5	2	3	9	0	2	23
Deception	1	4	2	1	3	4	23	38
Wounding	2	4	8	3	4	5	8	34
Obstructing Police	1	2	1	1	2	0	0	7
Fraud	0	2	0	0	1	0	4	7
Robbery	0	1	0	0	1	3	1	6
Obstructing Highway	0	3	0	1	0	0	0	4
Death D. D	0	1	0	0	0	0	0	1
False accounting	0	1	0	0	0	0	0	1
Manslaught	0	0	1	0	1	0	0	2
Disorderly Conduct	0	0	1	0	1	0	5	7
Pitch invasion	0	0	1	4	0	4	0	9
Breach S.S.	0	0	0	1	8	0	0	9
Riot	0	0	0	0	6	1	1	8

OFFENCE	HOOLIGAN GROUP							
Off Agnst person	0	0	0	0	1	0	0	1
Rape	0	0	0	0	2	0	0	2
Obst Gangway	0	0	0	0	1	0	0	1
Arson	0	0	0	0	1	0	0	1
Indecent Assault	0	0	0	0	0	4	0	4
Off Language	0	0	0	0	0	1	0	1
Con Riot	0	0	0	0	0	0	8	8
Con Violent Dis	0	0	0	0	0	0	6	6
Perverting Justice	0	0	0	0	0	0	2	2
Blackmail	0	0	0	0	0	0	1	1
Resisting Arrest	0	0	0	0	0	0	1	1
Absconding Bail	0	0	0	0	0	0	1	1
Unlawful Assbly	0	0	0	0	0	0	1	1
Sexual Offences	0	0	0	0	0	0	3	3
Total	121	386	153	140	343	164	290	1597

The majority of offences listed in Table 6.2.2 can be classified as being primarily related to violence or dishonesty. More than twice the overall number is for violent offences. At a club level there was little difference in terms of the number of convictions for dishonesty, yet interestingly there were differences in the number of violent convictions associated with members of each club, (F=2.37; p<0.05). The reasons why these differences exist are difficult to uncover without examining the individuals involved in a little more depth. A detailed examination of each hooligan's criminal background would provide an indication of the football hooligans 'criminal career', this information may provide an insight into the way in which individuals are socialised into each hooligan group, e.g. do they come from a predominantly violent or dishonest background.

From the information available it was decided that age of first conviction, together with details of such convictions should be examined for each hooligan group separately. In addition it was hypothesised that those individuals who had served a custodial sentence, either as a juvenile or as an adult may tend to be more persistent offenders, possibly also more violent. This is linked to the theory of prison as the 'University of Crime', e.g. prisoners learn their trade from other inmates whilst serving their sentence. Differences between the seven hooligan groups examined with respect to: age at, and type of first conviction; and number of members who served a custodial sentence as a juvenile or adult, may allow a preliminary classification to be made in terms of the extent of criminality. Table 6.3 provides a breakdown of age at, and type of first convictions for each hooligan group.

Table 6.3 Age at, and Type of First Conviction for Members of Each Hooligan Group

CLUB	% WITH 1st CONVICTION FOR: VIOLENCE	DISHONESTY	OTHER	AGE AT 1st CONVICTION: M	SD	RANGE
1 (N=17)	50	38	12	18.4	2.9	15-25
2 (N=32)	59.4	34	6	18.3	4.5	12-34
3 (N=22)	47.4	47.4	5.2	19	3.4	10-28
4 (N=9)	66	22	12	18.7	4.3	16-29

CLUB	VIOLENCE	DISHONESTY	OTHER	M	SD	RANGE
5(N=27)	74	22	4	18.7	4.1	13-34
6(N=13)	54	38	8	17.7	4.0	11-27
7(N=20)	40	50	10	18	4.8	10-32
TOTAL (N=140)	57	35.4	7.7	18.2	4.0	10-34

As Table 6.3 shows, age of first conviction ranged from 10 (club 7) to 34 (club 2). Individuals in all clubs except 3 and 7, had a higher percentage of violent first convictions, this was especially true for club 5. Club 7 was the only club with more first convictions for dishonesty, this may reflect a different socialisation process for members entering this group. Statistical analysis examining differences between clubs based on first convictions for dishonesty and violence was not significant. It would be useful in future research to conduct interviews with known football hooligans to establish the true age they became involved in such activities, and to understand how they were socialised into hooligan gangs.

Sixteen hooligans had served a custodial sentence as a juvenile. The length of sentence ranged from six individuals who had spent 24 hours in an attendance centre to one individual who served 24 months in borstal; (M= 3.96 months; SD=6.44). There were no statistically significant differences between hooligan groups in this respect. Forty subjects served a custodial sentence as an adult, this ranged from one individual serving 1 day to another being sentenced to a total of 123 months (M=24.8 months; SD=36.5). Again there were no significant differences between hooligan groups. It should be noted that the figures quoted in this study refer to the actual sentence imposed; it is unlikely that these were the actual lengths of sentences served, however details of actual time served was not available for analysis. Future research may examine the percentage of those who have served a custodial sentence as a juvenile and adult, compared with those who serve only a juvenile *or* adult custodial sentence.

166 The Social Psychology of Crime

It would also be interesting to examine the length of sentences actually served and compare these figures against base rates for other crimes. Comparisons between the type of offences that did or did not receive a custodial sentence would also be useful. Trivizas (1981) conducted a study to find out whether football hooligans were treated more leniently, more severely, or in the same way as those committing similar offences outside football. It was concluded that: "Persons committing offences in football crowd disorders are punished more severely than offenders committing the same kind of offence in political demonstrations". (p.348).

The results presented in the first part of this chapter have been discussed in depth for two main reasons. First, as the author had unprecedented access to such detailed information it seemed imperative that this should be utilised optimally, especially when one considers the severe lack of detail in the few studies that have been conducted. Second, it was considered essential that one attempts to understand the nature of the hooligans at an individual level before trying to explore the phenomenon at a group level. The second part of this chapter is concerned with developing a greater understanding of the nature and structure of 'hard-core' football hooligan groups.

Examining Football Hooliganism at a Group Level

Football hooliganism is essentially a group crime, and thus it is important to understand the nature, structure and pattern of associations within hooligan groups. The aim of the work presented in the remainder of this chapter was to examine the group structure, and cohesiveness of each hooligan group. There were several inter-related questions in this respect. First can we identify a structure within any of the hooligan groups and if so does this suggest the existence of a hierarchy? If there is evidence of a hierarchy, can the leaders and followers, or central and peripheral members be identified? If so, do central and peripheral members differ with respect to criminal backgrounds, or any demographic information such as age? Second, how cohesive are members of each of the hooligan groups. Hooligan groups whose members are highly interconnected are hypothesised to be more cohesive than those who are more diverse. Cohesive groups may be more difficult to penetrate as there may be less chance of an individual becoming an informer if he is located within a highly cohesive group.

Van Limbergen et al. (1989) conducted one study, which presents preliminary evidence of a hierarchical structure to football hooliganism. Examining the structure of hooligan groups they noted a "graduation in the intensity of hooliganism". The hard-core comprised the most central members; this group was aged between 18 and 23 years and saw themselves as 'professional hooligans'. This group tended to organise and plan the violence and was involved in other forms of delinquent behaviour. They also observed various individuals associating with the hard-core, yet who had little interest in the game itself. These individuals appeared to have been invited by friends from the hard core to participate in the expected trouble. Surrounding the hard-core was a less intense group which Van Limbergen et al. called 'stagiaries'; this group were younger (20 years), not quite delinquent, continuously associated with the central hard-core with the aim of eventually being part of it. When violence occurred, this group was the first to take part. The final group were ordinary adolescents who were motivated by the macho image and behaviour. However when the physical violence began they backed off.

One of the main hypotheses of the Van Limbergen et al. (1989) study was that football hooligans are attracted to the so-called 'near group' because of their social vulnerability. As they have few socially accepted prospects, association with other individuals faced with similar situations helps them to gain status by provoking society, making themselves visible, and thus providing a feeling of self esteem. Results of their study showed the 'hard-core' and 'stagiaries' were from "unstable working class families" had a short and frustrating school career, were unemployed and tended to be involved in delinquency and non football related crime.

The study, which is reported in the remainder of this chapter, was based on the hypothesis that the application of the principles of Social Network Analysis (Scott, 1991), may provide a basis for the investigation of a structural hierarchy within each of the hooligan groups.

Sociograms and Social Network Analysis

The sociometric or social network analysis conducted in this study was based on the ideas developed by Moreno in 1953, although he first described his sociometric test in 1934. This test is an instrument used to identify association preferences. The basic idea is that subjects are asked to nominate which members of a specified group they prefer to associate with. From the results of such tests, the structure of social relationships within the particular group may be examined, through the construction of a sociogram. There is a range of typical structures found in a sociogram, which are described in detail by Thomas (1979). The main weakness of the traditional sociogram is that:

> There is no structuring principle or system of co-ordinates to determine where any subject is to be placed in the sociogram, two people constructing a sociogram from the same sociometric data might draw two sociograms that at first glance appeared fundamentally different.
>
> (Thomas, 1979, p. 9).

The nature of the data in the current study did not lend itself to a direct sociometric test, as there was no direct contact with the subjects. Thus the associations had to be inferred from the observational data of 'known sightings' based on police intelligence reports relating to each of the identified football hooligans. The technique used in this study has been used by American criminal investigators (Swanson et al. 1992). Swanson et al. (1992), also use the term "Social Network Analysis" (SNA) and suggest that it is a useful technique in situations where police officers need to identify key participants and understand the associations among them to determine the extent of illicit operations. The rationale used is essentially the same as that used in sociometric tests. However, data collection involves observations, usually as a result of a surveillance operation.

Using Smallest Space Analysis (SSA) as an SNA measure provides a visual indication of the overall structure of each group, and the relationships within it. The explicitness and clarity of this visual representation allows an interpretation to be made, requiring little technical knowledge. Analysis of these visual relationships may allow the most central and/or peripheral members to be identified. The network diagram also provides a representation of the cohesiveness of each group.

Social network analysis as an investigative technique has a great deal to offer in terms of providing a deeper understanding of the various football hooligan groups based upon the relationships amongst members. It maintains all the advantages of earlier sociometric techniques, yet developments in computer software have alleviated the main problem of the sociogram; the positioning of people relative to one another in terms of distance may now be overcome.

Social Network Analysis of Football Hooligan Groups

The coded police intelligence information and criminal records referred to earlier, was used to conduct the SSA. The intelligence records contained details of the known associates of each individual, together with more specific details pertaining to actual sightings of members of each hooligan group. Two data matrixes were constructed for each of the seven hooligan groups. The first set of matrixes were constructed by recording in dichotomous form whether or not each of the identified members in the sample for every club were reported as 'known associates' of each other.

The second set of association matrixes was constructed by examining the intelligence information in further depth. Information was recorded regarding how often individuals had been seen in the company of other known football hooligans. For example, although person A may not be recorded as a known associate of person C, he may be spotted on different occasions with person C. The actual number of times an individual had been seen with another hooligan was recorded in the second set of matrixes. Cross-referring between intelligence logs, reporting on each subject checked the 'completeness' of the 'known associates' and the 'actual sightings' data. The results showed that information relating to actual sightings was more accurate than proposed associations. For instance, actual sightings of person A with person B were more likely to be correctly recorded in the intelligence reports of both A and B. However the intelligence information on 'known associates was more likely to only be recorded on the file of A or B, not both. Thus it was decided that using the 'sighting' data to record associations between members of each hooligan group was more accurate.

Construction of Social Network Diagrams

Smallest Space Analysis was conducted on data relating to six hooligan groups; the seventh group was excluded at this stage due to a lack of intelligence information. The use of SSA within the present study was somewhat unconventional in two respects. First, both the rows and columns of the data matrix represented people, whilst in most previous work, the columns represent variables and the rows subjects. Second, the matrixes used were in triangular form, representing actual sightings between people. However the principle is essentially the same, with the SSA simply comparing the number of sightings for each individual with the number of sightings for all other individuals, the rank ordering of numbers of sightings determining each individuals' position in Euclidean space. The SSA therefore produced the framework for the sociogram. Co-ordinates representing each individual signify their positioning in multidimensional space. To convert these plots into social network diagrams, lines (based on sightings) are added to connect the individuals.

The data used for the construction of the matrixes in this part of the study, referred to the actual number of times individuals had been sighted together. The data in each matrix was recorded as two columns per subject. Any subjects who were never seen with any other members of the group were excluded from the matrix. This resulted in 10 hooligans being excluded from the analysis at this stage: four from hooligan group 6; three from group 5; two from group 2; and one from group 1.

SSA was conducted on each of the six triangular matrixes. The results of each SSA are shown in detail in Johnston, (1994). The next stage of the analysis involved, referring back to the original matrixes and adding lines to represent the number of times each of the individuals had been seen together. Figures 6.1 to 6.6 show the results of this analysis in terms of sociometric linkages between members of each hooligan group.

Riot by Appointment 171

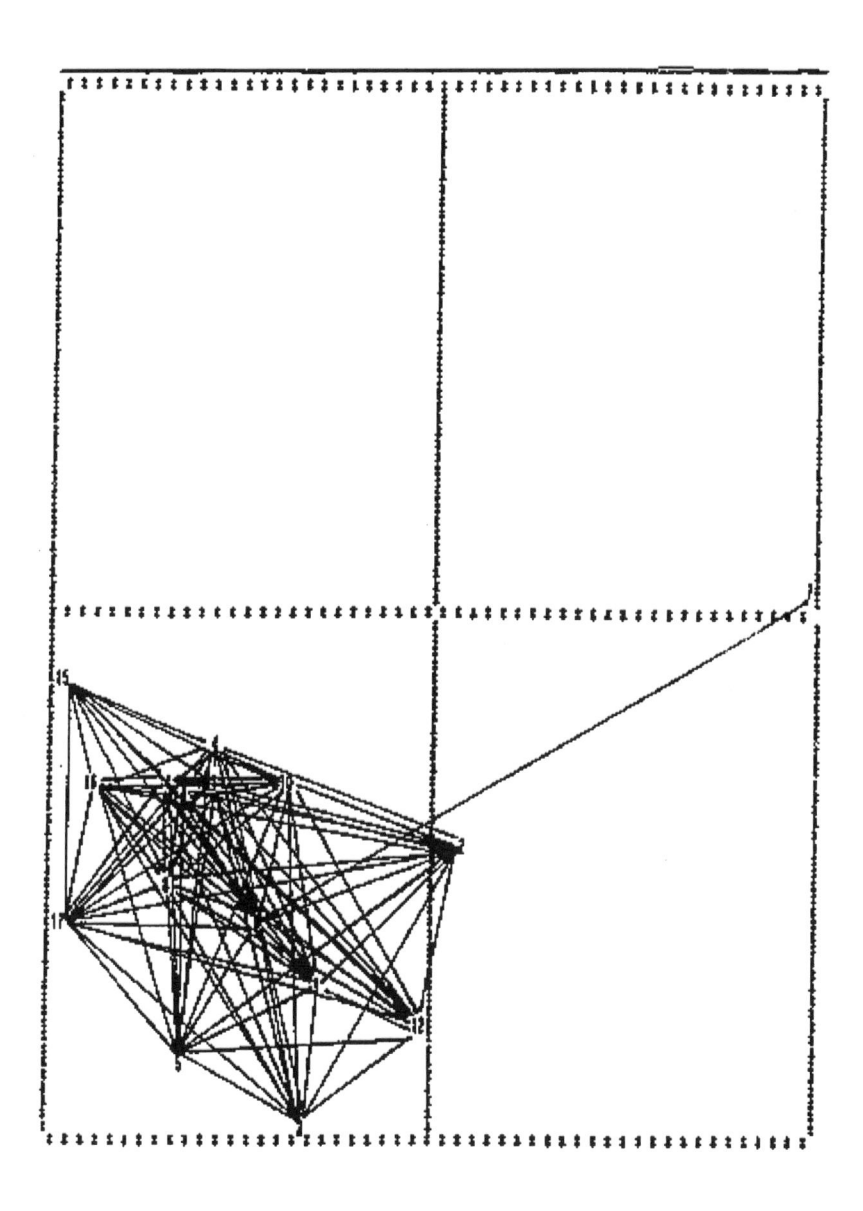

Figure 6.1 MSA of a Football Hooligan Group
(Guttman – Lingoes Coefficient of Alienation = 0.13237)

172 *The Social Psychology of Crime*

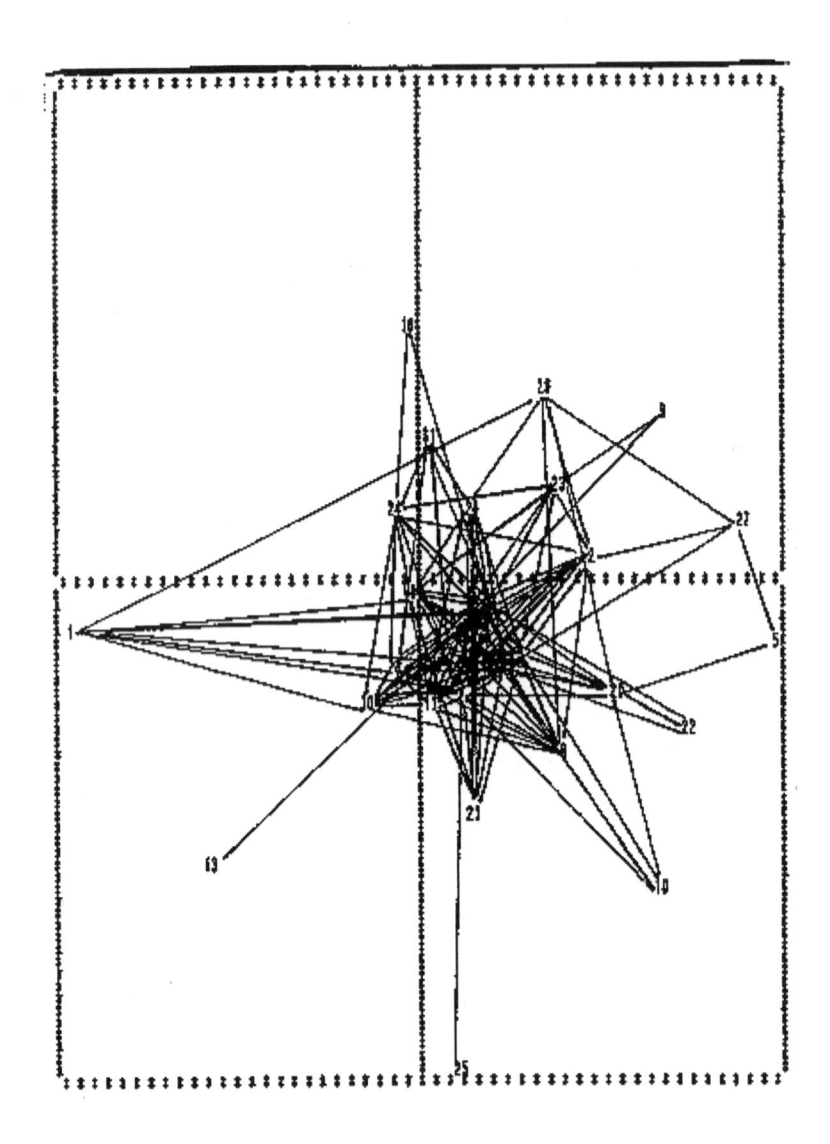

Figure 6.2 MSA of a Football Hooligan Group
(Guttman – Lingoes Coefficient of Alienation = 0.20207)

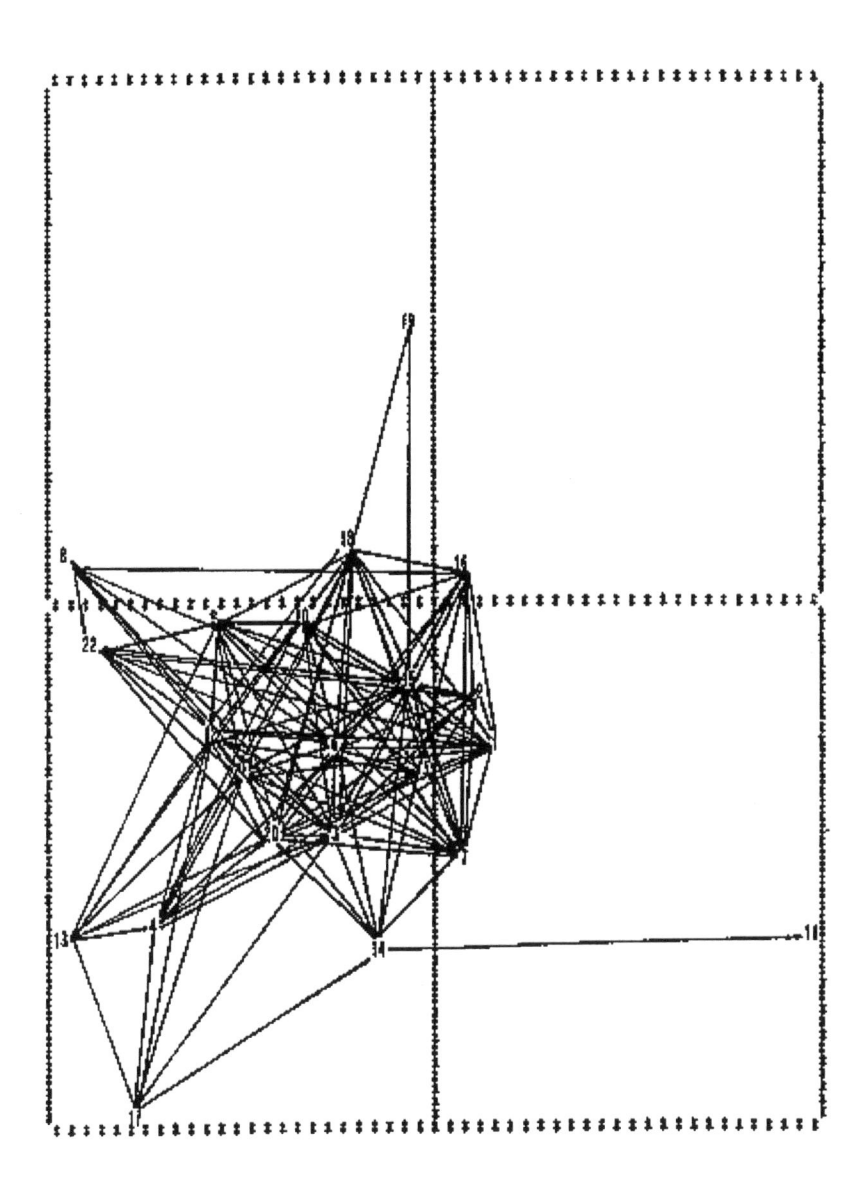

Figure 6.3 MSA of a Football Hooligan Group
(Guttman – Lingoes Coefficient of Alienation = 0.18219)

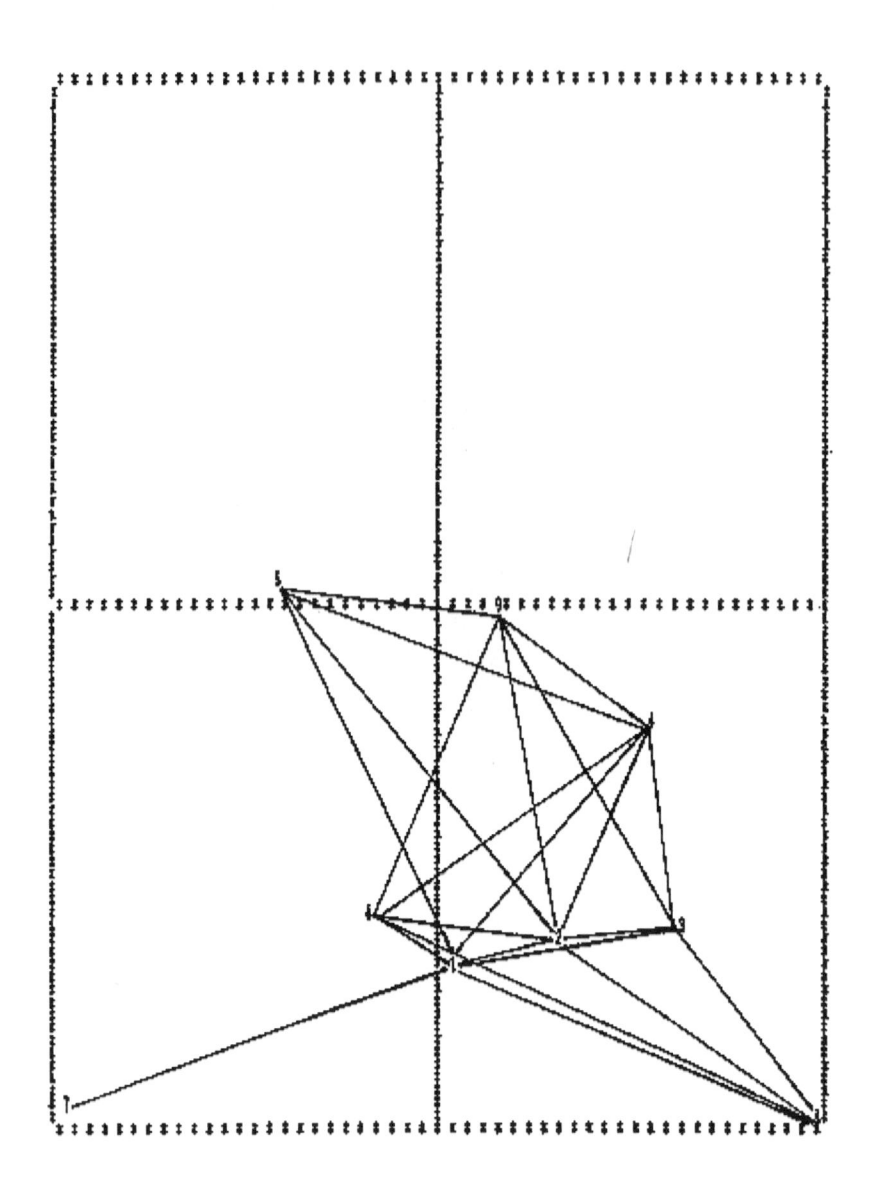

Figure 6.4 MSA of a Football Hooligan Group
(Guttman – Lingoes Coefficient of Alienation = 0.12523)

Riot by Appointment 175

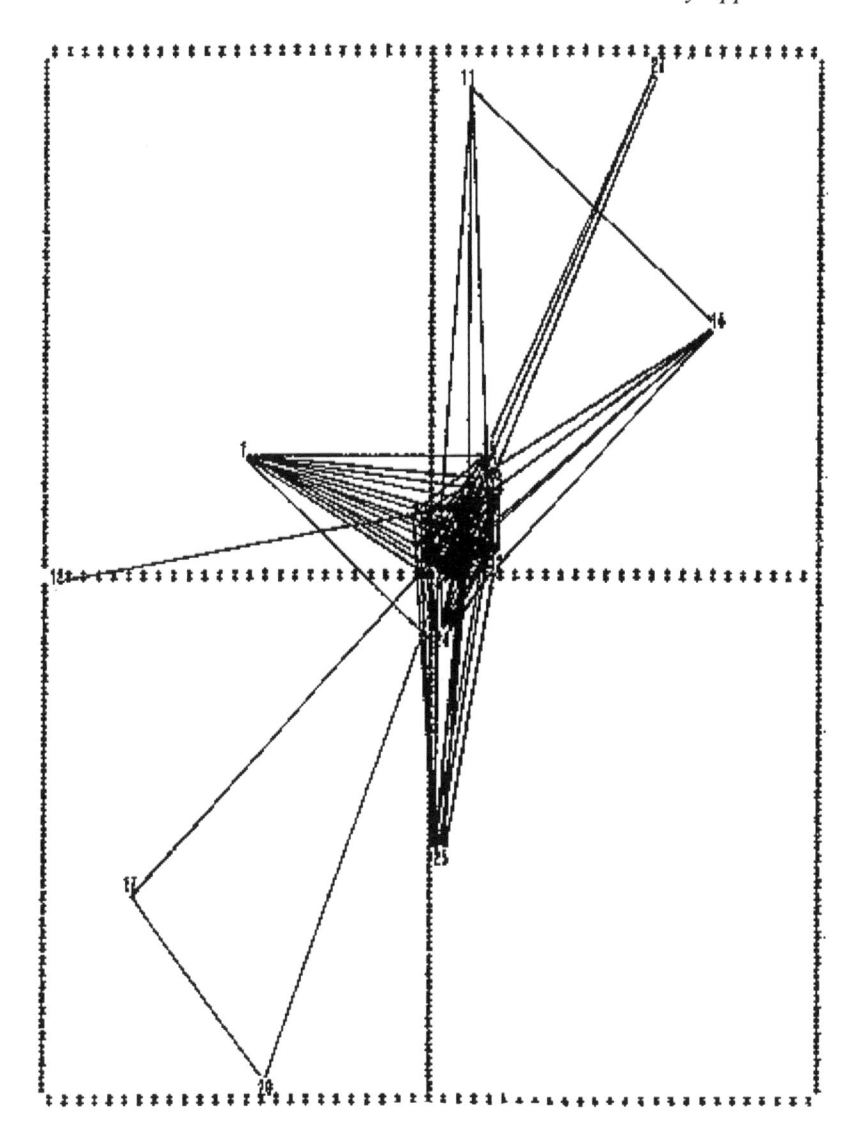

Figure 6.5 MSA of a Football Hooligan Group
(Guttman – Lingoes Coefficient of Alienation = 0.09654)

176 *The Social Psychology of Crime*

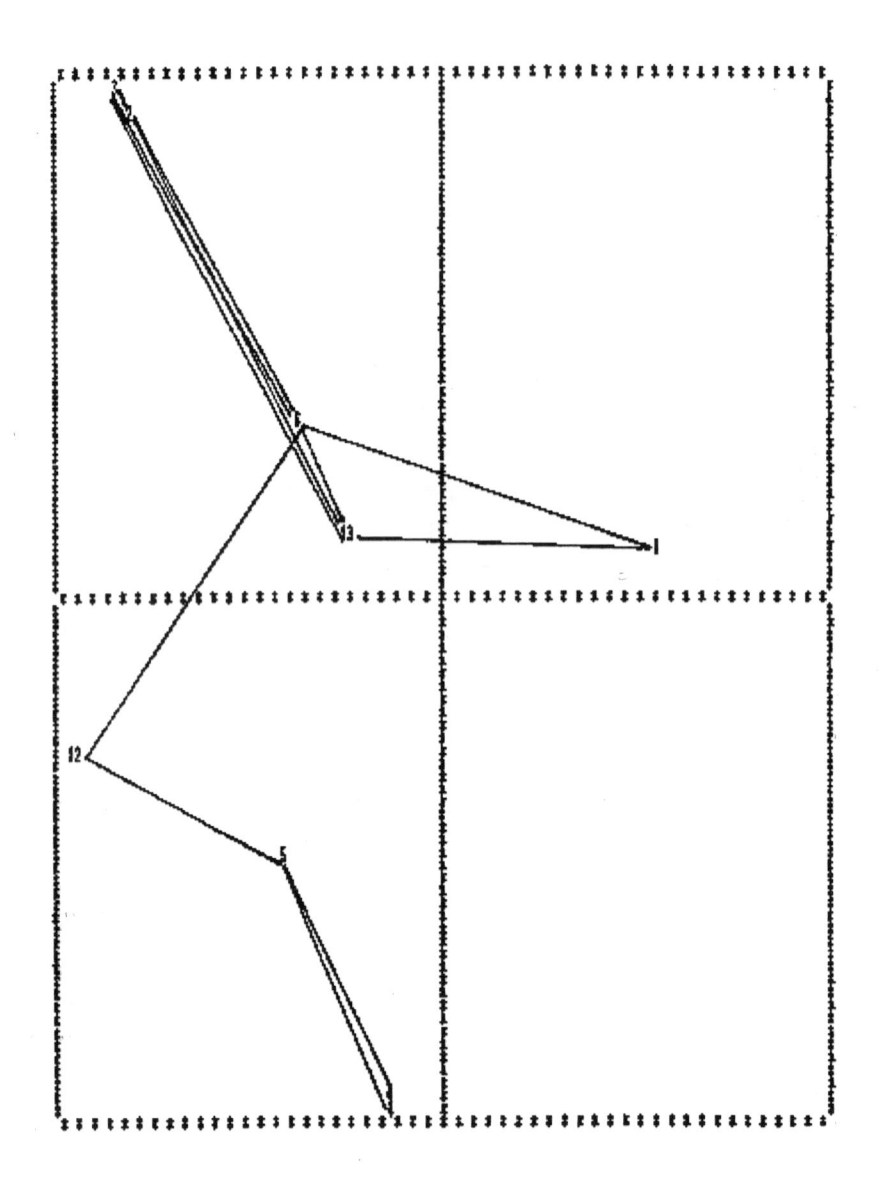

Figure 6.6 MSA of a Football Hooligan Group
(Guttman – Lingoes Coefficient of Alienation = 0.02551)

Figures 6.1 to 6.6 show that the individuals located within the centre of each diagram are those with the most associations. Moving outwards from the centre, the associations become less and less. Thus, those on the periphery of each plot are those with the fewest connections. The clearest structures may be observed in clubs 2 and 5, where it can be seen there is a definite central core, who have a high number of connections with each other, and with more peripheral members. Moving out from the central core, there is a second group, who has connections with members of the central core, but not as many as those in the centre, has with each other. This second group does not have as many connections with each other. This pattern may be observed as one moves further and further from the centre of Figures 6.2 and 6.5, where those with fewer interconnections are pushed away from the centre of the diagram.

Figures 6.2 and 6.5 provide support for the hypothesis that there is a hierarchical structure to football hooliganism. This may be conceptualised in terms of concentric rings moving outwards from the central hard core. The hierarchical structure is not so clear in Figures 6.1, 6.3, 6.4 and 6.6, as almost all members of these groups are interconnected. However the beginnings of a structure may be observed in Figures 6.1 and 6.3. One of the problems with directly comparing Figures 6.1 to 6.6 is that there were unequal numbers of subjects in each group. Those with the clearest structure had the highest number of subjects. It may be the case that the sample of individuals included in clubs 1, 3, 4 and 6 are the most central members of these groups, and that had more peripheral members been included, those in the present sample would have been pushed closer together towards the centre of each plot. Thus, this would produce a similar hierarchical structure to that found in Figures 6.2 and 6.5. Future research should aim to analyse a larger sample of football hooligans for each club.

Figures 6.2 and 6.5 help explain the problems with attempting to infer the cohesiveness of this group. If there is a hierarchical structure to hooligan groups, one must be clear which sub-group within this hierarchy is being examined. It seems the most productive means of assessing the cohesiveness of the group is to firstly clarify the structure of the group and then focus on the central '*core*' members. Restricting the measurement of cohesiveness in this way would have allowed a more direct comparison between the groups in this study.

In summary Figures 6.1 to 6.6 provide a preliminary indication that there is in fact a hierarchical structure to football hooligan groups. This structure may be described in terms of concentric rings moving outwards from the central 'hard core'. However we still do not know anything about the characteristics of those located within the different structural positions of the structure. For instance, are those in the centre more committed; are they the known leaders; and what sort of criminal background do they have? Additional analysis was thus conducted to examine the characteristics of individuals located within different positions in each of the structural positions.

Relationship between Structural Position and Background Characteristics

Figures 6.1 to 6.6 were used as the basis for this analysis. The structure of each group was closely scrutinised and from this it was decided that by adding frequency contours to each figure, individuals within each hooligan group could be assigned to a group, depending upon their structural position. All individuals in each hooligan group were assigned to one of three structural groups based on their position. Group 1 related to the most central members (i.e. those with the most associations in each group); group 2, related to those with a middle frequency of association (i.e. within the second frequency contour- moving outwards). Individuals assigned to group 3, were those who were located outside the second contour; and those who had earlier been excluded from the triangular matrixes due to lack of known associations (based on sightings). Figures 6.7 to 6.12 show the two-dimensional SSA plots for each of the six clubs, with frequency contours added. From this each individuals structural position can be observed.

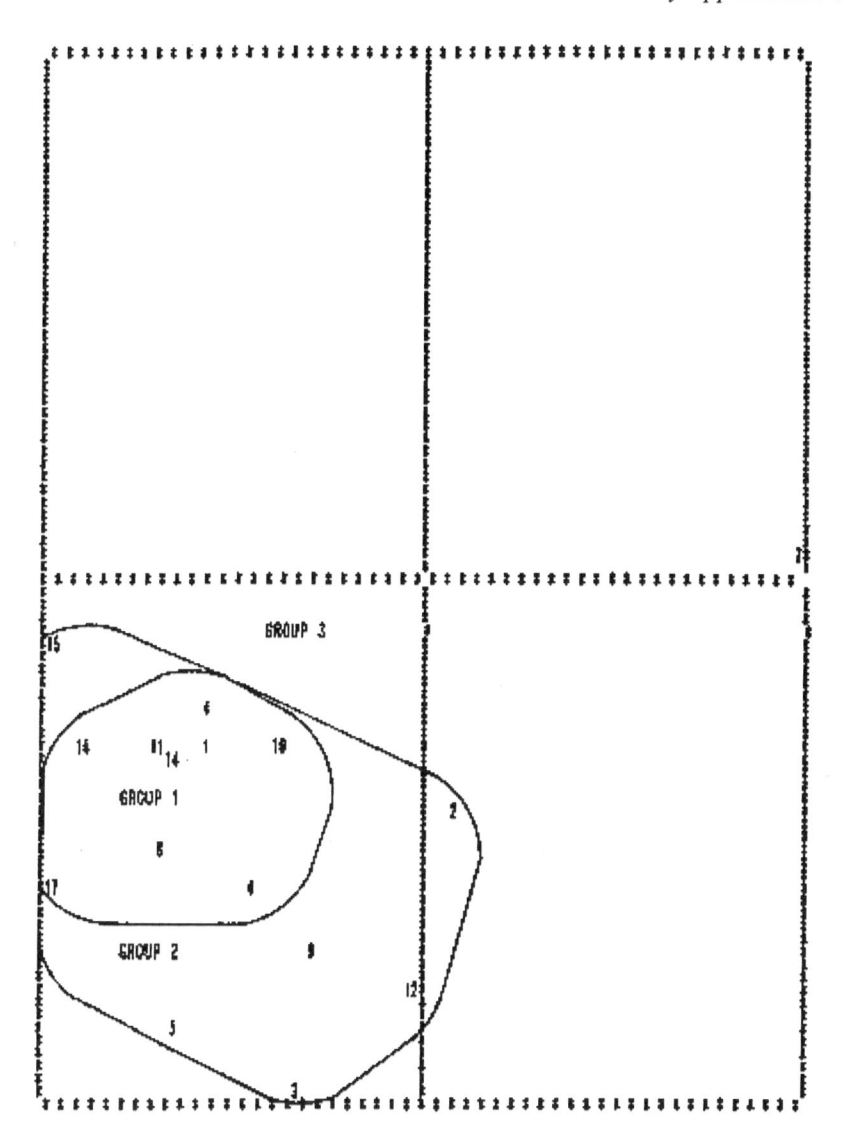

Figure 6.7 SSA outlining the Structural Frequency within a Hooligan Group
(Guttman Lingoes Coefficient of Alienation = 0.13237)

180 *The Social Psychology of Crime*

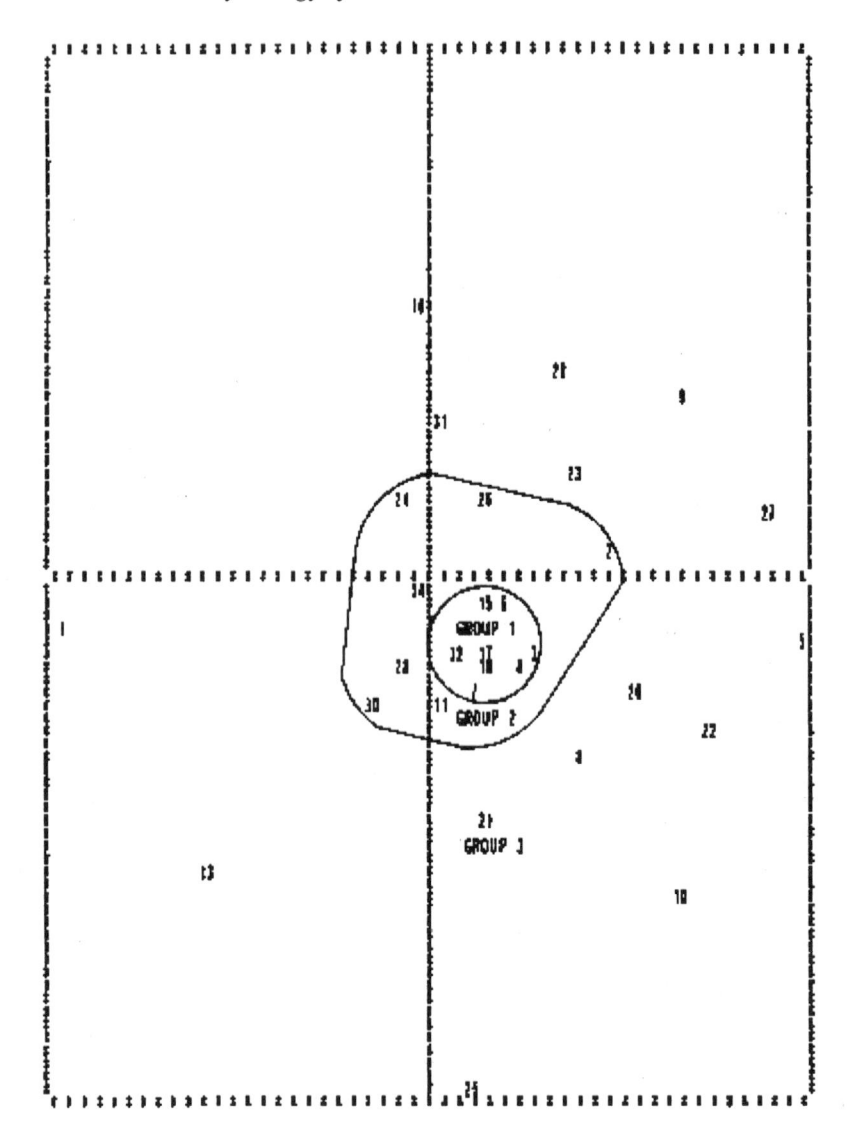

Figure 6.8 SSA outlining the Structural Frequency within a Hooligan Group
(Guttman Lingoes Coefficient of Alienation = 0.13237)

Riot by Appointment 181

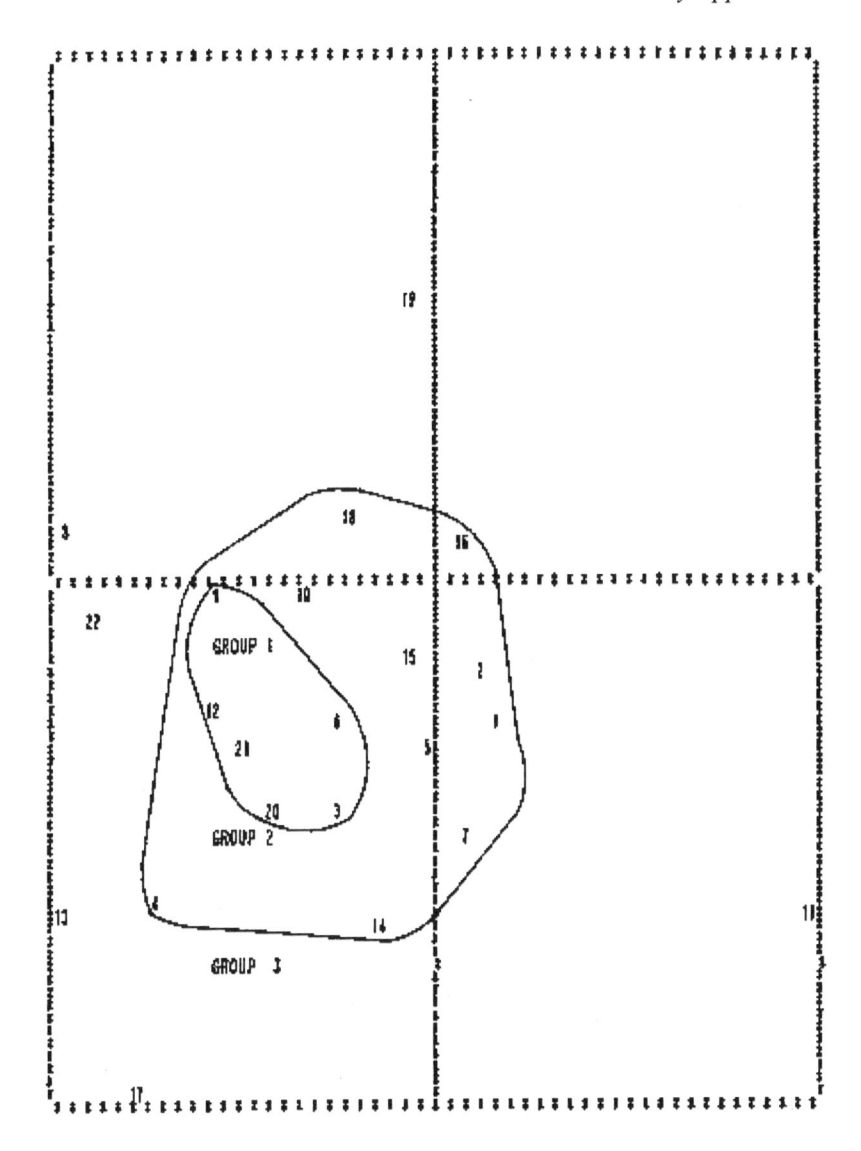

Figure 6.9 SSA outlining the Structural Frequency within a Hooligan Group
(G L Coefficient of Alienation = 0.13237)

182　*The Social Psychology of Crime*

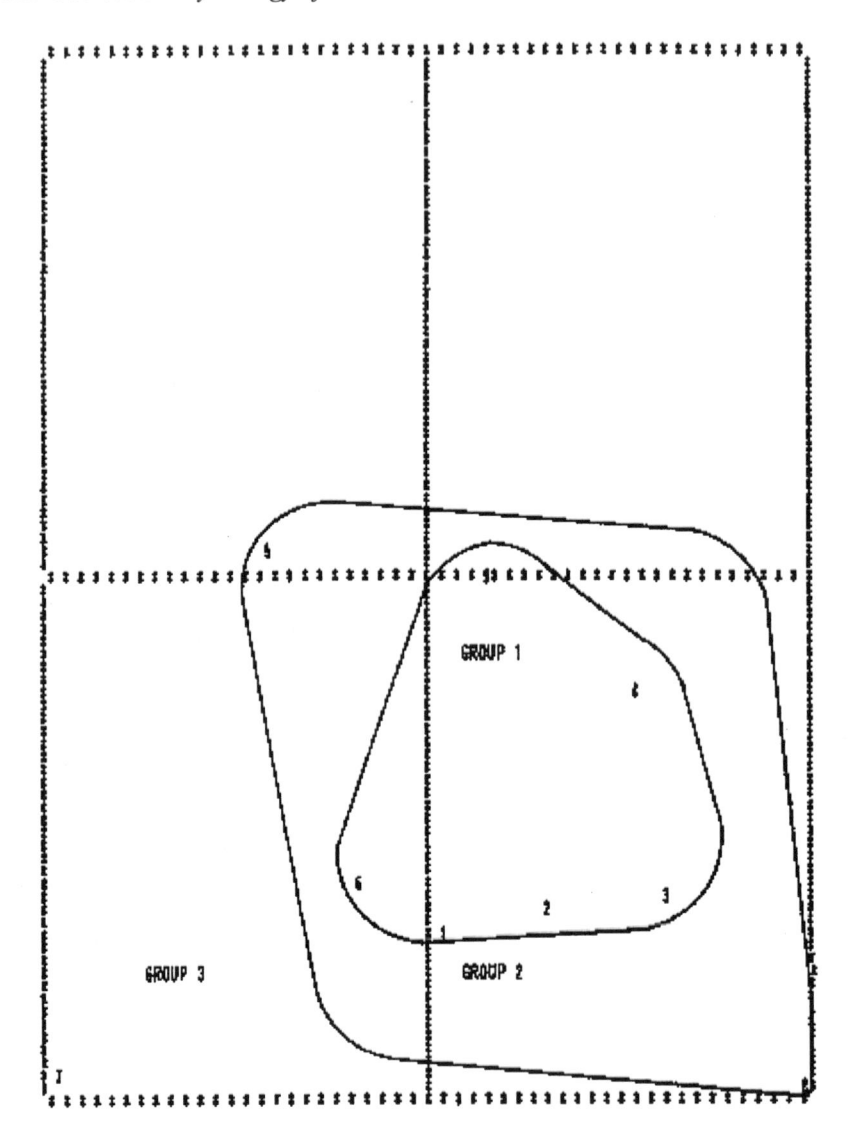

Figure 6.10　**SSA outlining the Structural Frequency within a Hooligan Group**
(Guttman Lingoes Coefficient of Alienation = 0.13237)

Riot by Appointment 183

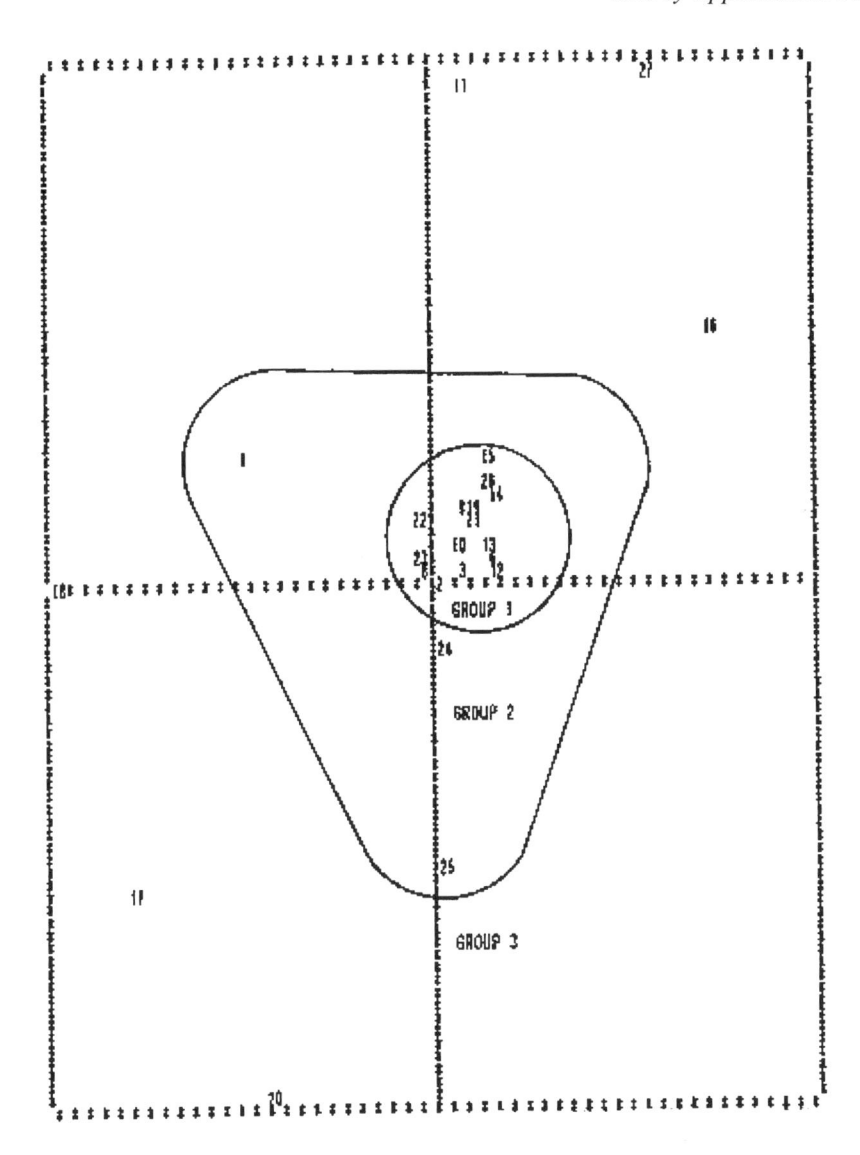

Figure 6.11   SSA outlining the Structural Frequency within a Hooligan Group
(Guttman Lingoes Coefficient of Alienation = 0.13237)

184 *The Social Psychology of Crime*

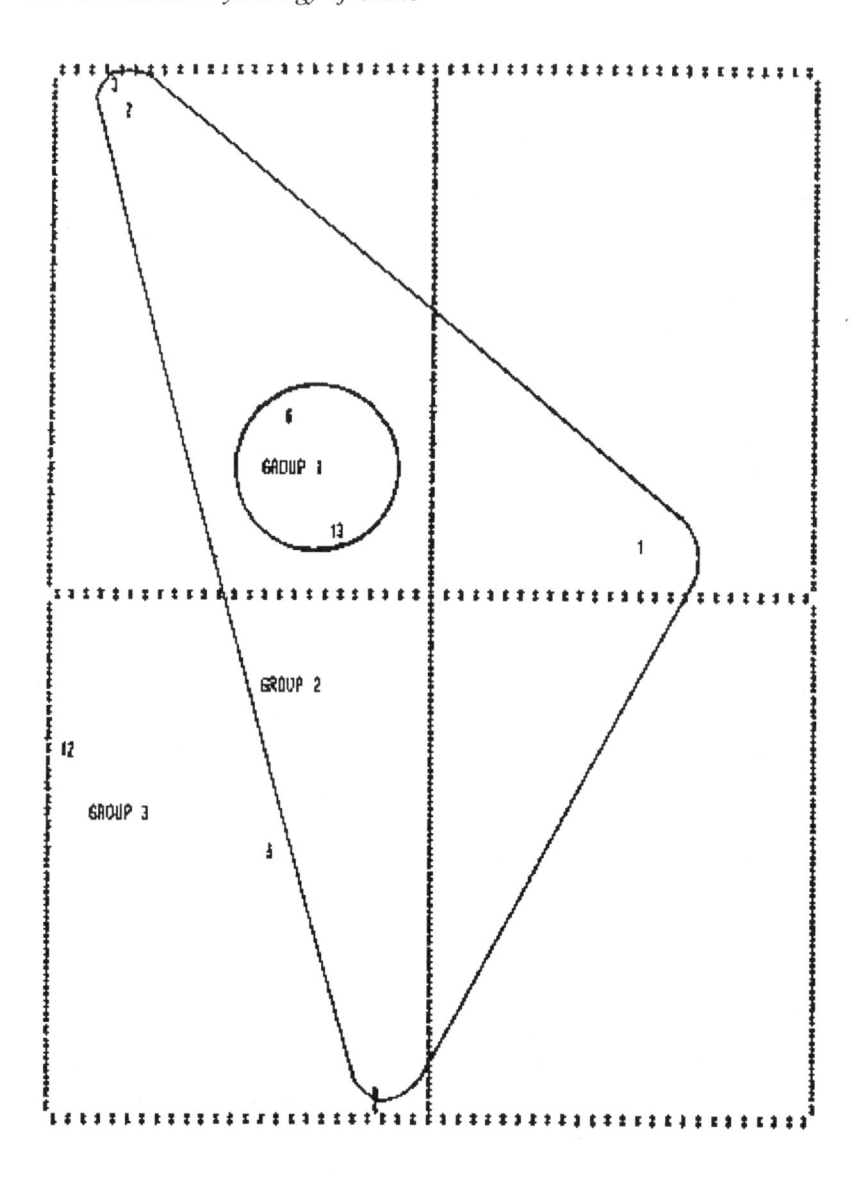

Figure 6.12 SSA outlining the Structural Frequency within a Hooligan Group
(Guttman Lingoes Coefficient of Alienation = 0.13237)

The next stage of analysis involved comparing the demographic and criminal backgrounds of individuals located within each of the three possible structural positions. No significant differences were noted between the structural position in the group and the following variables: age of first conviction; first convictions for dishonesty offences; total number of convictions; custodial sentence as a juvenile or adult; marital status; those who travel abroad; those who support the national side; those who support more than one club; and those known to be affiliated with the British National Party (BNP).

Significantly more people in position 1, (central), had 1st convictions for violence, (p<0.05). This offers preliminary support for the hypothesis that those who may be considered the most central hard-core members of each hooligan group may come into football hooliganism through a violent as opposed to dishonest background. In addition, analysis involving the total number of violence related convictions each individual had, approached significance, (F=1.87; P < 0.06). It seems likely therefore that those in the central position of each group do have a more violent criminal background than the more peripheral members.

It was hypothesised that the 'known leaders' of each group would be expected to occupy a more central position and the results confirmed this was the case, showing significant differences between the three possible structural positions (P<.05). Of the 23 known leaders in the sample 14 were positioned within the first frequency contour, two were positioned in the second, and seven in the outer contour.

Discussion of Results: Social Network Analysis

The study described in this chapter was concerned with developing a greater understanding of the nature and structure of 'hard-core' football hooligan groups, using police intelligence reports and criminal records. The use of SSA in this study provides a systematic means of determining where each subject is positioned in Euclidean space, thus overcoming the major weakness of the traditional sociogram. The SSA performed on six hooligan groups, allowed the structure of associations within each hooligan group to be easily interpreted and provided tentative support for the hypothesis that there is a hierarchical structure to football hooliganism, taking the form of concentric rings moving from the centre of the group. They provided a clear representation of each individual's structural position within the six hooligan groups studied.

This allowed the final analysis to be conducted; comparing individuals within different structural positions in each club on a variety of demographic and criminal background characteristics. Various structural differences were noted, providing preliminary support for the hypothesis that the leaders of each hooligan group are more likely to be located within the central core of the social network diagram, having many connections with both the other central members and more peripheral members. Those who are located within the centre of each group are more likely to have a predominantly violent as opposed to dishonesty background and they are also more likely to have first convictions for violence rather than dishonesty.

The main limitation of this study concerned the lack of comparable levels of intelligence for each hooligan group. Future research should aim to examine each group separately and to include larger samples. Samples of approximately 150 individuals from each hooligan group would seem appropriate. From this clearer differences between the true hard-core members and more peripheral members may be established, and the basis to the hierarchical structure which has been tentatively suggested may be further explored. If a clear structure can be identified, then further analysis examining the variables considered in this study may be conducted for each hooligan group separately.

Future research should explore alternative ways to represent the data. One way in which this may be done would be to represent each individual's associations on a separate diagram. Plots similar to Figure 6.1 may be used in the first stages of analysis to identify the key individuals. The next stage would merely involve a more detailed representation of the relationships involving the key individuals. If plots were produced for each individual separately, colour coded lines, arrowheads, broken and solid lines may be added to represent the associations in more detail. A more general implication for future research is that researchers should aim to extend this study by exploring the methodology used to develop a greater understanding of other criminal organisations.

A variety of software packages that visually represent relationships amongst organised groups of criminals are currently being used by various police forces world-wide. The notebooks visually represent relationships amongst organised groups of criminals. These provide a visual chart summary of the central features and links in a criminal organisation.

However, they suffer from the same limitation as the traditional sociogram, in that there does not appear to be any systematic structuring principle or system of co-ordinates as there is with SSA.

Conclusion

This chapter has provided a general profile of a sample of 140 known 'hard-core' football hooligans. This is arguably more comprehensive than previous research in this area and provides a more detailed insight into the characteristics of the type of individuals centrally involved, in hooliganism. The use of SSA was explored as a useful methodology for examining relationships between individuals involved in hooligan groups and for developing a precise understanding of the structure of such groups. The main limitation of this study concerned the lack of comparable levels of intelligence for each hooligan group. Future research should aim to examine each group separately and to include larger samples. It is hypothesised that if this is conducted, a clear differentiation between the various levels in the proposed hierarchy of football hooliganism may be observed.

References

Canter, D.V., Comber, M. and Uzzell, D.L. (1989), *Football in its Place: An Environmental Psychology of Football Grounds,* London: Routledge.

Centre For Leisure Research. (1984), *Crowd Behaviour at Football Matches: A Study in Scotland,* Edinburgh: Centre For Leisure Research.

Dunning, E., Murphy, P. and Williams, J. (1988), *The Roots of Football Hooliganism,* London: Routledge & Kegan Paul.

Harrington, J. (1968), *Soccer Hooliganism: A Preliminary Report,* Bristol: John Wright & Son Ltd.

Johnston, L. (1994), *Riot by Appointment: An Examination of the Nature and Structure of Seven Hard Core Football Hooligan Groups,* Unpublished MSc thesis. University of Surrey, Guildford, England.

Melnick, M. (1986), 'The Mythology Of Football Hooliganism: A Closer Look At The British Experience', *International Review For Sociology Of Sport,* **21 (1)**, 1-19.

Moreno, J. (1953), *Who Shall Survive? Foundations of Sociometry, Group Psychotherapy and Sociodrama,* Beacon, N.Y.: Beacon House Inc.

Popplewell, O. (1986), *Committee of Inquiry into Crowd Safety and Control at Sports Grounds; Final Report,* London: HMSO.

Scott, J.P. (1991), *Social Network Analysis: A handbook,* London: Sage.

Short, J. (1990), 'New Wine In Old Bottles? Change & Continuity In American Gangs', in C.R. Huff, (ed.), *Gangs In America,* London: Sage.

Thomas, K. (1979), *Sociometric techniques,* Nottingham: Nottingham University School of Education.

Trivizas, E. (1980), 'Offences and offenders in football crowd disorders', *British Journal of Criminology,* **20(3)**, 276-288.

Trivizas, E. (1981), 'Sentencing The Football Hooligan', *British Journal Of Criminology,* 21, 343-349.

Van Limbergen, K., Colaers, C. and Walgrave, L. (1989), 'The societal and psycho-sociological background of football hooliganism', *Current Psychology Research and Reviews,* **8(1)**, 4-14.

7 Ram Raiding: Criminals Working in Groups

IAN DONALD AND ANGELA WILSON

Enschewing the traditional social psychological approach to understanding group crime, the chapter examines the actions of commercial burglars - ram raiders - from the perspective of organisational psychology. One of the central questions asked is whether such offenders can be thought of as work groups in the same sense as more legitimate groups? Multidimensional Scaling (MDS) analysis of the behaviours and previous criminal records of ram raiders shows that group members develop a career that results in a degree of specialisation. Ram raid group structure resembles that of legitimate work groups, with members occupying and performing specific interdependent roles and tasks during the execution of the crime. The groups contain a clear leader as well as apprentices, who tend to go on to become leaders, and others who specialise in violence, driving and so on. These roles and tasks reflect the members' previous specialisation. The ram raiders fulfil most of the criteria necessary to define them as work groups. It is concluded that an organisational perspective is useful in developing an understanding of criminal activity, but also that organisational psychology can benefit theoretically and conceptually from considering non-legitimate work groups.

Ian Donald is a Senior Lecturer at the University of Liverpool. He teaches Applied Psychology and has responsibility research methods on the MSc course in Investigative Psychology. Since obtaining his PhD from Aston University Business School his main areas of research interest are within work and organisational psychology. He has advised major companies, the HSE, and the European Union on various industrial issues. Currently Dr. Donald has a number of research projects with international

Blue-chip companies looking at such factors as organisational climate and culture, organisational change, teamwork, and psychological aspects of industrial safety. He also has a long-standing interest in human behaviour in disasters, facet theory and psychological and emotional aspects of office design. Dr. Donald has published widely on social, environmental and organisational psychology as well as research methods. He has also presented his work at conferences and is invited to lectures around the world. In all he has presented and published over 100 papers. Dr. Donald is a chartered psychologist, Associate Fellow of the British Psychological Society, and a Member of the Institution of Occupational Safety and Health.

Angela Wilson is a Detective Chief Inspector with Thames Valley Police. She was awarded a BSc (Hons) degree in Psychology from St. Andrews University in 1984. She joined Thames Valley later that year. She studied with Professor Canter at Liverpool University in 1994/95 and was awarded the MSc in Investigative Psychology with distinction in 1995. Her Dissertation entitled "Do Birds of a Feather Flock Together" was a study of the criminal profiles of groups of offenders committing ram-raid offences. In 1996 she was awarded a Home Office, Police Research Group grant to study the geographic patterns and profile of domestic burglary offenders. She is currently reading for an MBA degree at Reading University.

7 Ram Raiding: Criminals Working in Groups
IAN DONALD and ANGELA WILSON

Introduction

Ram raiding, group commercial burglary, is legally defined as burglary, where "A person is a burglar if, having entered any building or part of a building as a trespasser he steals or attempts to steal anything in the building...". This is contrary to Section 9 of the Theft Act of 1968 and carries a maximum sentence of 14 years imprisonment. Despite this definition, ram raiding is behaviourally distinct from the usual images that people have of burglary and burglars.

Most people's image of burglary is of one, or perhaps two offenders breaking into a dwelling or commercial premises and quietly stealing property. Often such a crime is thought to involve relatively little planning and to be opportunistic. Ram raiding, on the other hand, is a professional crime that is usually well planned and overall requires a high level of skill and experience. Further it is a crime in which individuals work together in both planning and execution. As ram raiding appears to be a group activity, researching the area can draw on general psychological concepts, theories and findings relating to groups. Such research can also inform the study of groups from a perspective other than the more conventional social and organisational groups that have traditionally been the focus of research.

A Typical Ram Raiding Offence

While neither the police nor Home Office record ram raiding as a specific offence, incidents of ram raiding were seen as early as the 1930s when smash-and-grab raids, as they were then called, became common. Often several vehicles were used, with one smashing through part of a building to create an access point, another used during the raid, a third to make a getaway and sometimes a fourth to obstruct the police (Gosling, 1959). In the 1950s another variation was seen in which grappling irons were hooked to the grilles of jewellers shops, and then attached to the rear of a car, which was driven off at speed.

Today, typically and almost exclusively, groups of male offenders commit ram raids. The target premises are commercial, being retail, wholesale or more recently private company offices. The group, which numbers usually three to five offenders, will arrive at the target premises in one or more stolen high performance vehicles. Then either the vehicle or, more recently, tools such as sledge hammers, crowbars and bolt croppers, will be used to effect entry through doors, grills and plate glass windows. Generally a driver will remain in the vehicle while the others load a large amount of goods into the vehicle. Often one member of the group will stand guard with a weapon, usually a wooden or metal bar.

Within about 3-5 minutes of arriving at the scene, the group will drive off, often at very high speeds, and recklessly if required to outrun the police. The nature of the target often varies but is most usually one that contains electrical goods, fashion or sports clothing, jewellery or cigarettes.

More recently, however, attention has turned almost exclusively to computer equipment. Offenders may commit more than one offence each night and will commit many each month. These are high value crimes. One offence can net tens of thousands of pounds worth of goods.

Thus modern ram raiding has several different stages, e.g. planning, preparation, target selection, stealing a vehicle, smashing entry, stealing a quantity of goods in a short time, standing guard, driving a getaway vehicle, disposal and realisation of goods. Carrying out all these activities is not physically possible for one person and so the offence is by necessity committed by a group.

Despite this type of crime being committed for sixty years there has been a dearth of research on ram raiders or ram raiding, with most criminological research being focused on domestic burglars (see Bennett and Wright (1985) and Maguire (1982)). To gain a better understanding of group commercial burglary, this chapter will examine the previous convictions of a number of ram raiders. It will also look at how these relate to their roles within the commission of a ram raiding offence, and general group related issues.

Groups and Group Behaviour

One obvious characteristic of ram raids is that they are carried out by a number of people rather than solitary individuals or dyads. A central question then, is what the nature of that collection of people is? For instance whether ram raiders represent a group or simply a number of co-offenders. A further question is, if ram raiders are a group, what type of group are they? For example, they could be an informal social group, or a work group. In answering these and related questions some insights into how ram raiders operate may be achieved. This is likely to have applied implications, for instance, in indicating the sorts of offender that should be investigated, including whether an investigation should focus on violent criminals, burglars or others.

Examining the nature of ram raiders will also have more academic implications for theories of groups. While investigative forensic psychology is an applied discipline, these theoretical and conceptual issues are no less important. Investigative psychology is also a relatively new discipline. As part of its developments it will draw on existing areas of psychology, but also contribute to them. Part of this contribution will be a consequence of researching different, often unusual, populations to those that have typically been examined by, for instance, organisational psychologists. How adequately theories and concepts from other fields can account for the actions of these different populations allows an assessment of those theories and indicates areas of weakness. In this way investigative psychology can draw on and contribute to other fields of psychology.

The concept of groups has historically received much attention in social psychology. More recently organisational psychologists have become predominant in the study of group behaviour. With this change has been a shift in focus from the impact of group membership on individual behaviour, to an examination of the impact of group activity on performance (Guzzo, 1996). The concepts used in both social and organisational psychology may be applied in investigative psychology and the study of group offending. Drawing on these two perspectives a number of dimensions can be used to characterise and classify groups, however, the present chapter will be limited to some of the most fundamental.

The Purpose of Groups

Groups form so as to be able to, *inter alia*, perform particular tasks that individuals working alone cannot achieve. Some advantages of groups include the ability to work on complex, interdependent tasks, and the possibility of training new members (Chell, 1993). From the description of a typical ram raid provided above, clearly committing such an offence would not be possible for a lone offender. The function of training new members is intriguing, and will be considered in relation to ram raiders later.

Formality of Groups

One of the most basic distinctions made in social and organisational psychology is between formal and informal groups. Dipboye, Smith and Howell (1994) describe formal groups as created by an organisation to achieve work goals or specific tasks. The organisation tends not to recognise informal groups, in contrast, nor do they constitute them. Rather, informal groups emerge out of the day-to-day interactions of people within organisations or wider social context often as a consequence of proximity. The clear goals of ram raiders suggest they are a formal group. Yet that they are not put together by an organisation suggests a degree of informality.

Structure, Roles and Hierarchy

One of the clear defining features of a group is that it has a purpose and structure. Beyond groups being intentionally formed to achieve a particular goal or carry out an activity, each member of a group will usually have a specific role with an associated task to perform. Such role differentiation is a common feature of all groups (Brown, 1988) and has several advantages. For instance, it helps to make behaviour within the group more predictable and so bring internal order to the group. Differentiation also facilitates the division of labour, increasing the probability of success (Chell, 1993). Role differentiation is reflected in the group having a structure, "an interdependent network of roles and hierarchical status's" (Sherif and Sherif, 1969 p.150). If roles are not interdependent, and tasks are carried out independently, members of a group are simply likely to be co-acting.

While it may be assumed that ram raiders share a common goal and are intentionally brought together, the issue about whether particular individuals perform different roles, whether the group has a structure, is much more difficult to take for granted. Role differentiation within ram raiding groups is therefore something that is necessary to establish from empirical investigation. One of the principal aims of the present chapter is to provide such an empirical examination of ram raiding groups.

Ram Raiding Groups as Work Groups

As will be seen in later discussion of criminal co-offending, attempts to understand crime related group phenomena have tended to draw on the sociological and social psychological literature. There has, however, been some criticism of social psychological work on groups in terms of both the ecological validity of the research (Hartley, 1996) and the broadness of its concepts (Guzzo, 1996). In looking at ram raiders, the interest is not really in their relation to wider society or the social psychological issues that relate them to their social context. Rather, ram raiding is, relatively unusually for studies of criminals, considered here as work or a job. A more useful approach, if crime is considered primarily as work rather than deviance, is offered by organisational psychology. Shifting perspective from a social psychological and sociological viewpoint to an organisational psychology one is in many ways shifting perspective from that of society, how it came to produce the outsider, to that of the criminal, how he effectively organises his work. It is perhaps by understanding the criminal perspective that many new advances in investigative psychology are likely to ensue.

Guzzo (1996) makes an observation that is of some theoretical relevance here, noting that "the term group has indeed been used very expansively in general social science, for example to describe social aggregates in which there is no interdependence of members. But this has not been the case in the organisational sciences" (p.9). Consequently the

196 The Social Psychology of Crime

more limited and specific concept of work group will be used to consider ram raiders.

From this perspective one of the most basic questions is whether ram raiders do operate as work groups. Guzzo (1996) defines work groups by the existence of five co-present attributes. These are that:

a. They are social entities embedded in larger social systems. Such a social system is seen as the organisation.

b. They perform tasks relevant to the social system's (organisation's) mission.

c. The task performance has consequences that affect others inside and outside the organisation.

d. The work roles of members are interdependent.

e. The membership of the group is identifiable to both those inside and outside the group (Guzzo, 1996, p.8).

These defining characteristics raise a number of implications in relation to what a ram-raiding group is, and what the definition of a work group should be. By Guzzo's definition ram raiding groups are not work groups. For instance, they will not necessarily meet the first three of the criteria. Ram Raiders are not necessarily part of a larger organisation. They do not therefore perform tasks that help achieve the organisation's mission, and they do not have consequences for people within the organisation. The only likely scenario in which a ram raiding team will fulfil these criteria is if they are part of a larger criminal organisation, such as the Mafia or triads.

It could be argued that although ram raiders are not part of an organisation as usually conceived, they are nonetheless "embedded in a larger social system", society. The main difficulty with this is that it is unlikely that ram raiders would be performing tasks "relevant to the social system's mission". In fact, offenders such as these are clearly doing tasks that are directly contrary to society's mission. If this were not so, politicians would not expend so much effort in the pursuit of law and order. The counter argument to this could be that it is a social system of deviance, a criminal subculture, of which they are a part. Nevertheless, what this implies is that to have a criminal group requires both a criminal subculture and for that subculture to be both organised and have a clear mission. This is unlikely.

Ram raiding groups however do fulfil other criteria. These indicate that considering them as work groups is perfectly reasonable. For instance, members do share a common goal, the groups may have a clear structure, differentiation and specialisation of roles, comprise 'professional' participants who engage in such activity as a significant source of income, have identifiable membership, and task performance has implications for those within and outside the group.

Surely then, if ram raiding groups fulfil these criteria, they may be considered to be work groups. This can be further emphasised by comparing them with other recognised and acknowledged workgroups. Parallels can be drawn, for instance, between aircraft crews and ram raid groups. Both may have clear role differentiation, a hierarchy, shared goals, are recognisable in terms of membership and come together for a relatively short time to do a specific task. The only difference is that ram raiders do not necessarily work within a larger organisation.

What this discussion suggests is that the definition, provided by organisational psychologists, of what a work group needs revision to allow for groups such as ram raiders. In particular it appears that it should not be necessary to the definition of a work group, that such a group is part of a wider organisation. Academically, that the groups operate outside the law and outside the framework of legitimate work groups should not preclude them being defined as work groups.

Teams and Groups

A distinction is often made between teams and groups. In examining this issue, Guzzo (1996) points to the writing of Katzenbach and Smith (1993) who, according to Guzzo, consider the difference to be that "a group's performance is a function of what members do as individuals, whereas a team's performance includes individual and collective or joint work products" (Guzzo, 1996, p.8). That is, group members co-act, but in teams output is a result of individual *and* group members' interactions. Steiner (1972), however, has rightly argued that output from exclusively co-action is rare outside laboratory studies. Further, other writers define groups in terms of interaction (eg. Chell, 1993; Hartley, 1996; West, 1996). After considering these issues Guzzo concludes that no "grand distinction" can be made between teams and groups and uses the terms interchangeably. Interestingly, in his preface to the *Handbook of Work Group Psychology,* West (1996) also uses the terms interchangeably.

Offending in Groups

The issue of criminal groups, especially in relation to ram raids, has not really been addressed beyond co-offending and the activities of juvenile gangs. Furthermore, the literature on group criminal behaviour that does exist provides a confusing picture. First, there seems no clear definition of what criminal groups are or of different types of groups. For instance, some studies treat group offending as synonymous with the criminal activities of gangs with well-defined structure and leadership (cf. Miller, 1975). Others contend that groups who offend together are not highly structured (cf. Morash, 1983). Yet others see the offending groups as social networks made up of pairs, triads and constellations of four or more persons (cf. Reiss, 1986) without fulfilling many accepted criteria for what constitutes a group. Again it would be of benefit for investigative and forensic researchers to draw on the organisational psychology literature.

Group or accomplice offending is also known as *co-offending* in most of the criminal psychology and criminology literature. Co-offending is the committing of offences in 'groups' consisting of two or more individuals. Co-offending, however, can include instances in which two or more people commit a crime, but with no clear differentiation of the roles played by the co-offenders. It would be possible to argue that co-offending is not, therefore, group behaviour. In essence, group crime requires co-offending, though co-offending may not *per se* fulfil the criteria for a group, and is therefore not group activity. Consequently psychological, organisational and social processes are likely to be involved in true group offending that are not present in co-offending. Therefore it is unlikely that the same concepts and models can be used to structure and understand both group and co-offending behaviour.

If co-offending is to be considered as group behaviour it is all the more important that group behaviour such as that displayed by offenders such as ram raiders be differentiated. Co-offenders should be considered as a *co-acting group* (cf. Chell, 1993), as distinct from a work group.

Even within the literature on co-offending few studies have been carried out. Those that do exist tend to have examined samples of juveniles (Breckinridge and Abbot, 1917; Maguire and Bennett, 1982; Reiss, 1980; Shaw and McKay, 1931). In a review of research on co-offending, Reiss (1988) concluded that co-offending was more characteristic of juveniles, often called in the literature 'delinquents', than of adults. This literature thus tells us little of the behaviour of adult groups such as ram raiders. Even longitudinal studies of criminal careers that have followed samples of youths into their adult years (e.g. Shannon, 1978; Wolfgang, 1978), have not examined patterns of co-offending into adulthood.

Adult Co-Offending

Selection of Co-Offenders

In establishing the nature of group or co-offending an important issue is the selection of co-offenders. As to practical implications, if co-offenders are sought foremost for their skills, the geographical area from which offenders are selected is likely to be as wide as necessary to find people with appropriate skills. This may be a broad geographical range, requiring a broad search by police in an attempt to identify suspects. If however, selection were based on convenience and proximity, then focusing on a limited area would be appropriate for investigation. At a more theoretical level, if proximity is the principal factor in the selection of co-offenders, by implication skill-based role differentiation is less likely. In such cases the co-offenders are less likely to comprise a genuine work group with the associated characteristics.

Gould et al. (1965) examined what they termed 'professional' criminals. They reported that networks of adult offenders were characterised by the fact that the offenders seemed to patronise the same types of places, make the same kinds of social transactions and often be linked by a common residential area. They conclude, "excepting recruitment for more sophisticated crimes, which require a variety of highly specialised skills, the daily round suffices to select accomplices" (p.25). They also noted that the typical co-offending relationship seemed transitory with continual searches for new accomplices. Gould et al. (1965) consequently also concluded "while a few professional criminals work for extended periods with the same accomplices, most work from day-to-day, or week-to-week, with whomever they can put together for a particular job" (p.51). Gould et al.'s research is to some extent supported by Shover (1973) who found that burglars work together with co-offenders being "Formed from the pool of available manpower which frequents the bars and lounges where thieves hang out" (p.502). The characteristics described by Gould et al. and Shover, suggest that while co-offending was evident from their research, who offended with whom was a matter of social geography and convenience, rather than specialisation of roles, unless a particularly sophisticated crime were to be committed. The results of this research would suggest that the co-offenders included in their studies at most formed informal groups as proximity seemed the main basis for collaboration with little in terms of specialised roles, and therefore, presumably, role differentiation.

Role Differentiation

Few studies that have examined roles during the commission of offences have direct relevance to understanding ram raiding. Two that do however raise some interesting questions are Shover's (1973) previously cited study of the social organisation of burglars and Einstadter's (1969) similar investigation of armed robbers.

Role differentiation is to some extent apparent in both burglaries and armed robberies, although more pronounced in the former. Shover identified several roles present in the interactions of co-offending burglars in terms of internal and external organisation. The internal organisation was the *crew* themselves. These are the group of individuals who commit the burglary offence. The external organisations are those outside the crews that have symbiotic social relationships with the crew members. Einstadter, however, found no external members or organisations; "There is no sharing with outsiders as they do not exist for the robber" (p.66). In looking at the internal organisation, Shover found that the characteristics of the crews were that there are usually two or three stable members who often remain together over a relatively long period of time. If additional manpower is needed, someone known to the group will fill in, usually fitting into a specialised role by, for example, being physically strong or technically skilled. There was also some slight indication of role differentiation with, for instance, one person usually acting as lookout. Further, people's roles seem to be relatively consistent from one burglary to the next. In relation to armed robbery, Einstadter provides a similar description, noting that most offenders operate in groups of three; "The typical career robbery triad consists of two men who enter the establishment armed; the third remains outside near an automobile, is usually armed but need not be. Of the two men who perform the actual robbery, one is considered the 'backup'. It is his function to watch any customers in the establishment, prevent any from leaving, and 'cover' those that might enter while his partner gathers the cash. At times he assists also in gathering the *take* if there are no customers or other conditions that need his attention." (p.74). If the size and complexity of the robbery require, more people may take part in it, but as Einstadter notes, they do not perform roles that are different from the basic triad. During armed robbery and burglary, then, the participants have clear tasks to do. Thus, role differentiation is evident, although this is perhaps less complex for armed robbers. However, some difference between the groups may exist about how they allocate roles and whether they are interchangeable.

Shover suggests that within groups of burglars there is a degree of task specialisation. For instance he argues that "Tasks during scores are allocated on the basis of personal strengths and weaknesses, or personal preference" (p.504). This can be contrasted with Einstadter. While noting that committing an offence with others allows for the differentiation of tasks, Einstader writes, "Assignments are made as to the role each partner is to play in the encounter. The strengths and weaknesses of various members may be assessed and conclusions reached as to the roles best fitted to each participant. At other times a more flexible arrangement is used with assignments shifting from robbery to robbery. A loose specialisation results that is flexible and adaptable according to circumstances" (pp.73-74). Both authors imply some specialisation based on skills, but for armed robbery, this seems weaker. One reason for this may be the more limited roles that are to be performed during a robbery. It can be concluded that role differentiation during armed robbery and burglary is evident. However, clear flexibility resulting in roles that are to a degree interchangeable and with only weak specialisation of tasks is present.

Hierarchy and Leadership

Two related issues that have received considerable attention from social and organisational psychologists examining groups are the role of leader and the presence of a hierarchy within groups. Both Einstadter and Shover found only limited evidence for hierarchy or leadership within the burglary and armed robbery crews they examined. In relation to armed robbers Einstadter concluded, "there is little discernible evidence of distinctive leadership roles, (although) previous experiences of members are given due recognition. The group then is a partnership of equals. No single individual gives orders or assigns positions without group or individual consensus" (pp.72-3). Similarly, Shover writes in relation to burglars "Such differentiation of authority as does exist is usually grounded in marked internal differences in age, criminal experience, or skill. Rarely, however, is there a formally designated leader. An easy informally arrived at consensus seems to be the rule here" (p.504). Thus, while there is some evidence of hierarchy, both authors characterise the groups as relatively consensual and democratic.

External Context

Earlier it was discussed that work groups operate within a wider social or organisational context. It was further discussed whether, for criminal groups, this context may comprise the wider criminal community within which they function. There is some, albeit limited, indication of this from Shover's work. External social relationships among Shover's (1973) burglars were known as *connections*. An offender who is well connected will have established and maintained a set of practical and profitable relationships. Connections that they make serve the purpose of easing problems the crew or group may have in committing their crimes or realising profits. An important contact therefore is most often the 'fence' or handler who will deal with the stolen goods and provide a 'safe outlet' for merchandise. Burglars in Shover's study also relied on external connections for information as to appropriate targets and links to others in legitimate society, such as attorneys, in the event of arrest. These people provide essential support for the effective operation of the burglars. It is clear, however, that they do not form a social or organisational system such as that required for work groups as characterised earlier. Rather, outside connections have a symbiotic relationship, otherwise being independent of one another. They therefore do not fulfil the particular criteria of the definition of a work group.

Teams, Groups and Co-Offenders

Given the preceding discussion, it is possible to suggest that criminal activity involving more than one or two individuals may be located along a continuum of, in essence, social structure. At one extreme there are teams in which people interact, with the outcome being individual effort plus the product of the interaction. At the other extreme there is co-offending or, more generally, co-acting in which there is little interdependence of structure and roles. Between these are groups of various kinds. Work groups would be toward the team end of the continuum.

Locating criminal activity along this continuum would potentially result in juvenile or delinquent gangs being at the co-offending end, with robbers somewhere in the middle and ram raiders toward the team end. It may well be that other criminal collaborators could also be located on this continuum, for instance well organised terrorist groups.

Specialisation and Versatility

Many of the criteria of groups would imply that there is a degree of specialisation by group members. The notion of specialisation in criminal activity over time has received more attention than group offending. From the perspective of trying to understand ram raiding groups, specialisation and versatility are of interest. This is because if the crimes are planned, the skill mix of the offenders will be part of that planning. The recruitment of people to take part in the crimes would therefore require that appropriately skilled individuals could be identified. Such identification would most probably be based on evidence that the individuals possessed the necessary skills. The most likely source for this evidence would be a history of criminal activity that would be compatible with the roles and related skills required for the crime. In looking at this a contribution can be made to understanding the area of criminal careers.

Criminal career researchers are divided over the question of whether offenders tend to commit crimes of the same or different types throughout their criminal career. That is, their degree of specialisation or crime-type switching. Klien (1979) proposed the concept of *cafeteria* style offending in which people select a variety of crimes, as one would a meal in a cafeteria. Several studies have supported this by demonstrating that specialisation does not appear to occur when looking at single crime classifications such as burglary, rape, robbery and so on. However, the notion of cafeteria style offending is not supported by other studies that have demonstrated that when broader crime type categories are examined, rather than exact crime classifications, there is a good deal of support for specialisation. These broader categories can be seen as *themes*. Thus, although the individual crimes may be different, they may belong to the same *theme* of behaviour such as violence, dishonesty, or sexual crimes.

Evidence for specialisation has been found in a number of studies including burglary (Maguire and Bennet, 1982; Shover, 1991), property crime (Kempf, 1986), and violent offences (Gutteridge, Gabrielli, Mednick and Van Dusen, 1983). Blumstein, Cohen, Das and Moitra (1988) carried out one of the largest studies of crime switching. They examined the crime-type switching pattern between 32,197 adults arrested during the four year period 1974 to 1977 for six of the most serious index offences; homicide, forcible rape, robbery, aggravated assault, burglary and motor vehicle theft. Two distinct clusters of offences emerged from their analysis - violent offences (murder, rape, use of weapons and aggravated assault) and property offences (burglary, larceny, auto-theft and fraud). Offenders exhibited definite tendencies towards increased switching *within* these crime type clusters and decreased switching *between* the two clusters. This finding thus gives support to specialisation within broad categories of offence types, themes, for violent and dishonest offences.

That specialisation occurs in relation to themes is perhaps not surprising when the legal definitions of offences and the altering fashions and attitudes of the judicial system are considered. For offences of, for instance, dishonesty (e.g. theft, burglary, deception) there may be only subtle differences between each offence. The actual offence an offender is convicted of may owe more to the burden of legal proof, than to what was in the mind of the offender at the time. An illustration of this is an offender who is arrested in possession of stolen property who will give no explanation of it. He is most likely to subsequently be convicted of "handling stolen property", although the offence he actually committed was that of theft, because the burden of proof is less for the former offence.

One interesting feature of crime type switching in criminal careers is that specialisation seems to occur later in people's criminal activity. This was evident in the research by Blumstein, Cohen, Das and Moitra (1988) who found that crime type switching took place mainly during the juvenile phase of an offender's criminal career. "The offender samples a fairly wide variety of offences during the early phases, and then converges on those he finds most appropriate to his taste and skills" (Blumstein et al., 1988, p.12). Linking this to ram raids, it would be expected that if there are clear, specialised roles within a ram raid and that identifiable specialists are recruited to fulfil these roles, they would most likely be adults. Juveniles are less likely to have exhibited a specialism. To be effective, then, it would be expected that ram raiders would generally be adults.

Research Questions

The discussion of groups, specialisation, versatility and so on leads to numerous interrelated questions. The first of these is the extent to which there is a social structure to the commissioning of ram raiding offences. That is, do ram raiders form a group, and in particular a work group, or are they another type of group such as a co-acting group? Several specific questions need to be answered in order to establish the nature of this social structure. Taking the defining characteristics of formal groups it can be asked whether there is evidence of diversification of roles during the offence, whether the roles that people perform are interchangeable, and whether particular individuals consistently perform the same roles?

If offenders do perform the same roles over time, this has implications for, and raises questions about, criminal careers, specialisation and versatility. A further question, then, is how do the roles performed in the commission of a ram raiding offence relate to the previous criminal activities of individuals? That is, are people specialists in particular sorts of crimes prior to occupying a specific role in ram raiding?

Empirical Examination of a Sample of Ram Raiders

To explore some of the issues discussed above, a study was carried out looking at a sample of ram raiders. The specific questions that were being addressed were whether evidence of consistent ram raider roles is present in each group? Whether evidence for diversity or specialisation is present in the previous convictions of a sample of offenders who co-offend? Whether there is consistency between the role an individual performs in an offence and the type of previous convictions he has? Whether offenders who perform a similar role will have similar previous convictions? Finally, and related to the other questions, whether the role an individual performs during the commission of a ram raid will be reflected in the crime theme he has specialised in?

Research Data

To obtain data related to the activities of Ram Raiders, investigating officers were contacted from police forces that had run an operation focusing on the offence of ram raiding over the previous three years. Details were obtained of individuals who were subsequently convicted of an offence (not necessarily the actual burglary offence) related to a ram raid offence. The individuals' criminal histories, in the form of official conviction records, were then obtained from the Police National Computer (PNC). Further information was obtained from the original prosecution files and through interviews with the original investigating officers. The original prosecution files were examined for police reports and offenders' statements referring to the role each offender played in the offences. This was followed through with interviews with the investigating officers. Where several offenders were involved in an offence, the police officers were asked to say which behaviours (e.g. driving the vehicle, smashing the window) related to which offender. This was crosschecked against the statements made by the offenders when interviewed by the police. Further reliability checks were made by interviewing four offenders and confirming the details obtained from their original statements and the investigating officers.

The types of offences that each offender had previously been convicted of before their conviction for an offence related to a ram raid offence were examined. The last conviction relating to the ram raiding offence for which they had been arrested was not included in the analysis. This was because not all the convictions had appeared on the official records at the time of this study due to delays in processing court data.

A total of 70 individuals were included in the sample. Twelve individual teams or groups were identified ranging in number from three to 12 individuals. Within the larger groups, individuals would team-up in different combinations on different occasions. The offenders geographic locations were in the South East, North East and North West of England covering five police areas: Merseyside, Northumbria, Thames Valley, Surrey and the Metropolitan police district.

General Description of the Sample

Looking at the basic population parameters of the sample is itself of some interest in understanding the people involved in ram raiding. For instance, although gender was not a predetermined parameter of the sample all 70 offenders were male. The mean age of the offenders at the time of their last ram raid-related conviction was 23, with a standard deviation of 5.06, and a range from 16 to 52 years. The mean age at their first ever conviction (not necessarily for a ram raid offence) was 15 with a standard deviation of 2.3 and a range of 10 to 20 years.

These figures suggest that ram raiding is not an offence committed by juveniles. Indeed in the sample of 70 offenders, only one individual was a juvenile at the time of committing a ram raid offence. He stole vehicles for the ram raiders and took no part in the raid itself. This finding points to an inadequacy of using the literature concerned with juveniles for understanding the activities of ram raiders.

The average age at first conviction suggests that offenders who go on to become involved in ram raid offences commence their offending as juveniles, but not at a particularly early age. It should be borne in mind that the police may have cautioned many of these individuals before their first conviction. Policies have changed over the years in relation to cautioning and are different around the country. Cautions are not recorded as criminal convictions and so do not appear on an offender's criminal record. Juvenile criminal records therefore may be misleading. There are grounds, however, for concluding that those involved in ram raiding have quite extensive criminal histories and that adults commit the offence, suggesting that it is a 'mature' crime.

Specialisation and Versatility

The first issue to be examined is the evidence for specialisation or versatility in the criminal histories of the offenders. This can then be related to the roles they perform during the ram raid. To explore this issue, the offences for which the ram raiders had previous convictions were considered. The previous convictions for the sample, along with the number and percentage of offenders in the sample who had a previous conviction for each type of offence, are shown in table 7.1. The main offences have also been classified under their broad crime types. The basis of this classification was knowledge of the crime types and other Multidimensional Scaling analyses carried out as part of a broader study of the sample, but not included in the present chapter (cf. Wilson, 1995). As there may be some question of whether some of these offences are dishonesty, rather than, for instance, theft, it is worth taking time to explain how some less obvious dishonesty convictions have come to be classified as they are here. Although the offence of disqualified driving is not an offence of dishonesty it is usually strongly associated with taking a motor vehicle without consent (TWOC) and thus is often an offence committed by car thieves. The offence of criminal damage is also often charged as an alternative to one of the dishonesty offences when the full act has not been completed and intent cannot be established. For example, when an offender breaks a car window but is disturbed or stopped before stealing the vehicle or anything inside the vehicle, and if it cannot be established that he intended to steal, then he will be charged with causing damage. The same will apply to attempting to break into a house. Although the offence of criminal damage may also apply where wanton damage is caused, an examination of the nature of each charge in the case of the current sample reveals that generally the criminal damage is of the former type.

Table 7.1 Number of Offenders having a Previous Conviction for Each type of Offence

Type of offence	No. of offenders with a previous conviction for type of offence (total 70)	Percentage of offenders with a previous conviction for type of offence	Classification of Offence
Taking a vehicle without consent	52	74.3%	Dishonesty
Theft	47	67.1%	Dishonesty
Handling stolen goods	47	67.1%	Dishonesty
Burglary non-dwelling	44	62.9%	Dishonesty
Theft from motor vehicle	37	52.9%	Dishonesty
Criminal Damage	34	48.6%	Dishonesty
Disqualified driving	33	47.0%	Dishonesty
Going equipped to steal	24	34.3%	Dishonesty
Burglary dwelling	21	30.0%	Dishonesty
Reckless driving	21	30.0%	Antisocial
Public order (s4/s5 POA, minor)	20	28.6%	Violence
Possession of Drugs	19	27.1%	Antisocial
Possessing an offensive weapon	13	18.6%	Violence
Robbery	13	18.6%	Violence
Actual bodily harm (minor)	11	15.7%	Antisocial
Assault on police	10	14.3%	Violence
Grievous bodily harm (serious)	9	12.9%	Violence
Deception	7	10.0%	
Indecent assault	2	2.9%	

Before discussing the details of the offences committed, note that a number of possible, serious offences do not appear in the previous convictions of this sample of ram raiders including murder, rape, possession of a firearm, arson, serious sexual offences, and forgery. One reason for this may be that these offences generally attract long prison sentences that may reduce the availability of the offender to commit ram raid offences. A further, more psychologically intriguing, reason may be that these serious offences are also generally solo offences and those involved in ram raiding may prefer group offences. While this is an interesting proposition, it is, unfortunately, not open to an empirical test here.

From table 7.1 it can be seen that the most common previous convictions among the sample are offences of dishonesty (except disqualified driving). In descending order, these are taking a vehicle without consent (74.3%), handling stolen property (67.1%), theft (67.1%), burglary of a non dwelling (62.9%), theft from motor vehicle (52.9%) and disqualified driving (47.0%).

This high frequency of dishonesty offences points to there being a degree of specialisation in that theme amongst ram raiders. This is further supported by nine of the nineteen offence types (57.0%) committed by the 70 offenders being dishonesty or closely associated with dishonesty; theft, burglary dwelling, burglary non dwelling, handling, robbery, theft from motor vehicle, taking a vehicle without consent, going equipped to steal, disqualified driving and deception.

A relatively small percentage of ram raiders had been convicted for other offences. Of these, five are offences of violence; GBH (12.0%), ABH (15.7%), possession of an offensive weapon (18.6%), assault on police (14.3%) and public order offences (where violence is threatened, if not actually carried through). Robbery can be considered an offence of violence. The Theft Act (1968) in describing robbery states that, "A person is guilty of robbery if he steals, and immediately before or at the time of doing so, and in order to do so, he uses force on any person or seeks to put any person in fear of being then and there subjected to force". Violence is therefore inherent in robbery. Two of the remaining offences are of an antisocial nature; possession of drugs (27.1%) and reckless driving (30.0%). Two offenders have a conviction for one type of sexual offence, indecent assault. This offence is of the 'less serious' sexual offences.

The frequency analysis of the data provides initial support for the hypothesis that the ram raid offenders in the sample were specialists rather than eclectic. The analysis reveals that the most frequent offences in the previous conviction histories of the sample were offences of dishonesty. Of lower frequency were offences of an antisocial sort, with the lowest frequency offences being those of violence and of a sexual nature. These results confirm the findings of other researchers who have shown support for specialisation by studying broad themes of criminal offending and categorising groups of similar offences together, for example, property offences (Kempf, 1986), sex, fraud and burglary (Stander et al., 1989) and violence, property and substance abuse (Nicks, 1993).

The specialisation of ram raiders in dishonesty offences is perhaps to be expected, given that the offence of ram raiding is itself a dishonesty offence. However, the ram raid offence also has the potential to contain violent behaviours if the offenders are disturbed and this may be reflected in some offenders having violent offences in their criminal histories.

It is possible, from the frequencies, to hypothesise that there may be several different career paths that an offending ram raider may follow. This may include the predominantly specialist dishonesty offender who commits primarily offences of a dishonest nature. There is the violent-dishonest offender who again commits dishonesty offences and whose violent tendencies cause him to lean towards committing crimes of robbery. Finally there is the antisocial-dishonest offender whose antisocial tendencies manifest themselves in the commission of, for example, burglaries of dwellings, rather than the less victim-associated offence of commercial burglary. An examination of these possibilities is what we turn to next.

Profiling Previous Convictions

The examination of basic frequencies of offending tells us little of the combination of crimes for which particular individuals have been convicted. That is, of the three main themes identified, do people have convictions from more than one theme? Answering this is necessary before going on to look at role differentiation during the commission of an offence. Thus we will now focus much more on individuals and their combinations or profiles of convictions.

A Brief Description of MSA

To address these issues, employing a multivariate method of data analysis is fruitful. Multidimensional Scalogram Analysis (cf, Wilson, 1995; Zvulun, 1978) is ideal for this task. The procedure focuses on individual profiles across a number of variables. Based on these profiles the analysis provides a geometric representation of the individuals as points in space such that the more similar their profiles the closer they are together. So, in the present case, the closer two points in the MSA space, the more similar the previous convictions of the individuals those points represent.

The MSA compares only unique profiles. Therefore, the procedure represents identical case profiles as the same point in the space. The resultant plot consequently contains only profiles that are different from each other. Thus, if a profile represents say 10 subjects, (that is 10 subjects have the same profile) it is treated, more or less, in the same way as a profile that represents only one subject.

The analysis results in the production of a plot that shows the calculated position of profiles, and then a plot for each variable included in the analysis. These later plots show the score that each individual or case has on that variable. In doing this, the position of the points remains constant. These plots are then partitioned into regions that contain the same score on that variable. Partitioning in this way shows how scores on one variable are related to scores on each of the other variables. If meaningful partitions can be made, the first plot can be partitioned into regions of, in this case, crime types. These regions then show offenders who have similar conviction profiles. Thus those offenders with more similar criminal histories will be represented by points that are closer on the plot than those with dissimilar profiles. The issue then becomes whether offenders who perform similar roles during the ram raid are represented as points in the same regions of the MSA plot.

Selecting Variables for the Analysis

MSA is designed to reveal similarities and differences between individuals in a sample. Therefore, the inclusion of variables that are either very frequent or very infrequent will not help this process. Variables that have a high frequency will fail to highlight the differences between offenders, and those variables that are of a very low frequency will be so idiosyncratic that they will fail to reveal any similarities between offenders. The high frequency offences omitted from this analysis were TWOC (74.3% of offenders in the sample had a conviction for this offence), theft (67.1%) and burglary non-dwelling (62.9%). The low frequency variables omitted were deception (10.0%) and indecent assault (3.5%). Variables that represented offences that could be seen as somewhat ambiguous in nature were also removed from the analysis. Those excluded on this basis are; criminal damage, going equipped to steal, and possession of an offensive weapon.

To ensure that sufficient coverage of all the conviction themes was achieved, at least two offence variables from each theme were included in the MSA. From the theme identified as antisocial offences, possession of drugs and ABH were included. From the dishonesty offences' theme the offences of theft from a motor vehicle (TFMV), burglary dwelling, disqualified driving and handling were included. Finally, from the violent offences theme, GBH, robbery and assault on police were incorporated in the MSA.

Twenty-three of the profiles were identical to other profiles, leaving 47 unique profiles to be included in the analysis.

Relationship Between Offences

The partitioning of the nine item plots, one for each offence variable, is shown in figures 7.1.1 to 7.1.9. To simplify the interpretation and explanation only schematic representations are given. The shaded areas cover regions in which the ram raiders portrayed have a previous conviction for the offence.

214 The Social Psychology of Crime

Figure 7.1.1 Item Plot for Offenders with Conviction for Burgling Dwellings

Figure 7.1.2 Item Plot for Offenders with Conviction for Robbery

Figure 7.1.3 Item Plot for Offenders with Cnviction for TFMV

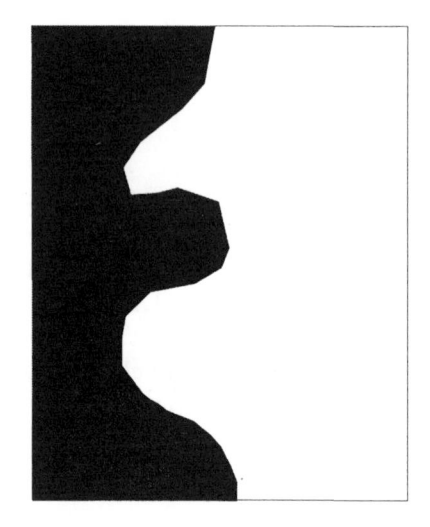

Figure 7.1.4 Item Plot for Offenders with Conviction for Disq. Driving

Ram Raiding 215

Figure 7.1.5 Item Plot for Offenders with Conviction for Drugs

Figure 7.1.6 Item Plot for Offenders with Conviction for Handling

Figure 7.1.7 Item Plot for Offenders with Conviction for ABH

Figure 7.1.8 Item Plot for Offenders with Conviction for GBH

216 The Social Psychology of Crime

**Figure 7.1.9 Item Plot for Offenders
with Conviction for Assaulting Police**

A number of interesting features are evident from the schematic representations. First, the plots for the offences of burglary of a dwelling, TFMV, disqualified driving and handling (figures 7.1.1, 7.1.3, 7.1.4 and 7.1.6) all partition vertically. In each case, offenders who have a conviction for the offence lie to the left of the plot. All of these offences are from the 'dishonesty' offences theme. Generally, the further a point (offender) is positioned to the left of the plot, the more dishonesty offences he has been convicted of. Thus if an offender has a previous conviction for burglary of a dwelling he is also likely to have previous convictions for TFMV, disqualified driving and handling.

The increasing propensity for offenders to have a conviction for one or more dishonesty offences is shown in figure 7.2. The numbers in brackets are the frequencies of different dishonesty offences of which the offenders have been convicted. It can be seen from figure 7.2 that those offenders represented to the left of the plot have a higher frequency of dishonesty offences than those on the right. Therefore, the dimension of the MSA running from left to right across the plot represents a continuum of dishonesty offences moving from high to low number of convictions.

The item plots for the offences of possession of drugs and ABH (figures 7.1.5 and 7.1.7) partition horizontally, although the region for possession of drugs is perhaps indicated more by a diagonal line in the top left of the plot. Both offences are from the theme of 'antisocial' offences and both form regions towards the top end of the plot with some degree of overlap. This indicates that offenders represented by points that lie towards the top of the plot have a conviction for one or both offences.

The item plots for GBH and robbery (figures 7.1.8 and 7.1.2), two of the offences from the 'violent offences' theme, partition diagonally in the lower part of the plot; GBH partitioning in the lower right of the plot and robbery in the lower left of the plot. There is a high degree of overlap between these two regions, indicating that many offenders who have a conviction for robbery also have a conviction for GBH.

The regions for GBH and robbery convictions are opposite to those for ABH and possession of drugs. Virtually no overlap exists between the regions. This shows that generally those offenders with convictions for GBH or robbery do not have convictions for ABH.

The item plot for assault on police (figure 7.1.9) partitions into two regions. One overlaps with the partition for GBH in the lower right of the plot. The other region overlaps with both the ABH and possession of drugs regions in the top part of the plot. This indicates that some offenders who have a conviction for assault on police also have a conviction for GBH. However, others have a conviction for ABH or possession of drugs but not GBH. This may be because the offence of assault on police can be either of a minor nature of, say, inflicting a scratch, or be where a more serious injury is caused. Similarly, an offender who assaults a police officer may do so out of immaturity and recklessness, thus conceptually being more akin to the type of person who would commit ABH or take drugs. Alternatively, he may assault the officer out of viciousness or continued violence more akin to the GBH offender. The two different regions then may be associated with two different *types* of offenders who commit this offence.

218 *The Social Psychology of Crime*

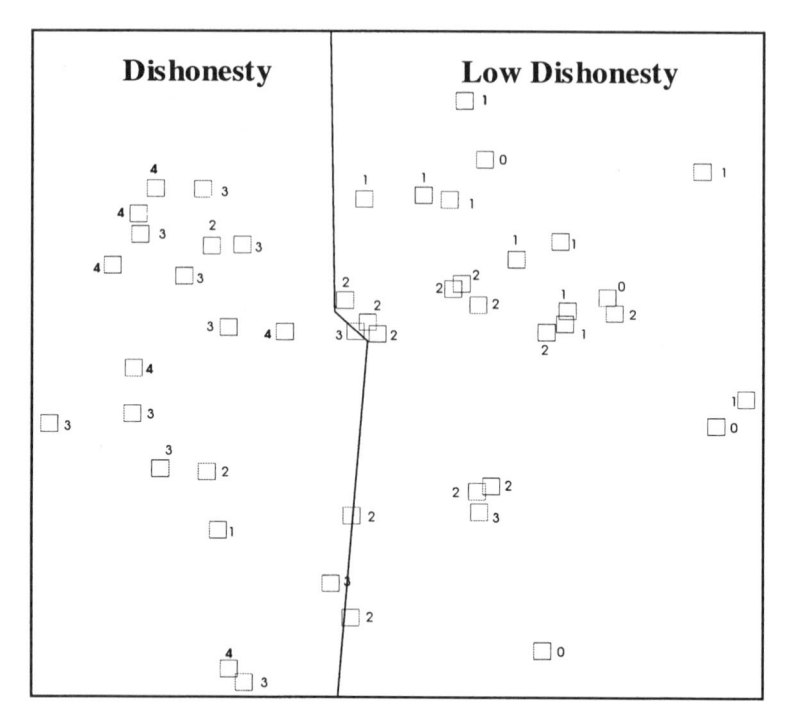

Figure 7.2 MSA Plot Indicating the Frequency of Dishonest Offenders
Coefficient of Contiguity = 0.903 for 7 iterations.

Types of Offence History

Taking all the offences together it is possible to divide the offenders into six groups depending upon where they are represented on the plot shown in figure 7.3. The numbers on this plot relate to individuals who have a particular profile. The roles of the individuals in the ram raid are shown in the appendix. The left of the plot represents offenders with the greatest number of convictions for dishonesty offences and the right side of the plot those with the least convictions for these offences. This represents a continuum. For convenience the plot has been partitioned into high and low dishonesty regions. The plot can further be divided horizontally. The top of the plot represents offenders with a conviction for one or more of the antisocial offences and the lower part of the plot showing offenders with a conviction for one or more of the violent offences. The central region represents offenders who have neither a conviction for an antisocial nor violent offence; the offences are purely of the dishonest theme. Offenders with a conviction for assault on police are represented either at the top or the bottom of the plot, but not in the central region.

For this sample of ram raiders there are interesting conclusions that may be drawn from the MSA. First it seems that the ram raiders who have been convicted of a dishonesty offence tend to have been convicted of a 'bundle' of such offences. The second interesting feature is that those who have been convicted for antisocial offences do not also have previous convictions for violent crimes, and vice versa. This is perhaps not what would be expected in the wider criminal population. Why it is so for these ram raiders can at present be only speculation. Nonetheless, it could well be that in selecting members of a team, there is no desire for a number of violent members, who could, perhaps, make the team more difficult to control.

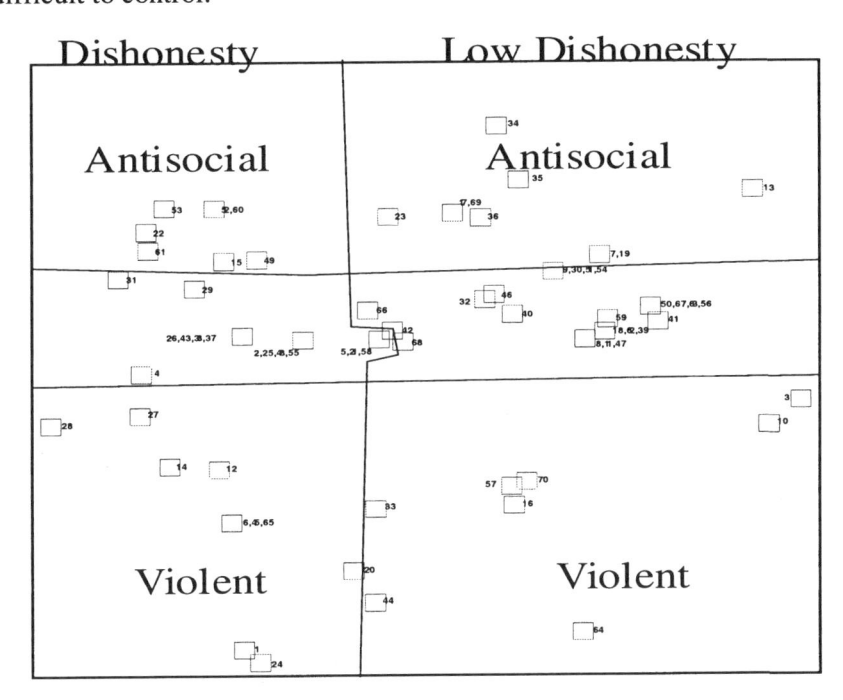

Figure 7.3 MSA Composite Plot of 70 Offenders using 9 Offence Variables
Coefficient of Contiguity = 0.903

Finally, while many ram raiders have convictions for offences from one or other of the themes identified previously, there are also offenders who have convictions from two themes demonstrating that the offenders cannot be placed into pure 'types'. None of the offenders are totally eclectic, having a conviction history that involves an offence from all three themes. Thus most of the offenders have a conviction from the dishonesty theme, but beyond that, some further specialisation is evident. This is subtler than other studies have shown, particularly those that use either/or typologies. In a sense there is a general factor, various levels dishonesty, common to all ram raid offenders, in addition to which some offenders exhibit other more specific offence traits.

The majority of current typologies place burglary offenders into strict dichotomous or tripartite *types*. These studies generally focus on aspects of the degree of sophistication of the offenders by examining levels of planning (cf. Bennett and Wright, 1984), experience (cf. Maguire and Bennett, 1982) and professionalism (cf. Cromwell, Olson and Avary, 1991). The level of sophistication exhibited by an offender can be examined by studying the types of offences he has previously committed. For example, has he committed offences that require high levels of planning, experience and professionalism, such as robbery, or offences that do not require such high levels of sophistication, such as ABH or possession of drugs?

It should be borne in mind when examining previous offences for levels of sophistication that legal classifications are crude approximations of behavioural groupings. Further, serious offences like robbery can be highly sophisticated (e.g. an armed robbery of a security van) or relatively unsophisticated (e.g. pushing someone off his bicycle and the stealing it). With these limitations in mind, the results of the MSA question the appropriateness of current classification systems for burglars when applied to ram raiders.

The ram raid offenders have previous convictions for offences from more than one theme. This lends support to the view that rather than classifying offenders in strict terms of typologies, they can be more fruitfully understood in relation to *themes* of behaviour.

Ram Raider Role and Previous Convictions

Similar to work groups, ram raid teams will be most effective when they are subdivided with individuals performing specific roles during the raid. Following on from this is the idea that people will be recruited based on their previously demonstrated skills or specialisation. To test this, the data were examined to establish whether there was any relationship between offenders' roles during the ram raid and their previous convictions. Achieving this requires the roles played by offenders to be established.

Roles within the Offence

An unpublished, detailed case study of ram raiding (Wilson and McCluskey, 1995) suggested that there were clearly defined roles performed by each member of the group. These roles were leader or planner, driver, heavy (who stands guard) and an apprentice. When the roles of criminals external to the immediate group, but necessary for the actualisation of the offence, are added this gives the additional roles of handler or fence, car thief and extra.

As noted earlier, information was gathered regarding the roles that each offender had played in the commission of the ram raiding offence. This information both supported the existence of the different roles, and allowed each offender to be assigned to a role group. These categories of roles also find support in the work of Shover (1973) described previously.

The roles occupied by the members of a ram raiding group are described below along with their criminal conviction histories. Figures 7.4.1 to 7.4.6 shows the same MSA plot as figure 7.3. Here, however, only the members of one role group are included on each plot. The numbers on the plots show the frequency of individuals occupying the role who are represented by each point. Where no number is included, the point represents only one individual. Overall, the plots clearly show a relationship between the role held during the ram raid and the offender's previous conviction theme. That is, people seem to be systematically assigned particular roles for the offence. In turn, this suggests some form of systematic selection. Unfortunately it is not possible from the current data and information to be firmer about such suggestions.

Leader/Planner

The leader is in overall charge of each offence. He arranges the group membership, decides the target premises, arranges the disposal of stolen property through a handler and distributes the gain from each offence, either as goods or money. The leader or planner will have the respect of the other offenders, but may not take part in every offence though he will co-ordinate the raids.

Offenders who perform the role of leader are represented by points located almost exclusively on the left of the plot shown in figure 7.4.1, revealing that they tend to have previous convictions for dishonesty offences. In fact, only two of the leaders have convictions for less than three of the four dishonesty offences. A number also have a conviction for the violent offence of robbery, as evidenced by the points in the left, lower region of the plot. Leaders, then, mainly display a high dishonesty - violent theme in their previous convictions, or purely a high dishonesty theme. A number of leaders have identical conviction profiles or very similar profiles suggesting some degree of homogeneity amongst them. The differences among the leaders may indicate that despite this relative homogeneity there is perhaps more than one kind of leader; dishonest-violent leaders and dishonest-non-violent leaders.

Heavy

Heavies assist in the raids by helping to smash an entry and may help in removal of goods. More commonly they stand guard outside the premises to warn off anyone who attempts to interfere with or stop the group. They will often be armed with a baseball bat or iron bar.

Not all groups incorporate a heavy in their structure; consequently there are fewer of these individuals in the sample. It can be seen from figure 7.4.2 that those offenders performing the role of heavy are represented by points in the lower right of the plot. Heavies can generally, therefore, be classified as low dishonesty - violent criminals having a conviction for GBH, but few of the dishonesty and none of the antisocial offences. These are perhaps the most specialised of the offenders in the sample. They are also one of the most homogeneous role groups.

Ram Raiding 223

Figure 7.4.1 Leader

```
Dishonesty          Low Dishonesty
┌─────────────┬─────────────┐
│ Antisocial  │ Antisocial  │
│             │             │
├─────────────┼─────────────┤
│      ■      │             │
│    2 ■  2 ■■│             │
│   ■         │             │
│    ■        │             │
│     ■ ■     │   ■         │
│       ■ 3   │             │
│ Violent     │ Violent     │
│         ■■  │             │
└─────────────┴─────────────┘
```

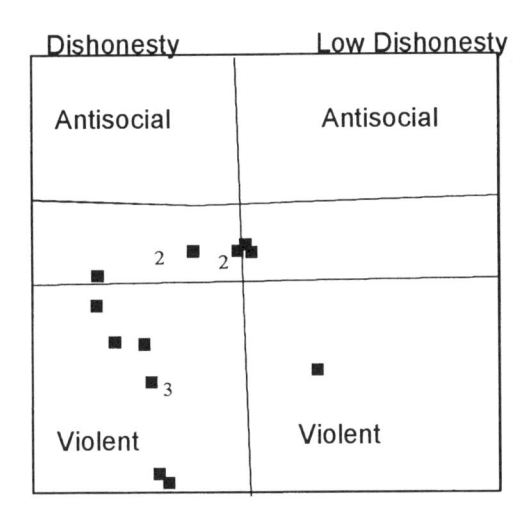

Figure 7.4.2 Heavy

```
Dishonesty          Low Dishonesty
┌─────────────┬─────────────┐
│ Antisocial  │ Antisocial  │
│             │             │
├─────────────┼─────────────┤
│             │             │
│             │          ■  │
│             │   ■         │
│         ■   │             │
│ Violent  ■  │ Violent     │
│             │     ■       │
└─────────────┴─────────────┘
```

224 The Social Psychology of Crime

Figure 7.4.3 Driver

Figure 7.4.4 Extra

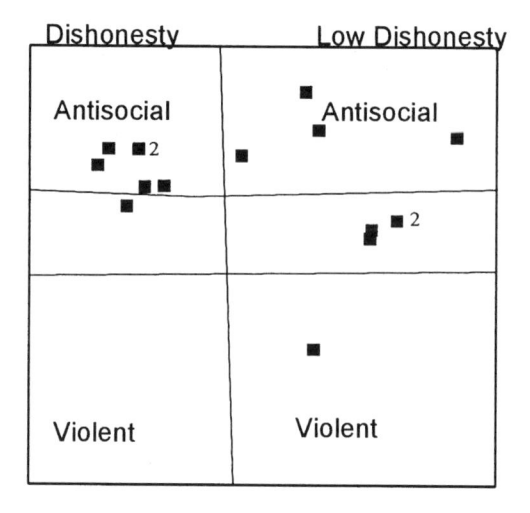

Ram Raiding 225

Figure 7. 4.5 Apprentice

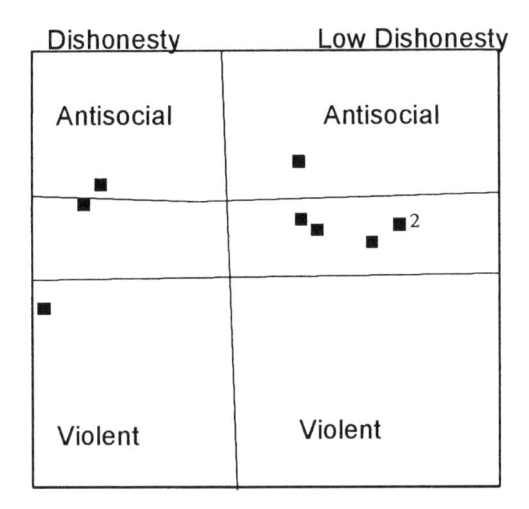

Figure 7. 4.6 Handler

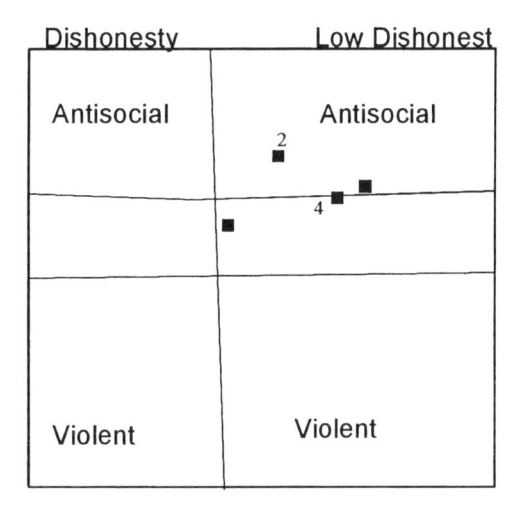

Drivers

With one exception, all of the points representing drivers on the plot shown in figure 7.4.3 can be found exclusively within the themes of either low or high dishonesty; they do not also have convictions for antisocial or violent offences. Again, several individuals have identical offence profiles, suggesting a degree of homogeneity. The previous offences of drivers allow them to be on a relatively simple continuum of dishonesty. Some drivers have a conviction for a dishonesty offence such as handling, disqualified driving or burglary of a dwelling, a few offenders who undertake the role of driver do not have a conviction for any of these offences. All of the drivers have a conviction for TWOC. This crime was not included in the analysis due to its high frequency however.

Extra

These offenders, as the name suggests, are extra to the core ram raid group. They may from time to time be included in an established group either for a raid that requires more individuals or to replace a missing member. Extras may steal vehicles for the group, help in disposing of the goods or generally act as assistants. Some extras will drift in and out of the fringe activities of ram raiding groups, while others may aspire to becoming permanent members of a group.

Examination of figure 7.4.4 shows those occupying the role of extra display varying levels of dishonesty in their offence history. They also generally have a conviction for one or more of the antisocial offences such as ABH or possession of drugs. With only one exception, none of the extras have convictions for any of the violent offences, for instance GBH or robbery, although they may have a previous conviction for assault on the police.

The lateral spread across the plot demonstrates that extras are less similar to each other than are some individuals who perform a similar role, for example, the heavies. This may be due to the extras being called upon to perform different, more general tasks, with some being required to steal vehicles, others to dispose of property and others to drive the vehicles during the offence. The propensity of extras to have convictions for antisocial offences may also indicate that they are petty criminals, or criminally immature. This may explain why they are not full members of the professional ram raid groups.

Apprentice

Apprentices usually assist in the entry to the premises and the removal of the goods. They can also be viewed as assistants to the leaders. Often, apprentices are closely connected with the leader, being a relative or longstanding and trusted friend. On the occasions when the leader does not take part in a raid, this individual may take on the responsibility of decision making at the scene, deciding for instance whether to abort a raid, what goods to take, or when to leave the premises. In time these individuals may go on to lead their own groups or associate teams.

The points representing the apprentices mainly lie horizontally in the middle part of the plot shown in figure 7.4.5. The apprentices seem to form two relatively distinct groups in relation to dishonesty. On the left are those who have a history of dishonesty offences, and those to the right who do not have such a history. This represents much less of a continuum than is the case for the drivers, with individuals being represented at a number of points located along the dishonesty dimension. Generally the apprentices do not have a conviction for violent offences, including GBH or robbery, but occasionally have a conviction for antisocial crimes such as possession of drugs or ABH.

This suggests that there are perhaps two types of apprentices, those with convictions for many types of dishonesty and those who have few types of dishonesty in their criminal career. It was noted earlier that many apprentices aspire to, and often succeed in becoming ram raid leaders. Further, apprentices are selected from the leaders' close, well-established friends or from amongst his relatives. Although they may not be formally groomed or trained in relation to their future leadership role, there was evidence from the interviews with offenders that this process occurs informally. For instance, leaders said that they might point to errors made by apprentices, and that they might also, later, teach them how to avoid such mistakes in the future.

The notion that apprentices are being trained to be a particular sort of leader can be supported by the MSA. For example, those that lie close to the left-hand side group of leaders in the plot may be being trained as future dishonesty-violent leaders. As they continue their training, they may commit more violent offences thus making them more like the dishonesty-violent leaders. The others may be being trained by the dishonesty-non-violent leaders to be more like them. As they are trained, they may commit more of the dishonesty offences giving them a profile that is more akin to the current dishonesty-non-violent leaders. Unfortunately the present study does not include data that can test this conjecture. However some support is evident when the relationship between apprentice and leader is further examined later in the chapter.

Handler

The final role is that of an offender who is not an immediate member of the group, but is an integral part of the criminal process of ram raiding. The handler or fence, as he is often colloquially referred to, disposes of the stolen goods and/or converts them into money. The role of the handler is extremely important, as unless stolen items can be exchanged for currency, such as money or maybe drugs, the group will not gain from the raids. Handlers will often arrange in advance with the group leader what goods he can dispose of and for what price. The group will then steal to order. The arrest of a particular handler may considerably change the group's selection of targets. For instance, if a handler who deals mainly in electrical goods is arrested, there is no point in the group continuing to steal such goods unless they can find another handler of them. Each group will often deal with more than one handler perhaps as a way of reducing this problem. Likewise, each handler may 'fence' for more than one ram raiding group.

The handlers, as is apparent from figure 7.4.6, can be characterised as having a low dishonesty theme evident in their previous convictions. These offenders have a conviction for handling but not necessarily any of the other dishonesty offences. Also, they do not have convictions for violent offences. Some handlers display an antisocial theme in their criminal history. While none of these include possession of drugs, some handlers have a conviction for ABH. As with some other offenders, a number of the handlers have identical previous conviction profiles, providing more evidence for homogeneity of offence history being associated with particular ram raiding roles.

Connections between Group Members

Analysis of the ram raiders' roles and previous convictions has revealed several interesting patterns. The analysis has shown that people's criminal histories are related to the roles they perform during a ram raid. But, so far, it tells us little about the make up or structure of the ram raiding groups in terms of the combinations of people that form each group. The difference between co-offending and group offending is that groups have differential tasks. The different tasks require different skills to be brought to bear. The groups should therefore be heterogeneous rather than homogeneous in their membership. This heterogeneity should be reflected in a mix of previous convictions amongst the group members. In this section the variety of previous convictions of the members of groups will be examined.

Connections within the Whole Group

If groups of ram raiders aim to improve effectiveness by having differential roles and skills, it would be expected that the members of any one group would differ in relation to the themes evident in their previous criminal convictions. They will not all be experienced in the same type of crime. Figures 7.5 and 7.6 show the same MSA as previously. In this case, arrows show the connections among all members of four of the largest offending groups in the sample of ram raiders.

These examples illustrate the mixed nature of the groups. Each group shown consists of individuals who differ in the themes of their previous convictions. Two of the groups have members from four crime conviction themes. The other two groups include individuals from five of the previous conviction themes. Further, each of the four ram raid groups also has individuals from a variety of the identified roles.

230 *The Social Psychology of Crime*

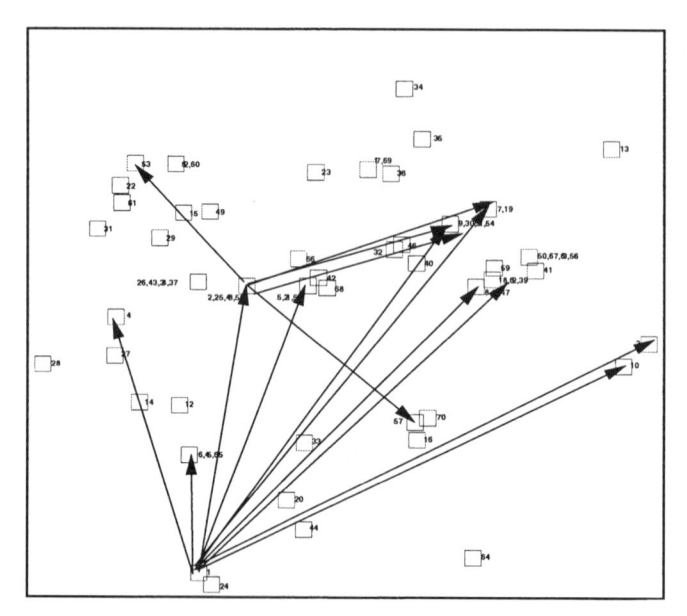

Figure 7.5 MSA Plot Showing the Links between Two Ram Raid Groups Coefficient of Contiguity = 0.903

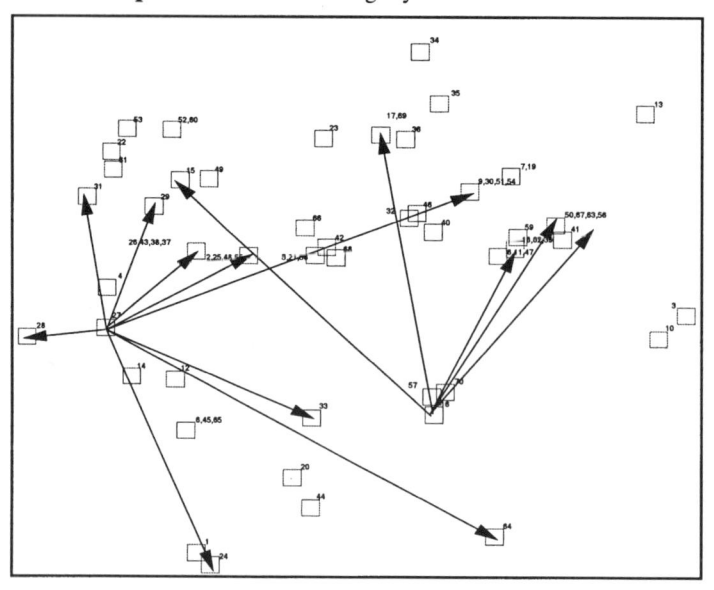

Figure 7.6 MSA Composite Plot showing the Links between Leaders and Apprentices Coefficient of Contiguity = 0.903

These findings are in keeping with theory, and research on groups that propose group structure involves an interdependent network of roles and argue that role differentiation is common to all groups and increases the probability of success (e.g. Brown, 1988; Chell, 1993; Sherif and Sherif, 1969; West, 1996). The groups examined in the present study all demonstrated role differentiation. Further, the role an individual performed is related to the experience he had obtained through the commission of other offences, as reflected in his previous convictions. The MSA thus revealed that the groups consisted of a network of individuals who performed different roles and had different skills. It is possible that the Leaders who initially form the groups recruit individuals who have the appropriate offence theme to fulfil a particular role in the offence. However, from the current data the nature of recruitment cannot be elucidated with certainty. Nonetheless, of particular interest concerning recruitment by leaders, and worth consideration, is the relationship between leader and apprentice previously mentioned.

Leader and Apprentice

Earlier it was suggested that apprentices may be divided into two groups, and that apprentices from different groups may be associated with particular types of leaders, as defined by their previous conviction themes. Some suggestion in the literature supports this hypothesis. For instance, West's (1978), study of high-rate juvenile thieves, found that serious thieving involves training through repeated contacts with experienced offenders in loosely structured social settings or encounters. Some juveniles learn through the observation of older more experienced thieves. Further, for some individuals there is an anticipatory apprenticeship in which there is some modelling by the juvenile of an older offender and the learning of skills during the commission of crimes.

The notion that apprentices are being trained to be of a particular sort is an interesting one, but also one that can be examined further using the MSA. If it is the case that apprentices are similar to the leader with whom they work, it would be expected that the points representing the leader and his apprentice would be quite close on the plot, and within the same conviction themes. If systematic selection or some form of training had not taken place, an arbitrary relationship between the conviction histories of apprentices and leaders would be expected.

Only five of the leaders have apprentices. Three of the five have more than one apprentice. This is possibly because these three leaders are part of large, extended groups that consist of a number of smaller subgroups, each having its own apprentice. Using the same MSA plot as before the relationship between these leaders and apprentices can be examined.

Figure 7.7 shows the MSA plot with lines connecting leaders with their apprentices. It can be seen that the apprentices and their leaders share similar profiles; points representing them are relatively close together on the MSA plot. That is, leaders and their apprentices have similar criminal backgrounds. In particular, viewing the dishonesty theme as representing a continuum, leaders and apprentices tend to be at similar points along the continuum, although leaders generally have more dishonesty convictions. The main difference between leaders and their apprentices is that they differ in relation to the dimension that runs from top to bottom of the plot. If this dimension is considered to run from petty, immature crimes at the top, to serious crimes at the bottom, it can be seen that in general leaders tend to have performed the more serious crimes, and apprentices the more immature. The connections, therefore, give some support to the hypothesis that the apprentices are being trained or recruited by different types of leaders. This is clearly an area that would benefit from more direct, focused attention. The results of the MSA also raise questions about the progression of apprentices. For instance, whether in future they will progress to the more serious crimes displayed by the leaders with whom they are associated.

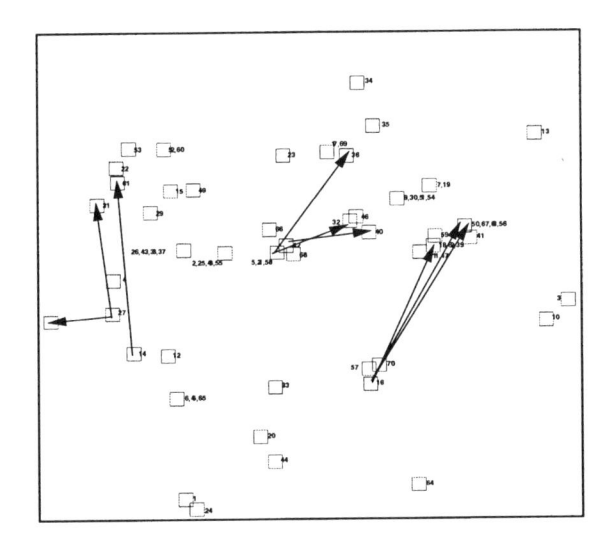

Figure 7.7 MSA Plot showing the Links between Leaders and Apprentices
Coefficient of Contiguity = 0.903

Implications and Conclusions

Ram Raiders as Work Groups

One fundamental issue discussed in the introduction to the chapter was what, in essence, organisationally, ram raiders are. A basic question posed was whether ram raiders form a group, and in particular, can they be considered to be a work group? The research described in this chapter has answered that question. Ram raiders clearly do constitute work groups. This has in turn resulted in some questioning of the concept of work group as used in organisational psychology.

In more detail, from the interviews carried out as part of the research it is evident that each group had a hierarchy. The groups had leaders who made the important decisions and brought the group together. Beyond this, they often had apprentices who would take on the role of deputy to the leader. Further, there was other clear evidence of role differentiation and interdependence. Moreover, the roles occupied by particular individuals do not seem to have been interchangeable. This is supported by analysis of the criminal histories of the ram raiders, which showed that the roles occupied were systematically related to their skills as reflected in their previous convictions. The group members, of course, had a shared purpose.

The ram raid groups have most of the characteristics required to be a work group. However, as was discussed earlier, according to accepted definitions of work groups, the ram raiders do not constitute such a group. The main reason for this is that they are not part of a recognisable organisation. The current research suggests that extending the concept of work groups, as defined by writers such as Guzzo (1996), to include those that may not be a part of an organisation, would be of value. This would allow the more ready inclusion of criminal groups including ram raiders.

At present non-legitimate groups, such as ram raiders, generally do not seem to be considered by organisational psychologists. For instance, West's excellent *Handbook of Work Group Psychology* (West, 1996) makes no consideration of criminal groups. This is understandable. However it is likely that many intriguing theoretical and applied issues would grow out of incorporating groups who, though not legitimate, nonetheless carry out their work in groups. This generation of interesting questions can be illustrated by consideration of other group related issues, *inter alia*, the nature of leaders and leadership.

A Short Digression on Leaders and Leadership

Within organisational and social psychology the issue of leadership has received much attention. In the present chapter, the important role of leader has been identified. It is not possible, however, to identify from the present data is exactly how the leader performs his role, and what charactcristics he displays. Beyond selecting the members of the group, the leader has the task of influencing the other members' behaviours, perceptions, or attitudes (Dipboye, Smith and Howell, 1994). The extent to which a person can do this is their degree of *social influence*, which relies on their on social power.

One of the more influential works in this area proposes five types of power (French and Raven, 1959) *reward, coercive, legitimate, referent and expert power.* Some of these are seen as more effective and appropriate in achieving success than others. Including criminal groups raises a number of questions. For example, does the definition of what is meant by each of these make sense if applied to criminal groups? Coercive power is exercised when one person can punish others in some way. Typically this means sanctions such as isolation or rejection. In criminal groups it may also include real violence or threats of violence. Could such behaviour realistically be considered similar to isolation and other social sanctions? The inclusion of criminal groups is likely, perhaps, to lead to the generation of more types of influence and power.

Related to types of power are the tactics that may be brought to bear to achieve influence. Yukl and Tracey (1992) proposed nine such tactics. The use of tactics will depend on whether a person is attempting to influence a subordinate, peer or superior. Dipboyle et al. (1994) has summarised these tactics. In essence they are:

- *Pressure* tactics (where threats and intimidation are used).
- *Legitimating* tactics (in which claims of authority are made).
- *Exchange* (promises or rewards are given).
- *Coalition* (where the support of others is used).
- *Ingratiating* (in which influence is sought by trying to get people to like them).
- *Rational* (which involves the use of logical argument).
- *Inspirational* (in which emotional appeals are made).
- *Consultational* (where participation is sought).
- *Personal* (in which appeals to loyalty and friendship are made).

There are indications that in most groups or organisations consultation, rational persuasion and inspirational tactics are most common. Again, there are questions as to whether these findings can be generalised to criminal work groups in which, perhaps, violence may be more acceptable. It is also possible that consultation and rational persuasion are most effective in criminal groups also. It will help develop a fuller understanding of work groups if these types of question are addressed.

It could be speculated that in heading a group of offenders it would be necessary for a leader to exercise a degree of coercion. However, examining the past offence histories of both the leaders and other group members suggest that this may not be the case and that there may be some similarity between leaders of criminal groups and those of more 'legitimate' groups. First, only one of the leaders has a conviction for a violent offence. This suggests that the leaders may not be particularly coercive. Further, each team includes only one offender who performs the role of heavy and has convictions for serious violent offences. It may be possible that this feature of the make up of the group is an attempt to produce a group that is easy to lead without threat or intimidation.

One final issue that has implications for investigation relates to the life history of effective leaders. In most 'legitimate' organisations leaders can often be characterised as having a pattern of being successful in other areas of their life, such as performance and achievement at college or university (e.g. Campbell, Dunnette, Lawler and Weick, 1970). Criminals, on the other hand, are often unsuccessful in many spheres of 'normal' life. There is the question of whether this is the case for leaders such as found in ram raid groups. As this also cannot be answered from the current data, it is perhaps time to return to further discussion of the questions that can be answered.

Co-Offending and Group Offending

The findings of the current research show that ram raiding is a crime carried out by adults. The work has also shown that a high degree of organisation exists in the commission of the crimes. Moreover, the inclusion of particular participants in the crime is based on their skills. Convenience and proximity are not necessarily the primary factors in determining group membership. Overall, different social processes are involved in the offending of ram raiders than is the case for co-offenders. The research on co-offending described earlier in this chapter consequently has limited value for understanding the type of crime that is ram raiding.

Clear differences and similarities are evident between the ram raiders considered as part of the present research and the burglar and armed robber studies by Shover (1973) and Einstadter (1969). For instance, to some extent all three sets of offenders show some role differentiation. The greatest is for ram raiders, followed, to a lesser extent, by burglars then armed robbers. Both Shover's burglars and the ram raiders exhibited similar internal and external structures with comparable functions and role groups.

The armed robbers of Einstadter are assigned tasks based on skill and experience to a lesser extent than is the case for burglars and ram raiders. Both burglars and armed robbers differ from the ram raiders in hierarchy and leadership. While little evidence of these two characteristics is apparent in co-offenders, leaders were clearly present in the ram raiding groups and played a consistent role.

While similarities between co-offenders and ram raiders exist, they do seem different in terms of social structure. The evidence from the current study and those of Shover and Estandter, as well as others, suggest that a dimension may exist along which different sorts of crime can be located in relation to the degree of social or organisational structure they exhibit. For instance such a dimension may run from formal, task/goal oriented groups to informal groups. In effect this is at least, in part, similar to distinguishing between social groups and work groups. Thus, delinquent gangs can be seen as social groups, with ram raiders as work groups at the other extreme, and robbers as co-offending groups somewhere between the two extremes. The co-offending groups would, in relation to ideas from organisational psychology be similar to what Chell (1993) terms *co-acting* groups. Again, this is an area that may be fruitful to explore further and link in to research in organisational and social psychology, not least because it would help to clarify definitions.

Specialisation, Consistency and Crime Types

The research clearly provides support for the notion that, within themes, offenders display a degree of specialisation. In terms of the concept of cafeteria style offending proposed by Klien (1979), the current study again demonstrates that there is little switching between themes. However, it is reasonable to suggest that once the cafeteria or theme has been selected, there is some variety of offence. The sample of ram raiders exhibits similar specialisation characteristics found by numerous other researchers (e.g. Blumstein et al., 1988; Gutteridge et al., 1983; Kempf, 1986; Maguire and Bennet, 1982).

The study revealed that it is possible to classify offenders in relation to offence themes. The themes are reflected in both the offenders' criminal history, and in the role they occupy in the commission of a ram raid offence. The role reflecting the experience and skills each ram raider has acquired through his previous offending. There are therefore several different career paths that may be followed by a ram raider. However, ram raiders sharing similar roles will be likely to have similar criminal careers. Clearly, this knowledge is of benefit to the police.

For example, an offender who displays the theme of Low Dishonesty - Violence has experience of committing violent offences but has little or no experience of dishonesty offences. Such an individual would probably have difficulty breaking into premises, disposing of stolen goods or planning a difficult dishonesty offence. The individual is capable and has previously been willing to inflict injury on another person and thus, for ram raids, is suitable to perform the role of Heavy but not suitable for performing any of the other roles. Extras do a variety of subsidiary tasks, usually involving stealing vehicles or filling in for absent members. They generally display themes of High Dishonesty - Antisocial and Low Dishonesty - Antisocial, showing that these individuals do not have experience of violent offences and have varying experience of dishonesty offences. The individuals with the theme of High Dishonesty - Antisocial may be those who 'fill in' for absent group members and the others may be the individuals who steal vehicles and assist to dispose of property for the group. It may be the propensity for antisocial offences that precludes these individuals from being included in the groups on a permanent basis, the commission of such offences being seen as less professional and more juvenile by other offenders.

The results suggest that the traditional typologies are not wholly appropriate to type ram raider offenders because they seek to place individuals into one type *or* another. The current typologies would classify all the offenders according to the overall behaviour involved in the current offence. Thus all the offenders would be typed as professional (Scarr, 1973; Cromwell et al., 1991), high level (Maguire and Bennett, 1982), planners (Bennett and Wright) or career burglars (Walsh, 1980). This study has revealed that the offenders are not all the same and do not all possess the same level of experience and skill in relation to the ram raid offence. It may be more appropriate to classify other sorts of offenders according to the six previous offence themes revealed in the MSA. It certainly seems a more appropriate and meaningful way of classifying the particular offenders involved in the commercial burglary.

This would give a classification of six types of offenders that could be simplified by proposing that two dimensions underlie the criminal activity. The first dimension is from high to low level of dishonesty. The second dimension is more challenging in its definition. At one extreme are the antisocial offences. These tend to be quite immature, petty crimes. They are mainly crimes that break social rules, such as possessing drugs.

The next set of crimes is the dishonesty offences. These tend to be more serious and require some skill and perhaps criminal maturity. While they are against particular people, they are generally not directed towards the person themselves, they do not threaten them. Instead these crimes are against inanimate objects, such as property. The final set of offences are the most serious, some, such as robbery, are quite sophisticated and so perhaps mature. The crimes also usually involve threats or violence directly to the victim.

Considering these factors, the dimension can be proposed as ordered from petty, immature crimes that are social and in a sense abstract. At the other extreme are more serious, mature crimes that are of a personal, concrete level.

The location of other crimes in relation to the two dimensions is open to question. It would be assumed that offenders with convictions for murder would be found further down the second dimension, below such crimes as GBH and robbery. Sexual crimes introduce a further interesting possibility and raise the question of whether they could be accommodated within this dimensional structure, or whether they would generate a third dimension. Dimensions that have been identified for sexual crime, (cf. Canter, 1994) to some extent have a potential relationship with those here. In particular the idea that one of the dimensions runs from social and abstract to personal and concrete has potential to be related to those identified by Canter. The inclusion of sexual crimes may also help in clarifying the second dimension, as there would be a more apparent indication of whether a part of this dimension is personal.

Immature, Petty, Abstract, Social

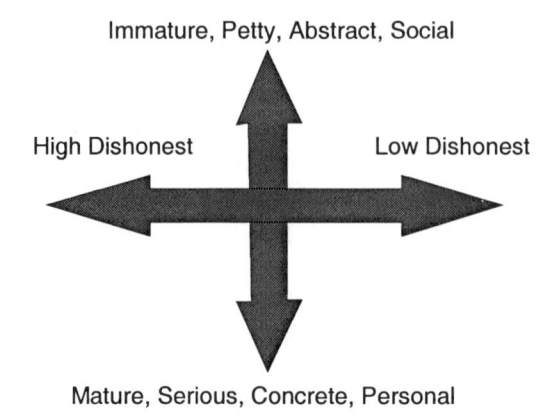

High Dishonest   Low Dishonest

Mature, Serious, Concrete, Personal

Figure 7.8 Dimensions of Crime Themes

Predicting Offender Characteristics

The results of this study lend scientific support to the theoretical challenges of the process of offender profiling; predicting offender characteristics and details from their criminal activity. Consistency has been shown within both the actions and the characteristics of ram raider offenders. Consistency in actions has been demonstrated through the role that offenders perform during the offence. An individual performs the same role each time the ram raid offence is committed. Consistency in the characteristics of the offenders has been shown through the examination and analysis of their previous convictions. It has been revealed that rather than being eclectic in their offending, these individuals commit similar offences that can be seen as falling into a distinct theme of similar offence types. It has also been demonstrated that differentiating between offenders who are involved in the same offence is possible in relation actions during the crime (the role they perform) and their characteristics (previous convictions).

The possibility of being able to predict an offender's previous offence theme from their role in an offence or their role in an offence from their previous offence theme, is important to the developing science of investigative psychology. Pragmatically these possibilities can be used by investigators to prioritise suspects when investigating crimes of this nature.

Conclusions

While the research has raised many questions about criminal groups, and pointed to the need for clearer definition in relation to groups in investigative psychology, it can be concluded that ram raiders can be considered to be a work group. Consequently it is more appropriate to draw on work in organisational psychology than sociology or social psychology to provide a framework for understanding their behaviour.

The results also show that there is a consistency in the offence themes as shown by the conviction histories of the study participants. Further, the themes appear to reflect specialised offenders who can be brought into a group to fulfil particular roles in an offence. This specialisation may be one aspect of ram raiders that can be used to assist the police with their enquiries.

There is a question of the degree to which the results of this study are generalisable to other groups of ram raiders. Those used for the present research were all unsuccessful in that they were in custody. So, perhaps, the characteristics displayed by the groups studied lead to their failure. The final point to be made is that while the research reported here has provided some insights into ram raiders by using police records, much would be gained from an expansion of other information and data gathering techniques, in particular interviews with the offenders.

References

Bennett, T. and Wright, R. (1984), *Burglars on Burglary,* Aldershot: Gower.

Blumstein, A., Cohen, J. and Farrington, D.P. (1988), 'Criminal Career Research: Its value for Criminology', *Criminology,* **26**, 1-35.

Blumstein, A., Cohen, J., Das, S. and Moitra, S. (1988), 'Specialisation and Seriousness During Adult Criminal Careers', *Journal of Quantitative Criminology,* **4**, 303-345.

Breckinridge, S.P. and Abbot, E. (1917), *The Delinquent Child and the Home,* New York: Russell Sage Foundation.

Brown, J. (1985), 'An Introduction to the Uses of Facet Theory', in D. Canter (ed.), *Facet Theory: Approaches to Social Research.* New York: Springer Verlag.

Bursik, R.J. (1980), 'The Dynamics of Specialisation In Juvenile Offenses', *Social Forces,* **58**, 851-864.

Campbell, J., Dunnette, M., Lawler, E. and Weick, K. (1970), *Managerial Behavior, Performance and Effectiveness*. New York: McGraw Hill.

Canter, D.V. (1994), *Criminal Shadows*, London: Harper Collins.

Chell, E. (1993), *The Psychology of Behaviour in Organisations: Second Edition*, London: Macmillan.

Cromwell, P.F., Olson, J.N. and Avary, D.W. (1991), *Breaking and Entering: An Ethnographic Analysis,* report to the US Dept. of Justice, National Institute of Justice.

Delieu, J.J.W. (1994), 'The Consistent Criminal Specialisation and Escalation in Criminal Careers. Do They Exist?', Unpublished Masters dissertation in Investigative Psychology, University of Surrey.

Dipboye, R., Smith, C. and Howell, W. (1994), *Understanding Industrial and Organizational Psychology: An Integrated Approach*, London: Harcourt Brace.

Donald, I. (1985), 'Cylindrex of Place Evaluation', in D.V. Canter (ed.), *Facet Theory: Approaches to Social Research,* New York: Springer Verlag.

Donald, I. (1995), 'Facet Theory: Defining Research Domains' In G. Breakwell, C. Fife-Shaw and S. Hammond (eds) *Research Methods in Psychology.* London: Sage.

Einstadter, W. (1969), 'The Social Organisation of Armed Robbery', *Social Problems,* **17,** 64-82.

Erikson, M. (1971), 'The group context of delinquent behaviour', *Social Problems,* **19,** 114-129.

Farrington, D.P. (1989), 'Self-reported and Official Offending from Adolescence to Adulthood', in M.W. Klein (ed.), *Cross-National Research in Self-Reported Crime and Delinquency,* Kluwer Academic Publishers. pp.399-423.

Farrington, D.P. (1992), 'Criminal Career Research in the United Kingdom', *British Journal of Criminology, 32,* 521-536.

Farrington, D.P. (1994), 'Human Development and Criminal Careers', in M. Maguire, R. Morgan and R. Reiner (eds). *The Oxford Handbook of Criminality,* Oxford: Clarendon Press.

Farrington, D.P. and West, D.J. (1989), 'The Cambridge Study in Delinquent Development: A Long-Term Follow-Up of 411 London Males', in G. Kaiser and H.J. Kerner (eds) *Criminality: Personality, Behaviour, Life History,* Heidelberg: Springer Verlag.

Fiedler, F.E. (1971), *Leadership,* New York: General Learning Press.

Foa, U.G. (1965), 'New Developments in Facet Design and Analysis', *Psychological Review,* **77,** 262-274.

French, J. and Raven, B. (1959), 'The Basis of Social Power', in D. Cartwright (ed.), *Studies in Social Power,* Ann Arbor: University of Michigan Press.

Gibbons, D.C. (1988), 'Some Critical Observations on Criminal Types and Criminal Careers', *Criminal Justice and Behaviour,* **15,** 8-23.

Gosling, J. (1959), *The Ghost Squad,* London: W.H. Allen.
Gottfredson,R. and Hischi, T. (1986), 'The True Value of Lambda Would Appear To Be Zero: An Essay On Career Criminals, Criminal Careers, Selective Incapacitation, Cohort Studies, And Related Topics', *Criminology,* **24**, 213-234.
Gottfredson,R. and Hischi, T.(1990), *A General Theory Of Crime,* Stanford: University Press.
Gould, L., Bittner, E., Chaneles, S., Messinger, S., Novak, K. and Powledge, F. (1965), 'Crime as a Profession: A Report on Professional Criminals in Four American Cities', *President's Commission on Law Enforcement and the Administration of Justice,* Washington D.C.: U.S. Government Printing Office.
Gutteridge, P., Gabrielle, W.F., Mednick, S.A. and Van Dusen, K.T. (1983), 'Criminal Violence in a birth cohort', in K.T. Van Dusen and S.A. Mednick (eds), *Prospective Studies of Crime and Delinquency,* pp.211-224.
Guzzo, R. (1996), 'Fundamental Considerations About Work Groups', in M. West (ed.), *Handbook of Work Group Psychology,* Chichester: Wiley.
Hartley, J. (1996), 'Inter-group Relations in Organisations', in M. West (ed.), *Handbook of Work Group Psychology,* Chichester: Wiley.
Hazlewood, R.R. (1983), 'The Behaviour-orientated Interview of Rape Victims: The Key to Profiling', *FBI Law Enforcement Bulletin,* September 1983.
Hill, W.C. (1955), *Boss of the Underworld,* London: Naldrett.
Hindelang, M.J. (1976), 'With a little help from their friends: Group participation in reported delinquency', *British Journal of Criminology,* **16**, 109-125.
Hogg, M. (1992), *The Social Psychology of Group Cohesiveness: From Attraction to Social Identity,* London: Harvester Wheatsheaf.
Hood, R. and Sparks, R. (1970), *Key Issues in Criminology,* London: World University Library.
Jacques, C. (1994), 'Ram raiding: the history, incidence and scope for prevention', in M. Gill (ed.), *Crime at Work: Studies in Security and Crime Prevention,* I, Perpetuity Press.
Janis, I. (1971), *Victims of Groupthink,* Boston: Houghton Mifflin.
Johnston, L. (1994), *'Riot by Appointment: An Examination of the Nature and Structure of 7 'Hard Core' Football Hooligan Groups',* Unpublished Masters dissertation: University of Surrey.
Katzenbach, J. and Smith, D. (1993), 'The Discipline of Teams', *Harvard Business Review,* Mar - Apr, 111-120.
Kempf, K. (1986), 'Offence Specialisation: Does It Exist?', in D.B.Cornish and R.V. Clarke (eds), *The Reasoning Criminal. Rationale Choice Perspectives on Offending,* London: Springer-Verlag.
Kirby, S. (1993), *'The Child Molester. Separating Myth from Reality',* Unpublished PhD thesis: University of Surrey.

Klein, M.W. (1984), 'Offence Specialisation and Versatility Among Juveniles', *The British Journal of Criminology,* **24**, 184-194.

Klein, M.W. and Crawford, L.Y. (1967), 'Groups, gangs and cohesiveness', *Journal of Research in Crime and Delinquency,* **4**, 142-165

Klein, M.W.(1971), *Street Gangs and Street Workers,* Englewood Cliffs: Prentice Hall.

Lingoes, J. (1973), *'The Guttman-Lingoes Non-Metric Program Series',* Ann Arbor: Mathesis Press.

Lingoes, J.(1969), 'The Multivariate Analysis of Qualitative data', *Multivariate Behaviour Research,* **3**, 61-94.

Maguire, M. and Bennett, T. (1982), *Burglary In A Dwelling: The offence, the offender and the victim,* London: Heineman.

McClintock, F.H. and Gibson, E. (1968), *Robbery in London,* London: Macmillan.

Miller, W.B. (1975), *Violence by Youth Gangs and Youth Groups as a Crime Problem in Major American Cities,* Washington, D.C: U.S. Government Printing Office.

Morash, M. (1983), 'Gangs, Groups and Delinquency', *British Journal of Criminology,* **23**, 309-331.

Nicks, K. (1993), *'The Differentiating Factors of Delinquent Offence Type: Estrangement, Self Esteem, Differential association and Self-Report Juvenile Delinquency',* Unpublished Bachelors dissertation: University of Surrey.

Peoria Crime Reduction Council (1979), *Criminal Activity of Juvenile Residential Burglars,* Peoria, Illinois: City of Peoria.

Petersilia, J. (1980), 'Criminal Career Research; A Review of Recent Evidence', in N.Morris and M. Tonry (eds), *Crime and Justice: An Annual Review of Research,* 2, Chicago: University of Chicago Press.

Petersilia, J.W. Greenwood, P.W. and Lavin, M. (1977), *Criminal Careers of Habitual Felons,* Santa Monica, CA: Rand.

Reiss, A.J. Jr (1980), 'Understanding changes in crime rates', in S.E. Fienberg and A.J. Reiss Jr (eds), *Indicators of Crime and Criminal Justice: Quantitative Studies.* Washington, DC: Bureau of Justice Statistics.

Reiss, A.J. Jr (1986), 'Co-offending Influences on Criminal Careers', in Blumstein, A Cohen, J Roth, J.A. and Viscter, C.A. (eds), *Criminal Careers and "Career Criminals",* II, 121-160.

Reiss, A.J. Jr (1988), 'Co-offending and Criminal Careers', in M. Tonry and N. Morris (eds), *Crime and Justice: A Review of Research,* **10**, 117-170.

Rennison, A. (1994), *'Understanding Burglars: The Facets of the Increasing Sophistication of Burglary Involving Unlawful Entry and Theft',* Unpublished Masters dissertation. University of Surrey.

Ressler, R.K. Burgess, A.W. and Douglas, J.E. (1993), *Sexual Homicide: Patterns and Motives,* London: Simon and Schuster.

Sarnecki, J. (1992), 'Brottslighet och Kamratrelationer: Rapport 1982:5 Stockholm.' Portions translated in 1984 by Denise Galarraga as *Criminality and Friend Relations: A Study of Juvenile Criminality in a Swedish community,* National criminal Justice Reference Service, Washington, D.C.: National Institute of Justice.

Scarr, H.A. (1973), *Patterns of Burglary.* Washington D.C. National Department of Justice, National Institute of Law Enforcement and Criminal Justice.

Shannon, L.W. (1978), 'A longitudinal study of delinquency and crime', in C. Welford, (ed.), *Quantitative Studies in Criminology,* Beverley Hills, Calif.: Sage Publications.

Shaw, C.R. (1938), *Brothers in Crime,* Chicago, Ill: University of Chicago Press.

Shaw, C.R. and McKay, H.D. (1931), 'Male juvenile delinquency as group behaviour', in *Report on the Causes of Crime,* 13, Washington D.C.: National Commission on Law Observance and the Administration of Justice.

Sherif, M. and Sherif, C.W. (1969), *Social Psychology.* New York: Harper and Row.

Shover, N. (1991), 'Burglary', in M. Tonry (ed.), *Crime and Justice: A Review of Research,* Chicago: Chicago Press.

Shover, N. (1973), 'The Social Organisation of Burglary', *Social Problems,* **20**, 499-51

Shye, S. (1978), *Theory Construction and Data Analysis in the Behavioral Sciences,* San Francisco: Jossey Bass.

Shye, S. (1985), *Multiple Scaling: The Theory and Application of Partial Order Scalogram Analysis,* Amsterdam: North Holland.

Shye, S. Elizur, E. and Hoffman, M. (1994), *Introduction To Facet Theory: Content Design and Intrinsic Data Analysis in Behavioral Research,* London: Sage.

Stander, J., Farrington, D.P., Hill, G. and Altham, P.M.E. (1989), 'Markov Chain Analyses and Specialisation in Criminal Careers', *The British Journal of Criminology,* **29**, 317-335.

Stattin, H. and Magnusson, D. (1989), 'The Role of Aggressive Behaviour in the Frequency, Seriousness and Types of Later Crime', *Journal of Consulting and Clinical Psychology,* **57**, 710-718.

Stattin, H. and Magnusson, D. (1991), 'Stability and Change in Criminal Behaviour Up To Age 30', *The British Journal of Criminology,* **31**, 327-346.

Steiner, I. (1972), *Group Processes and Productivity.* London: Academic Press.

Sutherland, E. (1937), *The Professional Thief,* Chicago: University of Chicago Press.

Walsh, D. (1986), *Heavy Business: Commercial Burglary and Robbery,* London: Routledge and Kegan-Paul.

Walsh, D. (1980), *Break-Ins: Burglary from Private Houses,* London: Constable.

Weisburd, D., Chayet, E.F. and Warring, E.J. (1990), 'White Collar Crime and Criminal Careers: Some Preliminary Findings', *Crime and Delinquency,* **36**, 342-355.

West, M. (1996), 'Introducing Work Group Psychology', in M. West (ed.), *Handbook of Work Group Psychology,* Chichester: Wiley.

West, W.G. (1978), 'The Short Term Careers of Serious Thieves', *Canadian Journal of Criminology,* **20**, 169-190.

Wilson, A. (1995), 'An Examination of the Behaviours and Characteristics of Commercial Burglars who Offend in Groups', unpublished Masters. Dissertation, University of Liverpool.

Wilson, A. and McCluskey, K. (1995), 'Life on the Road: A Case Study of the Ram Raider', Unpublished course work submitted to Liverpool University in part requirement of MSc Investigative Psychology.

Wolfgang, M. (1978), *Overview of Research into Violent Behaviour,* Testimony to the Subcommittee on Domestic and International Scientific Planning, Analysis and Co-operation of the House Committee on Science and Technology, 95th Cong., 2nd Session.

Wolfgang, M.E., Figlio, R.M. and Sellin, T. (1972), *Delinquency in a Birth Cohort.* Chicago: University of Chicago Press.

Yuki, G. and Tracey, J. (1992), 'Consequences of Influence Used With Subordinates, Peers and the Boss', *Journal of Applied Psychology,* **77**, 525-535.

Zvulan, E. (1978), 'Multidimensional Scalogram Analysis: The Methods and its Application', In S. Shye (ed.), *Theory Construction and Data Analysis in the Behavioral Sciences,* San Francisco: Jossey-Bass.

APPENDIX.

Leaders: (4, 27, 12, 14, 6, 45, 65, 1, 24, 16, 42, 68, 2, 48, 21 and 58)

Heavies: (44, 33, 64, 70, 10 and 3)

Drivers: (26, 43, 38, 37, 41, 8,11,47, 20, 5, 25, 55, 39 and 46)

Extras: (26, 43, 38, 37, 41, 8,11,47, 20, 5, 25, 55, 39 and 46)

Apprentices: (28,31,61,36,32,40,67,63 and 18)

Handlers: (66, 17, 69, 7, 9, 30, 51 and 54)

8 The Social Structure of Robbery
KARYN McCLUSKEY AND SARAH WARDLE

Offender Profiling research has until recently concentrated on offenders operating in isolation. However, many crimes are committed not by an offender acting alone, but by a group of offenders working together.

The purpose of this research was to examine the possibility of determining the characteristics of an armed robbery team from their actions at the scene of the crime. The first step in this research was to define whether the criminal team acted in ways similar to many other groups. The study examined the group make-up of seventeen armed robbery teams. All of the participants in this study were convicted armed robbers who were serving sentences in British Prisons.

Using the 5-WH interview technique (McGuire and Priestley, 1985) and sociograms, we examined the armed robbery team over a number of areas such as communication, roles, planning, conflict, trust, leadership, recruitment, goals and norms.

The overall finding of the research is that armed robbery teams are similar in many ways to many other 'legitimate' groups. They are goal oriented, have a structure, have positions for their members, undertake planning and set rules for themselves in the commission of the offence. In addition, there is a symbiotic relationship between the team organisation and the groups' cohesiveness.

Membership of an armed robbery team was found to influence the behaviour, beliefs, and attitudes of the team members. This research highlights the importance of examining group characteristics in order to fully understand the nature of this crime.

Karyn McCluskey obtained a BSc (Hons) in Psychology and then completed a Masters Degree in Investigative Psychology at the University of Liverpool. She worked for two years with the Sussex Police as a criminal intelligence analyst, and was in charge of developing their offender profiling programme. She has previously worked in prisons in Scotland, is a registered nurse and is currently working in the Lancashire Constabulary. She maintains an interest in prisoner profiling and is currently researching this with the Lancashire Police.

Sarah Wardle obtained a degree in Psychology and Neuroscience at the Victoria University of Manchester before completing a Masters degree in Investigative Psychology at the University of Liverpool. It was at Liverpool where the research documented in the following chapter was conducted. Since leaving Liverpool she returned to London and started work for the Metropolitan Police as a Criminal Intelligence Analyst. After 18 months she transferred to work at the Special Intelligence Section at New Scotland Yard. She is currently working as a Senior Analyst, with responsibility for the personal development of all analysts working in central London and for identifying and undertaking strategic analysis projects on crime area of concern to the area. She is hoping shortly to continue her research into robbery, focusing particularly on street robbery offences.

8 The Social Structure of Robbery

KARYN McCLUSKEY AND SARAH WARDLE

Offender profiling revolves around the possibility of identifying the characteristics of an offender on the basis of his actions at the scene of a crime (Canter, 1993). However, many crimes are committed, not by an individual acting alone, but by a group of offenders acting together. Social and Organisational Psychology research has emphasised the influence of group membership on individual behaviour. This influence can induce individual members to change their attitudes and behaviours from those displayed under circumstances where they did not belong to a group. It is our hypothesis that the actions perpetrated by a criminal team at the scene of a crime are as much a function of its 'group characteristics' as that of its individual members characteristics. Further we hypothesise that in attempting to profile a group of criminals who operate together, one must first consider the influence of the group on the *collective behaviour* of its members. This research is the first stage of that process, which was to determine what group characteristics exist within criminal teams and how the criminal teams vary in relation to these characteristics.

Cattell (1948) postulated that if the laws of group behaviour were understood and the characteristics of the individual members and the internal structure (i.e. roles, status positions and communication networks) were known then it would be possible to predict the group's behaviour. If one interprets this more conceptually it could suggest that from a group's actions at the scene of a crime it may be possible to infer aspects of the group's internal structure and characteristics of the individual members and indeed this forms an integral part of our hypothesis.

When designing any research project, an essential early stage involves the definition of the research domain and the generation of hypotheses. Integral to the first stage is the examination of the relevant literature of any past research. However, within this study of criminal group characteristics, however, the literature is sparse and that in existence is often anecdotal in nature. Consequently, it was necessary to draw concepts over which to study the criminal groups from the social and organisational psychology literature conducted on "legitimate" or non-criminal groups. It was recognised that additional psychological processes may occur in a criminal group which may not be fully covered by the existing psychological literature. Thus the research contained within this paper is of an essentially exploratory nature, based upon the interviews of offenders who had committed Armed Robberies in a team of three or more.

The Psychology of the Group

It is important to highlight that within Social Psychology there are two opposing camps which debate the influence of the group on individual behaviour: Allport (1924) stated that there is no more to groups than the individuals that comprise them. In comparison, Warriner (1956) proposes that a group is understandable solely in terms of distinctly social processes and factors, not by reference to individual psychology. The latter position has been affirmed by the documentation of certain psychological phenomena that arise only from the interaction of the individuals within a group, for example, Groupthink (Janis, 1972), Risky Shift (Stoner, 1961) Deindividuation (Zimbardo, 1973), Conformity (Asch, 1951).

There is clearly some ground between these theorists, which has some relevance in addressing the armed robbery team and the individual team members' behaviour. We need to see group forces, for example conforming to group pressure, as arising out of the actions of individuals, and individuals whose actions are a function of the group forces that they themselves have brought into existence.

From the vast psychological literature on groups the following elements of group characteristics were recognised by the majority of researchers, for example, Gibson et al. (1988), Shaw (1981), to influence the groups functioning and the individuals' behaviour.

The concepts discussed below are the cornerstones of the social psychology of groups, and an abundance of research is available. However in the interest of clarity and brevity, it is proposed only to define

Social Structure of Robbery 251

the essence of the concepts for the reader. Although they are discussed individually, it should be emphasised that one concept cannot stand in isolation, and that all interact in a complex relationship.

Communication Network

Shaw (1964) stated that communication lies at the heart of the group process. If the group is to function efficiently its members should be able to communicate easily and efficiently. The paths of communication may determine the group structure, the attainment of group goals and resulting satisfaction with the group. There are a number of communication structures that can occur within a group, see figure 8.1, and each structure would tend to suggest differing organisation within the team. This may range from complete two-way communication between each of the team members to one individual within the team controlling the flow of information and thus may emerge in a leadership role.

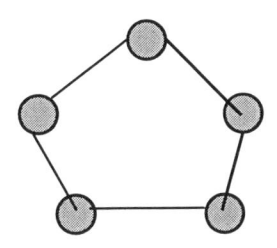

Figure 8.1.1
Circle

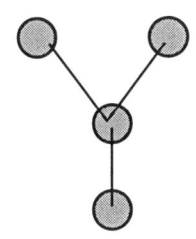

Figure 8.1.2
Y Configuration

Figure 8.1.1, 8.1.2 Group Structure

Shaw (1981) proposes that when the communication network is unrestricted as in the circle, it does not put one person in a highly centralised position, and the tendency is an 'each to all' organisational pattern. Importantly, Shaw (1981) states that "This is not merely a lack of organisation, as may be supposed; it involves a consistent procedure for ensuring that all members receive all available information". In figure

8.1.2 above information is funnelled to one person who solves the problem and distributes the answer to other group members.

Roles

In examining the roles of the individuals within a group, one is not referring to random differences between individuals but consistent differences in the behaviour of each individual member, which is expected and condoned by the other members.

There are a number of research findings regarding roles that are highlighted by Brown (1988). The most frequent finding is that roles imply a division of labour amongst group members, thus facilitating the achievement of the group goals. Secondly, roles help bring order to the groups existence. Brown (1988) states that "the emergence of task roles is essential in the organised groups as it means that group members will quickly learn who to look to and respond to in particular situations". Thus within the armed robbery team, the member who is elected to take the violent role, would be expected to counteract any resistance or violence from the victims in the offence location.

Additionally, from a profiling perspective, roles are one of the most potentially observable aspects of the groups' behaviour. Many researchers within Organisational Psychology have stated that the roles of individuals in small groups are observable and recognisable (Luckenbill, 1980). It is hypothesised that the actions of the individuals performing the roles will be apparent at the scene of a crime. Further, it is proposed that there will be role consistent behaviour within the armed robbery team, for instance the violent team member will be mainly responsible for controlling the victims at the scene of the crime. Consistency in the adoption of a specific role by each member of the team may be reflected in their individual criminal histories, for example, the driver within the team may have more vehicle related crime in his criminal history. Preliminary evidence to support this theory has been elicited from a study of ram raiding teams in the Thames Valley area, (Wilson and McCluskey, 1995)

Leadership/Structure

Organisational literature suggests that within the group there is usually some variation in the power associated with different roles. Leadership does not refer to a type of person, but to certain types of relationships in the groups. Leaders will by definition be the centre of interaction within the group, are commonly the most powerful person within the group and at the centre of the communication network.

There are a number of aspects associated with a leadership role. In examining the emergence of a leader, Wilson (1978), states that in the first instance one would need to look for the member who systematically influences the behaviour of others. Brown (1988) states that what characterises leaders is that they can influence others in the group more than they are influenced themselves. Cartwright and Zander (1969) state that it is the ability to initiate ideas and activities that are taken up by the rest of the group.

It is proposed that the approach to the commission of the offence will be influenced by the status structure defined by the team, and ultimately this may be observable at the scene of a crime.

The following two aspects of group behaviour are highly interrelated, but are examined separately as only the level of planning is observable within the offence, however the planning exists solely to facilitate the achievement of the group goal. A high level of planning would suggest a highly focused and goal orientated armed robbery team from which one could infer particular characteristics.

Goals

Perhaps most importantly the reason for formation of any group is to achieve a group goal, whether it is companionship, sport or financial gain. The attitude and commitment of the team towards the goal will influence the resulting structure of the team. This may also have considerable impact on the behaviour of the group members, and their desire to remain within the group to help it attain its goal. A very goal orientated team will be more satisfied with the group organisation, and in all likelihood will be more successful in the achievement of that goal.

Level of Planning

The level of planning within the offence of armed robbery is hypothesised to be related to level of goal orientated behaviour. Increased planning and a high level of forensic awareness can be indicative of the experience of the offenders and the commitment to the group goal. The level of planning within the offence is observable and may be inferred from the actions at the scene of an offence. Canter (1995) states that the level of forensic awareness can indicate the criminal experience of the offender and his likelihood of being within the police record system and for which type of offences.

Norms

Norms are the generally agreed rules of conduct of individual and group behaviour, which develop as a result of member interaction over time (Gibson et al., 1988). Importantly within the criminal group in this case Armed Robbery Teams, specific 'criminal' norms are hypothesised to develop to guide members' behaviour. An example would be the use of violence within the offence or the methods used in dealing with the police when arrested. Particularly with teams who are prolific offenders over a long period of time, the norms can become more apparent over time, and as such reflect on the group make up and the individual members.

The final two concepts of conflict and trust are in the main self-explanatory. However because of the high level of risk of Armed Robbery and subsequent long sentences on conviction, it was proposed that these concepts might be integral to the formation and endurance of the team.

Recruitment

The inclusion of recruitment within this study was to primarily address how and where the armed robbery teams originate. Although not a significant variable within the study of 'legitimate' group literature, it is hypothesised to be of some significance in the study of criminal groups. How the armed robbery team forms and whom it consists of, may considerably influence the groups offending behaviour. Although there is little literature on how individuals enter the criminal group, Anderson (1978) stated that amongst their peers, criminals acquire reputations based on their criminal performances and may be recruited for their specific skills. Whilst some of these peers may have fleeting relationships, many of these relationships can endure for many years. As offender profiling aims to identify the characteristics of the offenders, the recruitment into a criminal team and the population from which they are recruited will form part of any subsequent profile.

Cohesiveness

The resulting structure and organisation that emerges from the interaction of all the above facets of group organisation, were hypothesised to contribute to the cohesiveness of the group. Cohesiveness is the degree to which the group possesses a commonness of attitude, of performance and behaviour. It is derived from factors such as common goals, explicitness of goals, shared norms, values, and stability of membership.

The level of cohesiveness as a measure of group solidarity is ostensibly more useful than examining one individual concept, as it provides a global measurement of the nature of relationships among members.

Festinger (1950) states that cohesiveness is "the resultant of all forces acting on the members to remain in the group". Highly cohesive groups are those groups which are motivated to stay together, engage in more interaction, exert greater influence over their members and are more efficient in achieving goals set for themselves. In addition, the higher the cohesiveness of a group, no matter how it is measured, the more members depend upon one another for various rewards or satisfaction that come from participating in the group. Thus the level of cohesiveness is the level of interdependence among members.

Method

This present study examined the group characteristics of 17 armed robbery teams; for this purpose we interviewed one member of each team. Although ideally we would have liked to interview all the members of each team, it was practically impossible for a number of reasons. Firstly, all of the team may not have been convicted or even identified. Secondly, many members of the teams were imprisoned in geographically distant prisons, and finally recruitment of interviewees would have been non existent had all members of each team had to agree to talk to us, such are the confines of Real World research.

In 1982 Cressey defined a group as consisting of a "minimum membership of two people" - the more members a group has the greater the number of possible relationships that can exist between them and consequently the greater the structure and communication needed to operate the group. However, Einstadter (1969) supports the examination of the armed robbery team within the group of three, not only because they appear to be the most tactically efficient unit, but because the possible interactions are increased within the group. Further, Einstadter (1969) suggested that teams of two were most often friends or close relations. Therefore the criteria for recruitment to the study was that offenders should have committed their offences within a team of three or more. We did not specify an upper team size limit within our research.

The Interviewees were approached after having been identified from prison records as fitting the above criteria. The interviewees were assured of the confidentiality and anonymity of the interview and asked if they would volunteer.

The Interview

The interview of the offenders utilised a number of techniques:

1. The sociogram.
2. 5WH interview technique.
3. The use of police records as an additional source of information.

The Sociogram

The initial stage of the interview was the construction of the sociogram. Firstly, the interviewee was asked the to draw a circle on a piece of paper and put his name on the circle. Next, he was asked to repeat this procedure for the other members in the team, with those members he felt closer to drawn nearer to his circle.

In addition he was asked to represent the lines of communication within the team by using arrows.

Driver   Violent member

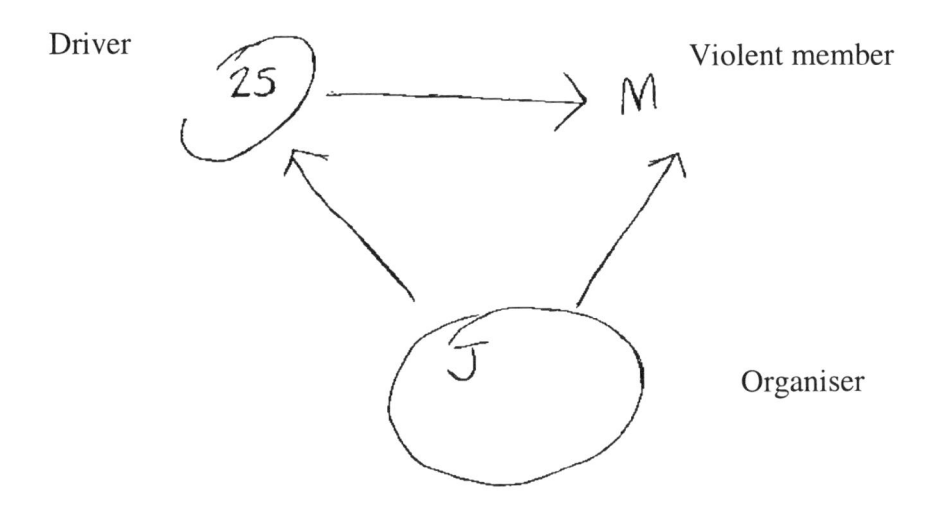

Figure 8.2 Sociogram of an Armed Robbery Team

The Sociogram is very beneficial within the interview in that it provides a visual representation of the team structure and members. In addition, it focuses the interviewee on the recalling the relationships between the team members and their role within the group, especially if the offender has been incarcerated for some time.

The 5WH Interview Schedule

The 5WH Interview Schedule (McGuire and Priestly, 1985) was originally devised to examine the actual offences people have committed to see what could be learnt from them. The 5WH is a simple technique known as situational analysis. It involves generating an exhaustive set of questions based around the following types of question:

Who, What, Where, When, and How?

The questions, when generated, can be asked in the form of a fully structured interview, whereby the interviewer asks a fixed set of questions in a fixed order. This has a number of advantages since they yield easily quantifiable data and ensure comparability of questions across the respondents (Breakwell, 1995).

However, it was decided to use a semi-structured approach for three reasons:

Firstly, because of the exploratory nature it was possible that a structured interview might miss some salient issues therefore an element of free recall was incorporated into the interview.

Secondly, Fisher, Geiselman and Redmond (1987) found that memory recall was impaired by frequent interruption and that short answer questioning was responsible for producing a less concentrated form of memory retrieval.

Finally, because of the sensitive nature of the information to be elicited it was decided a more conversational approach would help put the interviewee at ease.

Therefore the interview involved semi-structured schedule comprising free recall, open ended and specific questions. Each interview was conducted with two interviewers. One interviewer was predominantly concerned with checking that the interviewee had covered all the issues within the 5WH.

Once analysed the data was qualitatively analysed using Multi-Dimensional Scalogram Analysis (MSA: Lingoes, 1968). This technique is considered especially useful for revealing the structure to qualitative data. Analysing qualitative data reliably has historically been considered to be problematic particularly in relation to behavioural data due to the 'noise' associated with it. MSA allows the relationship between each of the group concepts such as roles, structure, planning etc., to be represented in a visual summary.

Results

Although the sample of seventeen robbery teams is relatively small and as such no conventional statistical methods would have been of little scientific utility. However, one is able to highlight some general trends from the interviews.

Collectively the teams admitted having perpetrated over three hundred armed robberies between them. All the teams had committed serious offences, which were reflected in sentences of between 10 and 25 years.

Descriptive Statistics

Team size- the teams interviewed varied in size being composed of between three to seven members with a mean team size of four members. That the most frequently occurring team size is three members, which would support Einstadter (1969) theory that a team of three is the most tactically efficient unit for this type of crime.

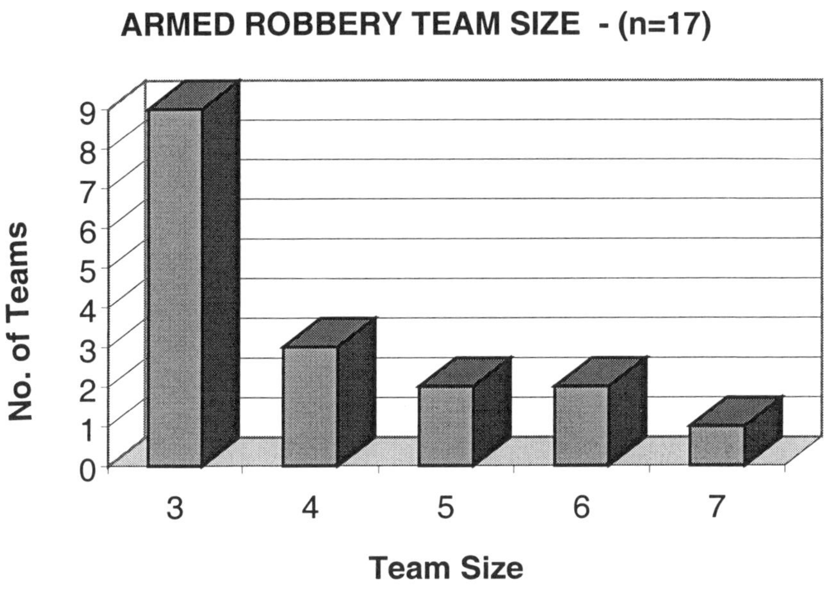

ARMED ROBBERY TEAM SIZE - (n=17)

Figure 8.3 Team Size in 16 Teams of Armed Robbers

Target Type

The armed robberies described in the interviews occurred on the following targets:

- Security vans.
- Banking premises, i.e. banks and building societies.

- Commercial premises, i.e. a safe in an area manager's office, an office of a public house, containing the takings.
- Person, i.e., in a private house.

ARMED ROBBERY TARGET TYPE (n=17)

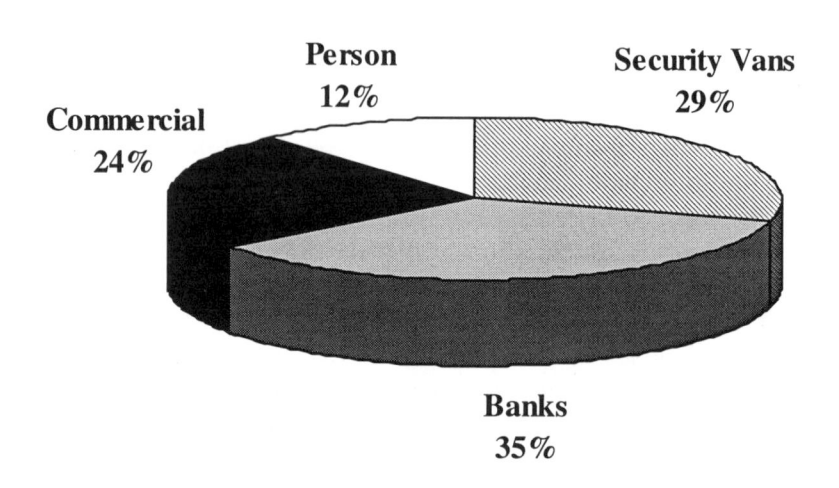

- Person 12%
- Security Vans 29%
- Commercial 24%
- Banks 35%

Figure 8.4 The Percentage of Target Types Chosen by the Teams

A correlation between the size of the team and the target chosen was not found, for example we did not find that targeting security vans required a larger team size. Although we had a small number of teams, the actual number of offences was large - over three hundred armed robberies, and teams appeared to specialise in certain types of target. One could tentatively suggest that those teams who targeted security vans were in the main more experienced criminals and expected a higher reward from them.

Distance Between Residences of Team Members

The members of each team lived, on average, within a 2.59-mile radius of each other; although one team shared the same flat and furthest distance between another team was 11 miles. It is difficult to compare these findings with other research as few studies have been conducted in this field.

Division of Haul

The money acquired from the offence was divided up by the offenders equally in 76.5% of the groups. This occurred mainly in the teams set up to commit more than one offence. This division of money was conducted after the information source had been paid (if there was one) and after cars or guns had been paid for. However, if an additional member was required to carry out a particular offence they were most often offered a set amount rather than an equal share.

Conversely, in those teams set up for one particular robbery the division of money was more unequal. This accounted for 23.5% of the teams. For example, in one offence 2 members worked out the logistics of the offence and got £75,000 each, another acquired the information about the offence and received £40,000 and the remaining 2 members, numbers 4 and 5, got £30,000. Number 4 worked for the security company and was driving the van and 5 had been previously sacked from the security company targeted.

In all of the offences the offenders targeted establishments or security vans for cash alone.

Ethnicity

The inclusion of ethnicity in this section serves only to confirm that the offenders involved in armed robbery are predominantly white. The team members interviewed described their team make-up as:

White	13 Teams
Mixed race	3 Teams
Asian	1 Team

Interview results

The following section highlights individual elements of the group characteristics; this serves to illustrate the similarities and differences between the teams in relation to their formation, their structure and resulting organisation. It also gives an indication of the richness of the interview material.

Specific Offences

This describes those teams that were formed for the perpetration of a single armed robbery. The specific armed robberies were all the result of inside information (100%) for example information from employees or ex-employees of a company. The targets predominantly included warehouses and other commercial premises and occasionally security vans and private houses, but did not include building societies or banks. Further, it becomes clear that much of the strategy for the armed robbery offence is devised from this inside information.

> *"This man here see (c), he was the security guard, but he got sacked for bad time keeping two weeks previous. He's passed the info to (a). The job was in ... These three were from ... (a) (f) (h). So as I've been done with this guy (f) before, he comes to me and says "I need a safe cracker, are you interested in doing it?" I says yeah I'll do it on two conditions, one, is there's no violence involved and two, I bring someone along with me. Cause I ain't gonna work with a team I don't know. So he says yeah no problem"*
> (Commercial robbery)

Social Structure of Robbery 263

Interviewee

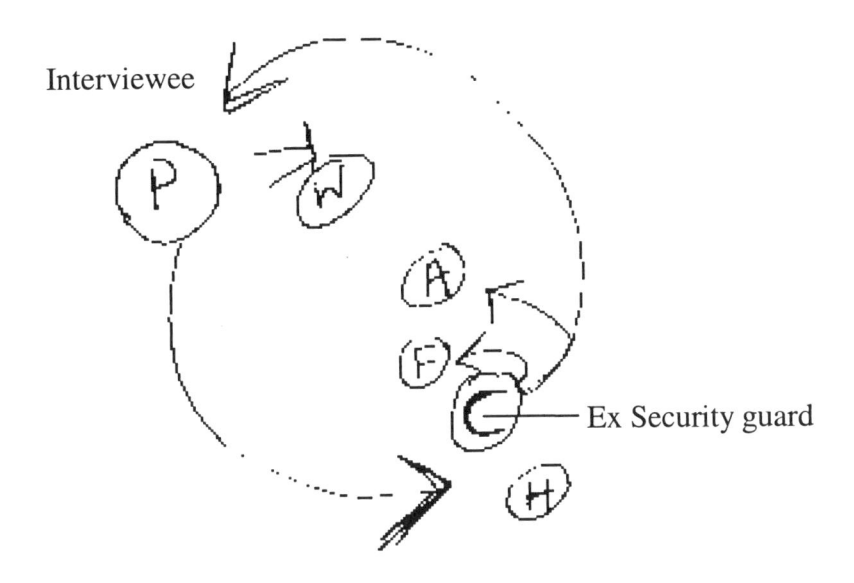

Ex Security guard

Figure 8.5 Sociogram of Robbery Communication

"We had this fella in the ...road branch of ... He'd worked in this other branch and he told us all about it, the whole run down, it was so easy it wasn't true."

(Commercial robbery)

The willingness of the offenders to take part in a robbery where there was inside information is all too obvious throughout the interviews. The expected yield of the robbery is known, as is the amount of planning needed to overcome the security in the premises or at the security vans. That these are robberies where there is less likelihood of having to overcome *unknown* obstacles, led many to view it as a "sure thing". This defined goal often led to a feeling of omnipotence within the offenders.

General Offending

This describes those teams that after an original offence have continued to commit offences in the same team arrangement. Those offenders who are members of teams set up for general offending are often motivated by one member within the team to commit armed robberies. The following quotes were in response to the question of how they got involved in the team.

> *"Well, there were three of us, Glaswegian as it goes, (a), he was at it already (armed robbery), me and (b) were burgling at the time, we had just been nicked, come out, and met (a) again. He was suited and booted and he's got untold dough, he's doing well, and he asks me if I know anywhere there's a likely target... I'd knocked a jewellers window out a few years previous and bulkheaded the grill out and like a smash and grab in a place called ... That seemed to me to be a nice hit and I took something like nine grand out of the window, so we went back and robbed it at gunpoint, and that was basically the first robbery, so it was like, we was in the pub (b) and me and was eager because of the money he was earning."*
>
> Bank robbers

> *"Me, personally, it was down to money, somebody came up with something in the region of half a million pounds upwards, yeah, I got interested... (2) came up with the idea, but at the end of the day nobody was no angel in the team, like, as much as I put myself back, like, I'm only doing it for the money - we're all the same you know...I was sort of em criminally that way inclined... So like there wasn't no convincing me."*
>
> Security vans

Morrison and O'Donnell (1994) state within their research on armed robbery, that they felt the robbers could rarely identify a single driving force that they felt made their behaviour understandable. Conversely, within this type of armed robbery teams one finds that an oft-cited theme for continued offending is that of greed. These individuals are primarily egocentric, and one could hypothesise that in being part of a team of like-minded individuals, served to reinforce these greed themes. Which would explain in part why they committed so many robberies, they had little intention of actually desisting from these robberies and said they felt that capture was eventually inevitable.

> *" We took to it, like fish to water after the jewellery raid, and there was a bit of panic with us being wanted, cos we think "cor armed robbery" that's a long time if we're nicked, but we got this buzz and thought fuck it lets go for it hammer and tongs."*
>
> Bank Robbery

Morrison and O'Donnell (1994) quote a Robbery Squad Detective who says "that robbers are intoxicated by the excitement of the activity of robbing". This may be an accurate reflection of the impression given to the police, however one would propose that, psychologically, the perceived reward is the "intoxicating" element. From a social learning perspective one could suggest that excitement and reward can be positive reinforcers of criminal behaviour.

"That was the thing with armed robbery, I think most of it was the amounts, I mean all crime is thievery, its always what you think you're going to get, but with actual armed robbery you know you was goin to get something. With burglary you might not or whatever, but with armed robbery you knew, cause there was money on the premises and it was always the final count that was the real buzz."

Commercial

Roles

Each position in the armed robbery team has an associated role that consists of the expected behaviours of the occupant of that position, for example the violent member obtaining the necessary weapons.

The roles the offenders took in the teams were allocated one of two ways; their roles were defined before they came into the team and thus they were recruited for their skills, or, they decided which role they would take when the group was already formed. Although organisational psychology literature indicates that a role cannot exist without the team, however many of the offenders within the teams were known for their skill in a certain area and were recruited for that skill. In many of the general offending teams the roles the offenders played within the team became more refined over time. Over a series of armed robberies the individuals enacting the roles within the team may modify their role behaviour depending on the success or failure of any particular action.

The identifiable roles within the team, in keeping with some of the research on roles, (Walsh, 1985), appeared to be the driver, the violent member, and the planner. It is proposed to examine the main roles in turn.

The Violent Member

A recurrent theme within the interviews is the role of the member who displays overt violence within the team, and deserves further comment.

> "(F) was the most violent, he tried to impress people, he was in the army, a P.E instructor and all this crap, you know what I mean, a real gangster...."

Bank Robbery

> " Yeah (A) he was good at demanding...he starts losing his rag, you know, what the fuck and all that, blaar blaar I want the fucking money now an all that crap...so he hits the safety glass with his shot gun at which point she's thrown her arms over her head and run off screaming...he shot him through the door, I thought he was going to kill him"

Security Vans

> "Yeah, I'd have to put myself in that sort of character really, because like I was with the weapon, I'd have to say if I wasn't violent why take up a weapon, plus I went to ...once got in an argument with this guy, ended up rucking with him and stabbing him..."

Commercial

> "No.1 had a magnum, he isn't crazy but wouldn't think twice about shooting someone.... No.2 had a loaded MNB he was like No.1"

Commercial

> "What can I say about (m), if you wanted a man to do a bit of torture - m's the person.... he was 5 foot 11, 19 stone and not an inch of fat on him. Would you argue with him...the bloke (victim) was resisting D's requests so m broke his leg with the butt of the gun...he gave the man a crack on the jaw, you could hear it break from upstairs"

Person

> "I'm the violent one, the others don't use it... I fired some warning shots at the police...I don't really aim for them"

Security Vans

> "D became very aggressive, hit the manager over the head with a baseball bat"

Banks

"I'm a gun toting gangster type of bloke"

Commercial

Within the armed robbery team, the role of the violent member seemed to be at the heart of the group. The other members in the team identified him without hesitation, and indeed there were a number of offenders who identified themselves as the violent team member.

In eight out of the nine teams which were set up to commit more than one armed robbery, the role of the violent member within the team was never taken by one of the other team members. This holds true for more than 250 robberies committed by these eight teams.

Although many groups can experience change and movement over time, there are areas that show some stability. Primarily this stability is reflected in the structure of the group and in particular the roles, and it is proposed that this consistency in role taking may be reflected in the criminal histories of the individual team members.

The Driver

The attitudes expressed by the interviewees regarding the driver in the group fell into one of three categories, which are illustrated below with quotes from the interviews.

Firstly, he was seen as an integral part of the team, highly important and much relied upon for his skills.

> *"No 4, he's the driver, he's the most important, a good man can go and get the prize, but can you go and get the right driver...no 4 was the best driver ever, you know we were on the 'redeye', you know, on the day we were caught, I heard "its the police", and a police car rams it from the back and then two rams it from the front, and they hold up guns to em, so he ducks down in the seat and flies down the road with seven police cars chasin him and he got away. The police told me he was a really great driver"*

Security Vans

> "T.D was a skilful driver. On the day we were caught, T.D reversed 400yards in reverse at 80mph round a corner. During the escape he drove at 90mph along a pavement and 150mph along the wrong side of the m ... During rush hour, he went 6 miles without hitting anyone."
>
> Security Vans

Secondly, he was drafted in to perform a driving role, paid a set amount but not informed about the planning and the set up of the team.

> "(D) was brought along to drive, we give him £5000 and he used his own car, he was recruited the night before."
>
> Security Vans

Finally, he was seen as taking less dangerous role in the offence and therefore getting easy money regardless of his driving prowess. Only one team expressed this last statement, although he received an equal share of the proceeds.

> "Yeah, (b) was a good driver...he used to get the cars...he wasn't as close as me and (a), (a) used to get the hump with him because we did think he was getting easy money really, as we were going through all the stress and strain.... (a) used to make him go in on a couple of jobs, just to make him come in"
>
> Banks/ Building Societies

The Planner

The identification of the planner in the offence was more frequently identified than a leadership role. Even those groups, which had an egalitarian structure, could identify a member of the team who was usually consulted by the rest of the team with regard to advice on the planning and commission of the offence. In the teams with a hierarchical structure this person was generally described as the leader.

One interviewee considered himself to be the leader, he had the information about the targets, and he felt he did most of the planning and considered things that could go wrong,

> "Always thought in what I does".

However he stated:

"We all take partnership - all know the outcome if we get caught."

"N.S. was the planner and gained information about the delivery of the money, he was in charge of getting the guns and getting the money. He had done time in the past for armed robbery and was an 'experienced criminal'"
Security Vans

"D was looked up to by the others, he wasn't really a criminal and was always cool and very calm. We were all involved in planning the offence, but we looked to D to see if we had missed anything important"
Commercial robbery

All the roles had a degree of planning attached to them. The driver usually acquired the stolen car and was responsible for making false numberplates if used. The violent member was in the main responsible for obtaining the weapons. Finally, the planner was often involved in obtaining equipment that wouldn't be readily available i.e. angle grinders for a safe, body scanners (scanners which are worn under clothing with an earpiece and can be tuned into police frequencies).

Our findings support the finding of many other researchers who have stated that the roles in small non-criminal groups are observable and recognisable (Brown, 1988; Luckenbill, 1980). The implications for offender profiling are obvious in that the roles will be apparent in the actions of the offenders at the scene of a crime. The logical progression of this research, having identified consistency in role taking behaviour within the armed robbery team, is to identify the associated repertoire of behaviours associated with each role.

Structure

The structure of the sociogram and the links between the individuals provides the researcher with a visual representation of the structure of the armed robbery team. Although it is essentially an egocentric view of the team, it nevertheless highlights the communication networks and how individuals see themselves within the group.

The structure of the team was considered in relation to whether it had a hierarchical or egalitarian organisation. The structure of the team has been touched upon when defining the roles. In looking at the structure of the

270 *The Social Psychology of Crime*

team, the use of the sociogram provided an ideal way of asking the offender to describe the team and the communication network within the team.

Generally within those teams who had a hierarchical structure, one found that they were made up of experienced offenders who had committed offences of this nature before.

The sociogram of team 4 illustrates the egalitarian structure of the group. Composed of friends who lived in the same flat they committed around 30 robberies in the same team.

(Team 4)

Figure 8.6 Sociogram of Egalitarian Structure

In comparison, the next team, below, was characterised by a strong and violent leader (M). He described the two other team members as reporting to him. M portrayed himself as omnipotent:

> *"I'm very volatile and can adapt to any situation I'm in....you have to be assertive to let people know where you are coming from.... I'm a robber, but I'm a nice robber"*

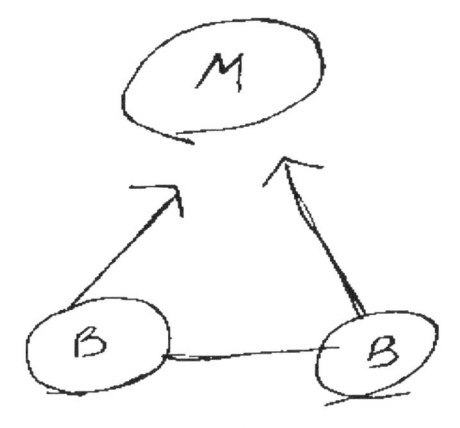

Figure 8.7 Sociogram of Strong Leader Structure

The offence carried out by the last team highlights the structure of the team set up for one offence as a result of inside information. Number 4 was a security guard, who was friends with No.5 who had been a guard in the same company but had been sacked. 5 fed information to 3 about the security van, and 3 in turn informed 1 and 2 who were experienced armed robbers. Although 3 (a loan shark) had no experience of armed robbery, he recruited the others to carry out the robbery of which he was to get a share. He controlled much of the information within the offence, but was not actually involved in the commission of the robbery. There was a great deal of mistrust within the team; it can be seen that a portion of the group had no contact with the van driver.

272 The Social Psychology of Crime

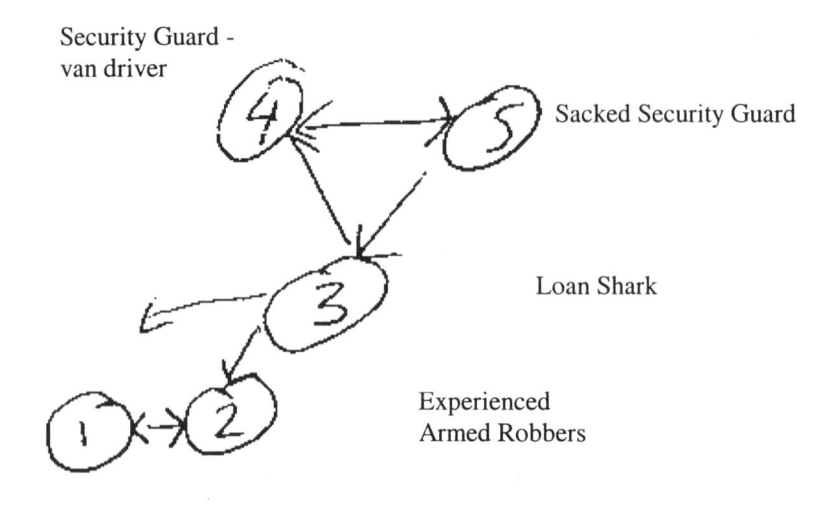

[Figure: hand-drawn sociogram with nodes labeled 1, 2, 3, 4, 5. Node 4 labeled "Security Guard - van driver"; Node 5 labeled "Sacked Security Guard"; Node 3 area "Loan Shark"; Nodes 1 and 2 "Experienced Armed Robbers". Arrows: 5→4, 4→3, 5→3, 3→2, 1↔2, 3→(left).]

Figure 8.8 Sociogram of an Inside Information Robbery

As opposed to the general perceptions of Armed Robbery teams, it is apparent that not all members of armed robbery teams have contact with each other prior to the offence. This has implications for Criminal Intelligence Analysis and the identification of suspects.

Communication

The communication network has been said to be at the heart of the group process. (Shaw, 1985). It was originally hypothesised that there would be three types of communication network.

1. Complete - complete two way communication throughout the group.
2. Partial - two-way communication between some members of the group and one way between others.
3. Directed - one member contacted all of the rest of the group and communication was not reciprocated.

Within the interview most of the teams had partial or complete communication networks, only one team referred to themselves as a directed network. This team was eventually removed from our analysis, as it typified the problems that occur when looking at crime as categorised by legal definitions. That is, that when one eventually looks at the behaviour within the offence one sees that although it is legally defined as armed robbery within a team, the behaviours are less definitive. In this case the central character in team 17 had picked up his two friends in a stolen vehicle, and when stopped by the police they hijacked the police car at gunpoint, and sped off in the stolen vehicle.

The examination of the communication network came both from the interviews and from the sociograms. Interestingly, a recurrent finding was that in the teams where the team was formed for a specific robbery, there was frequently a partial network, which often had interesting repercussions for the team members, as demonstrated in figure above. One can see that in Police Investigations, it may be difficult to identify all members of the team especially in those teams with partial communication networks. Indeed, in a substantial number of the teams interviewed, not all the members were identified and in most cases were protected by the group norms of non co-operation with the Police.

Planning

Norms within the literature were seen as standards shared by the members of the team. They are rules of conduct, which enable the individuals to predict the behaviour of the other group members. The existence of norms within the group is hypothesised to be apparent in two facets; firstly, role-taking and secondly in the planning of the offence. Norms serve to specify the roles of the members within the group and their subsequent associated role behaviour.

In planning, norms relate to the achievement of the group goal. Norms will emerge that encourage goal facilitative actions, for example, the dependence on the driver to have planned and be familiar with the escape route and discourage inhibitory behaviours, such as, deviating from the defined plan during the commission of the offence. This is worthy of some further comment to emphasise the importance of the development of norms in the planning phase of the robbery. It is hypothesised that a well planned and organised team who perpetrate an offence, where pre-planned strategies have been implemented to react to any situation that arises during the robbery, will have developed norms which relate to the roles of each member and guide the behaviour of the team.

Closely related to the facet of planning and the goal achievement is the forensic awareness of the group. Forensic awareness includes taking such precautionary measures as wearing disguises, using VHF scanners which can pick up Police radio frequencies, and taking care not to leave any traceable marks, for example, fingerprints or hair. The implementation of these measures requires prior planning. Canter (1994) stated that forensic awareness can often indicate the experience and history of an offender, and has revealed evidence for this in the investigation of sexual offences. Our hypothesis suggests that evidence of planning the forensic awareness of the group can indicate to the psychologist the experience and history of the group, for instance, the length of time over which the group has been formed and their experience of offending as a team. This information may be very useful to the investigator when prioritising suspects and looking for possible linking of other related offences.

It is proposed only to briefly illustrate the two groups:

> *"We had a fella in the supermarket, he nicked us the aprons, the badges, the little bow ties and the pink trousers, he told us the whole run down it was so easy it wasn't true...it was a funny turn but on the way in some fella asked a where the garlic sausages were, and he's gone " over there somewhere" sort of thing, he was such an abrupt little fucker...the customer said he'd already looked there...we were trying to calm a down...we went upstairs to the wages office to the two way mirror and a knocked.. She pulled back the mirror, and I said I've come about my wages. . she's having a go at him, you know, you low life shelf filler and he's proceeded to put the shotgun through..."*
>
> Team 9

> *"D broke into a police section house and stole 2 uniforms.... whilst we were at the job, we were to stand outside in the uniforms and walk around it a few times to act as lookouts...as we were standing out front this police van comes down the road, we could have legged it but we just waved at it, and it flashed its lights and the old bill waved back..."*
>
> Team 7

The other level of planning was infinitely more involved.

"All would have body scanners, expensive ones which could be pre set to 7 frequencies, they would leave their houses three days before their robbery to avoid surveillance, steal cars from a hire depot, the keys would be taken from the box outside, so the cars wouldn't be reported missing."

Team 14

It is thought that in conjunction with the other facets of the group structure, the inclusion of the level of forensic awareness will emphasise a qualitative difference between the teams.

Conflict and Trust

Much of the literature on groups states that interpersonal liking; shared norms and values contribute to group cohesiveness. However, when groups of like-minded people come together does the conflict within the group negatively influence the group in terms of the cohesiveness?

Many teams mentioned some degree of conflict within the group:

"Yeah, we had some screaming arguments even to the point of guns coming out, it was all front really I mean you knew he wasn't going to shoot me, it was all front I suppose we were like a lot of tarts living together sometimes pulling their hair out."

Team 10

" I had a row with 3 it was sort of violent...there was tension over the job, 3 was unhappy with me, he thought I was being too slack"

Team 5

Often in those teams where conflict existed, when asked if they trusted the other members there were some interesting comments:

"I trusted 2 more than 3, he was more on the same level, but its not so important to trust him but trusting his judgement...didn't trust 2 with a gun as he was ruthless, he's well known for violence and had a previous for kidnapping...you just need to respect what they are doing."

Team 5

" I trusted them with my life"

Team 4

" I didn't trust them because I didn't know them"

Team 11

" We trusted each other implicitly"

Team 1

Team 5 epitomised a theme that came out in many of the interviews, that interpersonal liking had little to do with the cohesiveness of the team, but what was important was that there was trust in their skills and their commitment to the goal. Even in those teams where there was some conflict, many still trusted each other in performing their role in the offence.

Other Facets of Group Behaviour

When asked about the robberies they had committed and the sequence of events, many offenders commented on the moments just before the event:

> *"We arrived at 7.30 am, the van was due at 11, we were just sitting in the van waiting, just brief conversation, reflecting, looking around, getting a bit paranoid cause you're seeing things you ain't supposed to see, but again, mens got this macho thing, like, I ain't gonna be the one who says I ain't doin this, so you sit back and hold your fear until the van comes...when we come to prison I said to 2 and 3 "why didn't you just say something, and they said like, "why didn't you say something", but its like you just can't judge your feelings."*

Team 4

> *"I had a funny feeling about that.... bank, I had a gut reaction, I didn't fancy it...on the way I got this strong feeling, for the first time ever I said stop the car, I want out of the car, and so I did, and I wanted to get a cab, but I'd waited 15-20 minutes on it, and a was short on patience sort of thing, and he said " fuck this, what's the fucking problem lets get back in the car, big mistake, straight into their trap...yeah I forced myself to do things I didn't want to do."*

Team 9

Although not a facet of organisational behaviour that we are presently discussing, this highlights some interesting processes occurring within the team. One can see from the above comments made by two individuals from two separate teams that, in belonging to a group, despite strong reservations about committing the offence, they were carried along with the general consensus and committed the robbery. The second member actually expressed his concerns but was persuaded to perpetrate the offence against his better judgement. We suggest that this is an integral influence of the effect of group norms on individual behaviour. As discussed previously in the planning aspect, norms develop to facilitate the achievement of the group goal. The achievement of the goal relies heavily on the full commitment of each member to fulfil the group expectations on him and indeed norms develop which discourage negative behaviours, for example, expressing fear or doubt.

Within the clinical treatment of these offenders one needs to address the ability of these individuals to understand the effects of group membership on their decision making. Equipping offenders with some insight into the group pressures on their individual behaviour, when involved in a criminal team, should form an integral part of any treatment programme and their eventual rehabilitation.

Group Analysis

As discussed in the introduction, the research was exploratory and through examination of the interviews we confirmed that the facets drawn from the psychological literature on the non-criminal group are valid concepts over which to study the criminal group. In addition, the groups were also examined over the facets of trust within the team and conflict. Moreover, it is understood that all the above concepts interact in a complex relationship, and it is this interaction of the concepts over which the teams are examined.

At its simplest, only by looking at how each individual concept interacts with each of the other concepts can we see the whole picture. Most conventional statistical methods would compare one aspect of group membership against another, for example, recruitment into the team against forensic awareness. By achieving a high correlation one could say that one variable influenced another. Unfortunately behavioural data, and even more so criminal behavioural data, is extremely 'noisy', the correlation described above may have been influenced by a third facet of group behaviour. As such it is only by looking at all the facets together that one may begin to see a pattern in our research data.

The most efficient way of looking for patterns in our data was by employing multivariate statistics, where each team is compared over all of the facets of group behaviour. The use of Multi-Dimensional Scaling (MSA: Lingoes, 1968) is a multivariate technique that enables the researchers to look at the similarities and differences between the teams.

The first stage in the process is the construction of a data matrix. Each team is scored as to the presence or absence of each of the discussed facets. For example, each team would be scored a 1 if their roles were defined before being recruited into the armed robbery team, i.e. they were recruited to be a driver, or a 2 if the roles were decided after the team was formed. Each team was scored over the 8 group facets and this results in a mathematical profile for each armed robbery team. For example, Group One's profile = 22122211.

The MSA will compare the mathematical profiles of each of the 16 teams and will plot them in 'geometric' space with the teams sharing similar characteristics plotted closer together in space.

The final MSA plot, as seen below, shows a series of squares, each of which represents an armed robbery team. It should be indicated here that although the teams are plotted in respect to their similarities and differences, the use of MSA requires the researchers to examine which group characteristics make them similar or indeed different.

Social Structure of Robbery 279

SPECIALIST

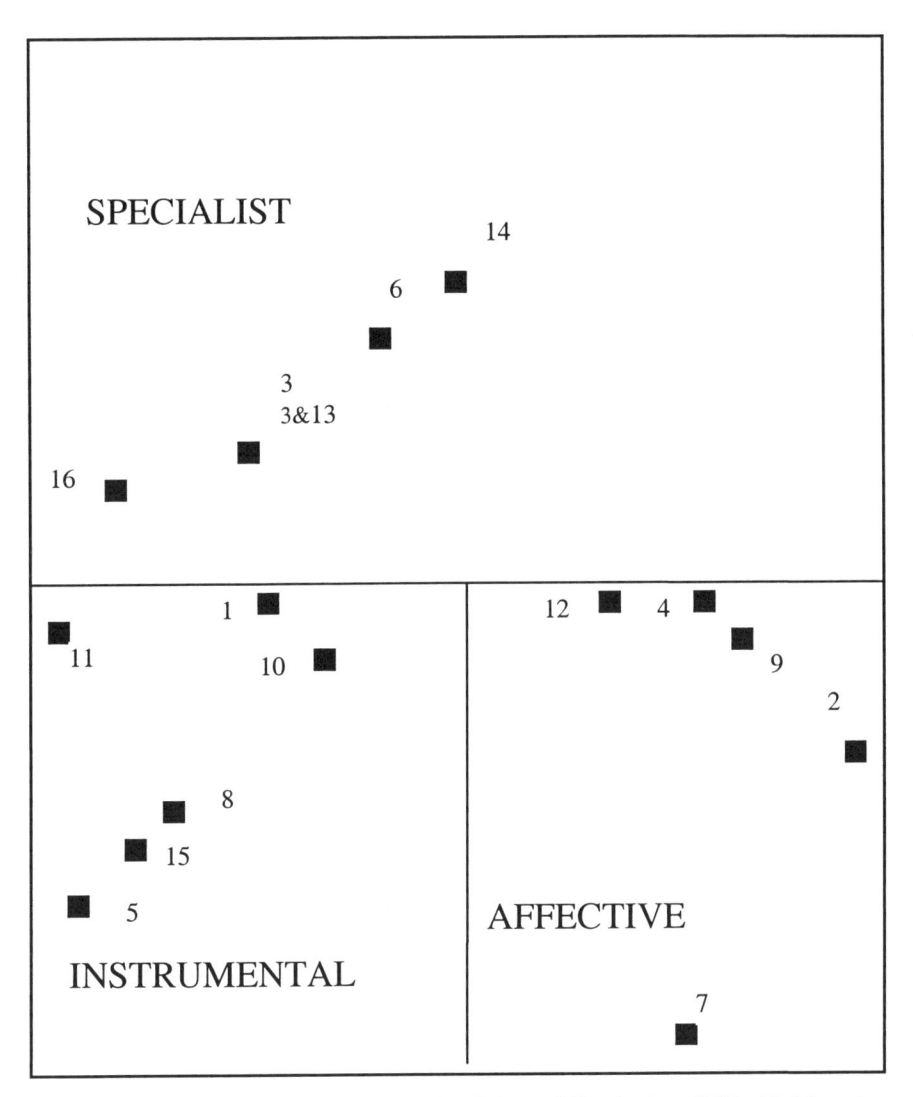

14
6
3
3&13
16

1
11 10
12 4
9
2
8
15
5   AFFECTIVE
INSTRUMENTAL
7

Coefficient of Contiguity = 0.97 with 3 iterations.

Figure 8.9 Multidimensional Scalogram Analysis of 16 Teams of Armed Robbers

The teams gravitating towards the top of the plot - termed the Specialist Region, can be differentiated based on certain group characteristics. The teams positioned towards the top of the plot are characterised by:

-A hierarchical structure.
-Roles that are defined before entering the team.
-A higher degree of planning and forensic awareness.
-No conflict between the team members.
-Full trust between all the members.

The teams positioned towards the bottom half of the plot are characterised by:

-An egalitarian structure.
-Roles that are decided once the group has formed.
-A medium level of planning.
-A degree of conflict.
-Only trusting some of the members.

Further to the distinctions made above one can also see a difference within this latter group. The teams positioned on the left-hand side of the plot - the instrumental region are:

-Set up for a specific offence.
-Had a partial communication network.
-Would consider themselves to be criminal acquaintances when the group formed.

The teams on the right of the plot - the Affective region, did not possess the above characteristics but instead:

-Were set up for general armed robbery offending.
-Had complete communication networks.
-Were friends before they decided to commit offences together.

Although MSA analysis does not impose an order on the qualitative data, it seems that the teams situated towards the top half of the plot were more organised and consequently more professional in their planning and their approach to the commission of the offence. These teams were more organised towards their achievement of the goal and they also appear to be more cohesive. That armed robbery teams are said to be cohesive is hypothesised to be related to their goal. Research has shown that the highly cohesive group is effective in achieving whatever goals its members establish (Goodacre, 1951: Shaw and Shaw, 1962). However, we have established, as did Klein and Crawford (1967) in their study of gangs, that interpersonal attraction in the criminal group does not necessarily lead to increased cohesiveness. Rather, that within the armed robbery team cohesiveness results, not from interpersonal liking, but from their perceived ability to perform their criminal role and achieve the ultimate goal. Further analysis would be required to confirm whether there was indeed a graduation in the level of organisation occurring within the teams.

Discussion

The overall finding of the research is that armed robbery teams are similar in many ways to other 'legitimate' groups - they are goal orientated, have differing structures and communication networks, have positions for their members, undertake planning, set rules for themselves in the commission of the offence. Membership of an armed robbery team influences the behaviour, beliefs, and attitudes of their members and therefore any valid explanations of the group must be at the level of the group.

What is the relevance of group characteristics within the armed robbery team and its utility to offender profiling?

Offender profiling revolves around the possibility of characterising differences between criminals on the basis of their actions in a crime (Canter, 1993). The first step is in identifying the similarities and differences between offenders. However it would be difficult to extract the individual from the armed robbery team and examine his behaviour in isolation. The psychological pressures evident within the group have inimitable consequences on the behaviour of those individuals that belong to it. Evidence has been elicited within this research that there are identifiable differences within these criminal teams in relation to their group makeup and it is further hypothesised that these differences would be identifiable in the commission of their offences.

To expand, there are elements of the group process that are observable and are apparent in the actions of the team members at the scene of the offence, for example, the role taking behaviour, planning, forensic awareness, and in some cases structure. From these observable group behaviours one could further infer other unseen group characteristics such as the possible communication networks between the individual members, the circumstances of their recruitment, how long they have been established as a team, and whether their offending is part of a series or a solitary offence. The offence specifics and the group characteristics can also allude to the geographical distance between the offender's home base and the offence location. For example groups set up for one specific offence where there was inside information, tended to travel longer distances and live further apart, and had little knowledge of the other team members.

There is an investigative requirement for further techniques in identifying Armed Robbery teams exemplified by a recent study by Wardle (1997) on behalf of New Scotland Yard. She found that out of 44 Armed Robberies involving teams of three or more on commercial premises in December 1996 only 3 offences had all of the team identified and an additional 3 had identified on 1 member of the team. Of those 3 teams where all the offenders were identified they were mainly as a result of informant information.

One must ask that if one was to examine the group actions at the scene of the crime could the characteristics of the team have resulted in additional information about the origins and background of the team, and for the investigators, help in the prioritisation of suspects and in the criminal intelligence process.

Although the relevance of looking at group characteristics of Armed Robbery teams has been established, the work also has implications for the investigative process at the scene of the crime. Historically within Armed Robbery offences there are a number of intrinsic problems. For example, the use of disguises by offenders, the effects of such a violent event on witness recall, and the number of offenders where there may only be one witness to the offence as in many sub post offices, can all influence the reliability and detail of the witness statement. In some cases this is being overcome by the use of CCTV within premises, which ultimately may have implication for the examination of criminal group behaviour.

As an example, role-taking behaviour was found in almost all of the teams, therefore indicating a degree of specialisation. One could hypothesise that the adoption of these roles may be related to the personal characteristics of the members and could perhaps be reflected in their criminal histories (Delieu, 1994; Wilson et al., 1995). The level of planning exhibited at the scene of the crime is observable and can be related to the group characteristics, for example, norms, leadership, goals, and the role of inside information. The type of target chosen can also be linked to the group organisation.

As an exploratory examination of the criminal group; the study has highlighted that for Police and professionals who deal in the treatment of violent offenders, the complexity and the influence of criminal group membership cannot be ignored. Instead, it must form an essential part in the investigation and eventual rehabilitation of these offenders.

References

Allport, F.H. (1924), *Social Psychology,* Boston: Houghton Miffin.
Asch (1951), 'Effects of Group Pressure Upon the Modification and Distortion of Judgements', in H. Guetzkow (ed.), *Groups Leadership and Men,* New York: Carnegie Press.
Anderson, L.R. (1978), 'Groups Would do Better Without Humans', *Personality and Social Psychology Bulletin*, **4**, 557-558.
Best, J. and Luckenbill, D. (1980), 'The Social Organisation of Deviants', *Social Problems*, **28 (1)**, 15-31.
Breakwell, G. (1995), 'Interviewing', in G. Breakwell et al. (eds), *Research Methods in Psychology,* London: Sage.
Brown, R. (1988), *Group Processes: Dynamics Within and Between Groups,* New York: Basil Blackwell.
Canter, D.V. (1993), 'The Psychology of Offender Profiling', Unpublished Manuscript (In Press) Department of Psychology, University of Surrey.
Canter, D.V. (1994), *Criminal Shadows,* London: Harper Collins.
Cartwright, D. and Zander, A. (eds) (1968), *Group Dynamics: Research and Theory,* 3rd edn, New York: Harper and Row.
Cattell, R.B. (1948), 'Concepts and Methods in the Measurement of Group Syntality', *Psychological Review*, **55**, 48-63.

Cressey, D.R. and Sutherland, E.H. (1992)[1970], Principles of Criminology, 11th edn, Dix Hills, N.Y.: General Hall.
Delieu, J. (1994), 'The Consistent Criminal: Specialisation and Escalation in Criminal Careers. Do They Exist?', M.Sc. Dissertation Unpublished, Department of Psychology, University of Surrey.
Einstader, W.J. (1969), 'The Social Organisation of Armed Robbery', *Social Problems*, **17 (1)**, 64-83.
Festinger, L., Schacter, S. and Back, K. (1950), *Social Pressures in Informal Groups,* New York: Harper.
Fisher, R.P., Geiselman R.E. and Redmond, D.S. (1987), 'Critical Analysis of Police Interview Techniques', *Journal of Police Science and Administration*, **15**, 291-297.
Gibson, J., Ivanchevich, J., and Donnelly J. (1988), *Organisations: Behcaviour Structure Processes,* Illinois: Homewood.
Goodacre, M. (1951), 'The Use of the Sociometric Test as a Predictor of Combat Unit Effectiveness', *Sociometry*, **14**, 148-152.
Janis, I.L. (1972), *Victims of Groupthink,* Boston: Houghton Mifflin.
Klein, M.W. and Crawford, L.Y. (1967), 'Groups, Gangs and Cohesiveness', *Journal of Research in Crime and Delinquency,* **14 (4)**, 142-165.
Lingoes, J.C. (1968), 'The Multivariate Analysis of Qualitative Data', *Multivariate Behavioural Research*, **3**, 61-94.
McCluskey, K. and Wilson, A. (1995), 'A Facet Theoretic Approach to the Criminal Careers of a Team of Ram Raiders', Unpublished Assignment as part of a Msc Course in Investigative Psychology, University of Liverpool.
McGuire, J.E. and Priesley, P. (1985), *Offending Behaviour: Skills and Strategems for Going Straight,* London: Batsford.
Morrison, S. and O'Donnell, I. (1994), 'Armed Robbery: A Study in London', *Occasional Paper,* **14**, Oxford: Oxford University Press.
Shaw, M.E. and Shaw, L.M. (1962), 'Some effects of Sociometric Grouping Upon Learning', *Journal of Social Psychology*, **57**, 453-458.
Shaw, M. (1981), *Group Dynamics: The Social Psychology of Small Group Behaviour,* New York: McGraw-Hill.
Shaw, E.W. (1964), 'Communication Networks', in L. Berkowitz (ed.), *Advances in Experimental Social Psychology,* **1**, New York: Academic Press.
Shaw M.E. (1955), 'A comparison of two types of Leadership in Various Communications Networks', *Journal of Abnormal and Social Psychology*, **50**, 127-134.
Stoner, J.A.F. (1961), 'A Comparison of Individual and Group Decisions Involving Risk', Unpublished Masters Thesis, Massachusetts Institute of Technology.
Walsh, D. (1986), *Heavy Business: Commercial Burglary and Robbery,* London: Routledge and Kegan Paul.

Warriner, C.H. (1956), 'Groups are Real: A Reaffirmation', *American Sociological Review*, **21**, 549-554.
Wilson, S. (1978), *Informal Groups: An Introduction,* New Jersey: Prentice Hall.
Wardle, S. (1997), Unpublished Research.
Zimbardo, P.G. (1973), 'A Priandellian Prison: The Mind is a Formidable Jailor', in *New York Times Magazine*, April 8, 38-60.

9 Criminology, Desistance and the Psychology of the Stranger

SHADD MARUNA

Research on personality and crime has concentrated on distinguishing the dispositional traits that separate offenders from non-offenders. Since, by definition, such traits are largely constant over time and social context, this emphasis implies that the "criminal personality" is a stable and permanent "thing" to be measured. In fact, considerable longitudinal and ethnographic research on crime over the life course indicates that "criminal careers" are sporadic, short-lived and largely shaped by social and developmental contexts. Therefore, criminologists need to use a richer, more dynamic framework for understanding the personalities of those involved in crime. Narrative psychology offers an ideal theoretical backdrop for understanding socially contingent and developmentally contextual behaviour over time. Self-narratives are shaped by experience, and then reflected in behaviour. An understanding of why individuals commit crimes requires an analysis and understanding of these internal stories.

Shadd Maruna completed his Ph.D. at Northwestern University in Chicago, USA, and is now an associate professor in the School of Criminal Justice at the State University of New York at Albany. He is the recipient of a Fulbright Scholarship and a Guggenheim Fellowship, and has recently been published in 'The Narrative Study of Lives'. His current research, with Professor David Canter at the University of Liverpool, involves a three-year study of how and why serious offenders desist from crime.

9 Criminology, Desistance and the Psychology of the Stranger
SHADD MARUNA

Research on the psychology of crime has concentrated on distinguishing the specific personality traits of offenders. Since, by definition, traits are largely constant over time and social context, this emphasis implies that the "criminal personality" is a stable and permanent "thing" to be measured. In fact, considerable longitudinal and ethnographic research on crime over the life course indicates that "criminal careers" are sporadic, short-lived and largely shaped by social and developmental contexts. Therefore, criminologists need to use a richer, more dynamic framework for understanding the personalities of those involved in crime. Narrative psychology offers an ideal theoretical backdrop for understanding socially contingent and developmentally contextual behaviour over time. Self-narratives are shaped by experience, and then reflected in behaviour. An understanding of why individuals commit crimes requires an analysis and understanding of these internal stories.

Dating back to the origins of the discipline, criminology has had a rather uncomfortable relationship with personality psychology. Though many criminologists have tried to isolate the psychological factors that differentiate offenders from non-offenders, the notion of a "criminal personality" or a "psychology of crime" has been ardently debated by criminologists with sociological backgrounds (see Andrews and Wormith, 1989). Nonetheless, over the last 20 years, personality variables have ascended to the foreground of popular and professional criminological thought (Flanagan, 1987).This would be in large measure thanks to their acceptance by influential criminologists outside of the field of psychology like James Q. Wilson (Wilson and Herrnstein, 1985) and Travis Hirschi (Gottfredson and Hirschi, 1990).

The vast majority of this research on criminal personalities involves the study of stable dispositional traits (Caspi, et al., 1994). For instance, in the influential *Crime and Personality,* Eysenck (1977) defines criminality as a "continuous trait of the same kind as intelligence, or height or weight" that is innate in a small minority of individuals (77). A short list of the traits that have been proposed as correlates to criminal behaviour includes: aggressiveness, assertiveness, dependency, egocentricity, emotional instability, extroversion, fearlessness, hostility, impulsiveness, insecurity, irresponsibility, low arousal, low empathy, low intelligence, obsession, pessimism, recklessness, unconventionality, and weak socialisation. Various combinations or constellations of these traits have been described as an "antisocial" or "criminal" personality. Criminologists have even formally operationalised "criminality" with a stable personality profile on the Minnesota Multiphasic Personality Inventory (MMPI), characterised by high scores in psychopathic deviation, schizophrenia and hypomania (Hathaway and Monachese, 1963; Rathus and Siegel, 1980).

According to Allport (1937) the personality trait is "a neuropsychic structure having the capacity to render many stimuli functionally equivalent, and to initiate and guide...behaviour". William James suggested that such traits are "set like plaster" after one reaches thirty years of age, and, in fact, the relative stability of trait scores over the life course is one of the most robust findings in personality psychology (Stevens and Truss, 1985). Costa and McCrae (1989) argue not only that traits remain consistent over the life course, but that they are also transcontextual. Using this framework for understanding personality, criminologists commonly view criminality from an ontogenetic framework, and the development into delinquency is viewed as an unchanging course of "maturational unfolding" set in one's early childhood years (Block, 1971; Dannefer, 1984; Sullivan, forthcoming). In fact, Loeber (1982) suggests that a "consensus" has been reached in favour of the "stability hypothesis" of criminal behaviour, and Sampson and Laub (1995) call the continuity of criminal traits over time "an impressive generalisation that is rare in the social sciences" (see also Huesmann et al., 1984).

Nonetheless, criminal trait theory has a serious problem to overcome. Though it is true that most adult criminals showed signs of being 'delinquent' children, the majority of juvenile offenders *do not* become adult criminals (Graham and Bowling, 1995; Robins and Rutter, 1990; Rutherford, 1992). By age 28, nearly 85 percent of former delinquents desist from offending (Blumstein and Cohen, 1987), with only a tiny fraction of delinquents progressing on to life-long "criminal careers" (Loeber, 1982; Moffitt, 1993). In fact, in the same article in which they suggest that there is "stability of offending over the life course", Gottfredson and Hirschi (1995) report that criminal behaviour "declines precipitously and continuously throughout life" (1995: 31). One of the perplexing paradoxes of criminology, therefore, is the simultaneous finding of *stability* in "criminal personality" or "criminality" over time and the marked *instability* of criminal *behaviour* as recorded by official criminal justice data and surveys (Katz, 1988; Matza, 1964).

Following McAdams in *Can Personality Change?* (1994a), I will argue that one way to provide insight into this apparent paradox might be to move beyond dispositional traits and view personality as a multi-layered process. Temperamental traits provide only what McAdams calls the "psychology of the stranger", or precisely the types of attributes one knows about a person she knows little about. McAdams describes a broader, three-level approach for understanding the "whole person" (Murray, 1938), involving not only dispositional traits, but also strategies or motives, and the narrative identity or self-concept (Becker, 1964, 1968; Denzin, 1987; Giddens, 1991). According to this theory, though dispositional traits like aggressiveness or low self-control may be stable over the life course, individuals can still 'change' -- the change simply takes place on a *different level* of their personality. This approach to understanding the person, a central component of what is being called 'narrative psychology', can have important ramifications in criminology, investigative psychology (see Canter, 1994), and corrections policy (see Lewis and Maruna, in press).

A Brief Review of Trait Criminology

Criminal trait theories can fall under the rubric of either 'nature' or 'nurture', and range from sociological explanations about 'delinquent subcultures', to genetic theories of the 'born criminal'. Historically, these trait theories can be broken down into three general and overlapping 'eras' (for a more comprehensive review see Blackburn, 1994).

1860-1950: The Search for the 'Born Criminal'

At the turn of the century, trait theories comprised the most influential strain of criminological thinking. According to the social Darwinism-influenced theories of Lombroso (1911) and Garofalo (1885), offenders tend to lack the intelligence, maturity, self-control and sensitivity of non-offenders. Foucault (1988) describes this early era of positivist criminology as involving the creation of a "new type of dangerous individual" - the criminal without a crime, who exhibits delinquent "tendencies" and "signs" but may not have broken any laws. This "psychiatrization" of criminality shifted the focus of crime studies "from the crime to the criminal; from the act as it was actually committed to the danger potentially inherent in the individual; from the modulated punishment of the guilty party to the absolute protection of others" (Foucault 1988, p.144). These early trait theories frequently either deny or question the possibility "rehabilitation". Lombroso (1911) writes, "Atavism shows us the inefficacy of punishment for *born criminals* and why it is that *they inevitably have periodic relapses into crime*" (p.369; emphasis mine).

Lange (1931), Hooton (1939), and Sheldon et al. (1940) further developed this understanding of the biological determination of criminal behaviour, but the most scientifically sophisticated early research into criminal personality was the work of Sheldon and Eleanor Glueck. Glueck and Glueck (1940) provide a comprehensive biosocial theory involving everything from physical and temperamental traits of delinquents to the emotional, disciplinary, and intellectual character of their families. Family environments, in which parents are either hostile or indifferent to children they argue, frequently produce children who score highly on measures of traits like hostility, narcissism and extroversion.

1930-1975: Environmental Traits

Beginning with the early Chicago School of sociology, these individualist theories of crime -- especially those based in genetic and eugenic concepts -- began to lose ground to sociological theories. Matza (1964) writes, criminologists began to "relocate pathology...from the personal to the social plane" (p.47). Moreover, several sociological criminologists began to systematically criticise earlier studies of the criminal personality during this time (e.g. Sutherland, 1947; Merton and Montagu, 1940). In their review of 113 studies of criminal psychology, for instance, Schuessler and Cressey (1950) conclude that most of the early personality studies lacked methodological rigour and failed to conclusively illustrate a link between crime and personality. Waldo and Dinitz (1967) review 94 studies of offender personality between 1950 and 1965, and reach similar conclusions.

Nonetheless, sociologists of this era did not abandon the notion of a criminal personality altogether. In fact, subsequent reviews have suggested that sociological criminologists merely 'disguised' the similarities between their social explanations and more psychological ones (Blackburn, 1994; see also Matza, 1964). In many ways, concepts like the 'culture of poverty' and 'culture of violence' (Wolfgang and Ferracuti, 1967) became trait-like substitutes for the stability of genetic explanations of behavioural differences. Foucault (1988) writes, though "The age of criminal anthropology with its radical naiveté's, seems to have disappeared with the 19th Century, ...a much more subtle psycho-sociology of delinquency has taken up the fight" (p.145).

Banfield (1968), for example, traces the crime and unemployment of impoverished communities to the inheritance of a 'present-time orientation' and a lack of an internalised work ethic among ghetto children. Rooted in the functionalist notion of 'cultural lag', this subcultural theory represented an explicit departure from most environmental theories of behaviour (Reed, 1992). The 'nurture' side of the nature/nurture debate traditionally represented the Enlightenment principle of human plasticity and adaptation. Yet, like nature itself, this new 'culture' produces bounded traits that are nearly as self-reproducing and resistant to change as genetic traits. For example, Lewis (1968) writes, "By the time slum children are age six or seven, they...are not psychologically geared to take full advantage of changing conditions or increased opportunities which may occur in their lifetime" (xlv).

1965-Present: Criminal Inventories

Aided by the development of reliable personality inventories like the MMPI, research on the personality characteristics of offenders was revitalised in the 1960s. These true-and-false questionnaires are designed to gauge the degree to which a person exhibits traits such as neuroticism relative to others. A majority of studies between 1966 and 1975 found a positive correlation between various traits and criminal behaviour (Tennenbaum, 1977). Gough (1965), for instance, reports on a large-scale, international study using a socialisation scale of the California Psychological Inventory, modelled after the MMPI. He found that the scores of criminal offenders have differed substantially from those of non-offenders across ten countries, and that offenders in every country scored in the same general range (Wilson and Herrnstein, 1985).

Eysenck (1977, 1989) focused primarily on extroversion, neuroticism, and psychoticism, and their roots in biology and genetics. According to Eysenck, an under-aroused cerebral cortex causes extroverts to seek out stimulation from the environment and makes these individuals more difficult to socialise than introverts. When this extroversion is mixed with an autonomic nervous system characterised by either neurotic or psychotic tendencies, the individual is even more likely to be difficult to condition and control. Eysenck's theory has received mixed empirical support, but increasing attention over the last 20 years (e.g. Mak, 1990).

Still, offender personality studies gained the most ground when the authors of two of criminology's most well known texts (Hirschi, 1969; Wilson, 1975) developed new arguments suggesting that personal traits were essential for understanding why some persons commit crimes and others do not. Both Wilson and Herrnstein (1985) and Gottfredson and Hirschi (1990, 1995) posit that 'impulsivity' or 'low self-control' differentiates those persons likely to commit crimes from those who are not. Gottfredson and Hirschi (1990) write, "People who lack self-control will tend to be impulsive, insensitive, physical (as opposed to mental), risk-taking, shortsighted, and non-verbal, and they will tend therefore to engage in criminal and analogous acts" (p.90).

Like the Gluecks, these authors suggest that young people with low self-control are generally raised in homes in which parents do not know "how to punish" (Wilson and Herrnstein, 1985). Delinquent behaviour, they argue, is the product of families who punish irregularly, sporadically and often unjustly. Again, though this is an environmental cause, these researchers suggest that the psychological effects of this parenting are highly intractable. Gottfredson and Hirschi (1995) write, "Enhancing the level of self-control appears possible in early childhood, but the record suggests that successful efforts to change the level later in life are exceedingly rare, if not non-existent" (p.33). These trait theories have received empirical support (Brownfield and Sorenson, 1993; Caspi, et al., 1994), and have inspired several personality researchers to develop more refined and integrative theories of "criminality" over the last decade (c.f. Farrington, 1992; LeBlanc, et al., 1988).

The Challenge of Desistance

The study of personality traits has helped criminologists understand why two persons with similar backgrounds and environments can have very different criminal histories. Still, many critiques have been made of this 'reductionist' emphasis on individual psychology over situational or macro-social causes of crime (see Currie, 1985; and G. Becker, 1968, for two very different approaches), and the empirical evidence has also been criticised (Gibbons, 1989).

Few critiques have had the effect of David Matza's (1964) argument in *Delinquency and Drift,* though. Matza faults trait theories for their tendency to vastly overpredict criminal behaviour, which he calls an "embarrassment of riches" (p.21). Though it is true that most adult criminals showed signs of being "delinquent" children, he argues, the majority of juvenile offenders *do not* become adult criminals. Matza suggests that most trait theories, from biological to sociological, fall apart when this notion of impermanence is introduced. For instance, if delinquency is the product of the behavioural norms of the ghetto, then why do forty year-olds seem to be so immune to these pressures? Or why do impulsive seventeen year-olds commit so many more crimes than impulsive thirty year-olds? Matza says, few positivist criminological theories can provide a coherent answer.

This critique remains highly salient today (DiClemente, 1994; Gove, 1985; Moffitt, 1993). Almost no one disputes the relationship between age and crime. Loeber (1982), West (1982), Caspi and Moffitt (1993), and others have identified a small percentage of "life-course persistent" delinquents, who seem to continue to engage in criminal behaviour throughout adulthood. Yet, the typical delinquent *does* change his behaviour in early adulthood. Moffitt (1993) writes, "In contrast with the rare life-course-persistent type, adolescence-limited delinquency is ubiquitous" (p.685).

Though the exact figures differ for various offences, criminal behaviours generally rise through adolescence, peak in the late teens and early twenties, then drop sharply throughout adulthood (Cline, 1980; Gartner and Piliavin, 1988). This pattern emerges in studies using various methods of measuring offending (Hindelang, 1981; Irwin, 1970; Rowe and Tittle, 1977; Sullivan, 1989) and has remained "virtually unchanged for about 150 years" (Gottfredson and Hirschi, 1990). As far back as 1913, Goring called this age-crime relationship a "law of nature" - the young simply commit the most crimes, and older persons desist from such behaviour. Similarly, many contemporary scholars, like Gottfredson and Hirschi (1990) argue that "the age effect is invariant across social and cultural conditions" (128). Though such claims are controversial (see Farrington, 1986; Greenberg, 1985), almost everyone agrees that some sort of reform or desistance process does seem to take place during early adulthood in contemporary Western society.

Yet, desistance remains an "unexplained process" (Gottfredson and Hirschi, 1990). In fact, in one of the most thorough analyses of the topic, Rand (1987) suggests, "The phenomenon of desistance has received no specific theoretical or empirical attention" (p.134). Though this is overstated (see Greenberg, 1981; Shover, 1985; or Trasler, 1979 for notable exceptions), studies of desistance do tend to be difficult to locate and seem to exist in relative isolation from one another. Wilson and Herrnstein (1985) conclude that the linkage of age and crime "resists explanation" (145), and Shover (1985) writes, "Although it is conventional wisdom that most offenders eventually desist from criminal behaviour, criminology textbooks have little or nothing to say about this process" (p.15).

Moffitt (1993) calls the "mysterious" relationship between age and crime "at once the most robust and least understood empirical observation in the field of criminology" (p.675). Gove (1985) argues, "All of (the major) theoretical perspectives either explicitly or implicitly suggest that deviant behaviour is an amplifying process that leads to further and more serious deviance" (p.118) in *direct contradiction* to the "empirical facts about the enormous amount of desistance from crime that happens soon *after* adolescence" (Moffitt, 1993, p.694). Mulvey and LaRosa (1986) conclude, "In short, we know that many youth "grow out" of delinquent activity, but we know very little about why" (p.213).

Maturational Reform and its Critics

One of the first criminologists to address the question of reform was Adolphe Quetelet (1833). Like other students of crime in this period, Quetelet takes a biological approach to delinquency. He argues that the penchant for crime "Seems to develop by reason of the intensity of man's physical vitality and passions". Criminality peaks when physical development has "almost been completed", then "diminishes still later due to the enfeeblement of physical vitality and the passions" (cited in Brown and Miller, 1988: p.13). Sheldon and Eleanor Glueck develop this into their theory of 'maturational reform', in which they argue that criminality naturally declines after the age of 25. Glueck and Glueck (1940) suggest that with the "sheer passage of time" juvenile delinquents "grow out" of this transitory phase and change their life goals. They find that "ageing is the only factor which emerges as significant in the reformative process" (p.105). Young adults "burn out" physiologically and can no longer maintain the type of energy and aggressiveness needed in delinquency.

Though the Gluecks (1940) explicitly urge future researchers to "dissect maturation into its components" (p. 270), Shover (1985) and others assert that criminology's "explanatory efforts have not progressed appreciably beyond (the Gluecks') work". Maturational reform continues, almost by default, to be one of the most influential theories of desistance in criminology (Gove, 1985; Graham and Bowling, 1995). For instance, using data collected by Rowe and Tittle (1977), Wilson and Herrnstein (1985) argue that none of the possible correlates of age, such as employment, peers or family circumstances, explain crime as well as the variable of age itself. "That is to say, an older person is likely to have a lower propensity for crime than a younger person, even after they have been matched in demographic variables", they write (p.145). Similarly, Gottfredson and Hirschi (1990), write, "We are left with the conclusion that (desistance) is due to the inexorable ageing of the organism" rather than any social variables (p.141).

According to each theory, ageing 'causes' desistance. Yet, as Sutton (1994) suggests, "To say that age influences everything is to say nothing" (p.228). Importantly, developmental psychologists have deemed biological age an "ambiguous" and "irrelevant" variable, with little meaning except that which is socially attached to it (Neugarten and Neugarten, 1986; Rutter, 1989). Few criminologists would be satisfied with the assessment:

"Criminal behaviour peaks at age seventeen, therefore, crime is caused by turning seventeen". Yet, ageing is seen as an adequate explanation for desistance.

Though age is certainly a very strong correlate of desistance, criminologists have generally failed to "unpack" the "meaning" of age (Sampson and Laub, 1992). Some efforts have been made to use normative patterns of adult development to explain desistance as a "natural" process of human development (e.g. Gove, 1985; Jolin, 1985), borrowing from the theories of Levinson and Erikson. Yet, much of this research also commits what Dannefer (1984) refers to as the "ontogenetic fallacy," by accepting that changes in behavior reflect the natural and universal "properties of the aging organism" rather than changes in social or institutional conditions (see also Greenberg, 1981). Like theories of "burnout" or "maturation," developmental theories of desistance generally re-name the age-crime relationship, but do little to increase or understanding of how this change takes place (Wooton, 1959). As Matza (1964) argues, a simple notion like 'burning out', "merely reiterates the occurrence of maturational reform. It hardly explains it" (Matza, 1964, p.24; see also Wooton, 1959).

Personality, Policy and Change

One reason for this lack of an explanation may be the dominant paradigm for understanding the psychology of crime. Criminology needs an understanding of criminal behaviour and personality that will allow for this sort of plasticity and change, while still acknowledging the role of individual differences in cognition and identity. Since personality traits are almost inherently static, trait theories cannot easily answer this challenge. Like Matza, Moffitt (1993) writes:

> (Psychological) theories typically rely on the stability of individual differences in traits such as impulsivity, neuroticism, autonomic nervous system reactivity, or low intelligence. Psychological theories cannot explain the onset and desistence of adolescent delinquency without positing compelling reasons for a sudden and dramatic population shift in criminogenic traits followed by return to baseline a few years later (694).

By definition, if personality traits changed radically over time, they would not be traits, but rather temporary states or phases, and would lose their predictive and theoretical value.

Consequently the *policy implications* of many trait studies also contrast sharply with the promising recent studies on offender rehabilitation and reintegration (Lipsey, 1992; McGuire, 1995). If persons are nothing but the sum of their stable dispositional traits, then why waste money trying to rehabilitate such populations? (Gibbons, 1989). In fact, dating back to the tradition's historic link to eugenics (see Gould, 1981; Rafter, 1994), criminal trait research leads almost inevitably to the pessimistic attitude of "lock 'em up" currently dominating the crime policy agenda. Lilly, et al. (1994) similarly argue that trait theories generally "lend credence to the idea that offenders are largely beyond reform and in need of punitive control" (p.219).

> To be sure, the conclusion that offenders are characterised by unchangeable bodily or psychological characteristics leads logically to the conclusion that offenders should be either eliminated, caged indefinitely (incapacitation), or altered physically through intrusive measures.
>
> (p.35)

In order to understand desistance, and design innovative new programmes for ex-offender reintegration, criminology must go beyond psychological traits in efforts to understand criminal behaviour (Lewis and Maruna, 1995).

Beyond Traits

McAdams (1985, 1992, and 1993) might suggest that one reason for the difficulty in understanding desistance is that the majority of criminological work dwells solely within the "psychology of the stranger". This involves the sort of simple, typological and comparative ways one "sizes up" someone he or she has met, but really does not "understand". One might say, for instance, "That woman seemed so shy and depressed, I wish I knew what she was *really* about", or "I wish I could get to *know* her". Her traits only give us the *beginning* of the "whole" personality, McAdams would argue.

Though some psychologists argue that personality is made up entirely of dispositional traits (Buss, 1989), research by Bromley (1977) and Thorne (1989) indicates that when most people talk about "who they are" they generally conceive of something very different than simple temperamental characteristics. Moreover, many of the most important theories of personality - including those of Adler, Erikson, Fromm, Jung, McClelland and Tomkins - cannot be broken down into the language of traits (McAdams, 1994b). Erikson and Jung saw the life span as involving a continual process of possible change. Similarly, according to developmental, social learning and interactionist perspectives, personal behaviour is guided by changing social expectations and norms as well as personal contexts and social environments (Hagestad and Neugarten, 1985).

McAdams (1994a) argues that to fully understand personality, we must move beyond stable traits to the "flesh-and-blood, in-the-world doer, striving to accomplish things, expressing himself or herself" through plans, tactics, self-understandings and life stories (p.306). Statistical differences on the "simple, comparative and only vaguely conditional" measures of extroversion or impulsiveness can be helpful "first reads" into personality, but they do not constitute the "whole person" (McAdams, 1994a). Though individual differences in traits might be relatively stable over time, therefore, there is more to personality than what can be measured on a series of linear continua.

This argument has considerable support from critics of criminology as well. Toch (1986), for instance, has argued that:

> Positivist approaches to classification help to produce explanatory theories, which in turn help us to 'understand crime'. These theories, however, do not permit us to 'understand criminals,' because they are segmental views rather than full-blooded portraits. ...These must be supplemented with portraits of offender perspectives, and with a review of unique personal histories.
>
> (p.162)

Citing Magnusson and Bergman (1988), Sampson and Laub (1993) suggest that criminology research should shift from a purely "variable-orientation" to include a "person-orientation" as well (see also Currie, 1993). And, Cairns (1986) argues that personal transitions in the life course are one of the "phenomena lost" by over reliance on large-scale quantitative research (see also Sullivan, 1989).

Essentially, what seems to be missing from most criminology research is "the person" - the wholeness and agentic subjectivity of the individual. Sartre (1963) argues that trying to explain behaviour, and individual change in particular, by relying on "the great idols of our epoch - heredity, education, environment, physiological constitution" allows us to "understand nothing". He writes:

> The transitions, the becomings, the transformations, have been carefully veiled from us, and we have been limited to putting order into the succession by invoking empirically established but literally unintelligible sequences.
>
> (p.24)

Sartre makes the same point as an expanding group of researchers in cognitive and personality psychology: we need a literally *intelligible* sequence, or a coherent "story" of the individual if we want to understand changes in behaviour such as desistance.

This growing new perspective, occasionally referred to as "narrative psychology" has been called "a viable alternative to the positivist paradigm" (Sarbin, 1986, p.vii). Kotre even argues that there is a "quiet revolution taking place in psychology" that is putting narrative ways of knowing and thinking at the foreground of the understanding of personality and cognition (cited in McAdams, 1993). According to this view, in order to achieve a contingent, temporally structured and contextualized understanding of human behaviour (Toch's "full-blooded portraits"), one needs to look at the self-narratives or subjective self-concepts of individuals (Bruner, 1987; Giddens, 1991; Hermans, et al., 1992; McAdams, 1985). In his narrative theory of psychological development, McAdams (1994a) argues that personality should be seen as a three-level process, involving traits, personal strategies, and identity narratives or self stories (see also Conley, 1985). Though traits are relatively stable over the life course, the second two, more contextualized domains leaves open the possibility of substantial personality change in adulthood.

Motives and Strategies

McAdams' second level of personality is the level that criminal investigators are typically trained to concentrate upon: the person's central motives. What does the person want? What plans or goals is she trying to accomplish?

Psychological research on this second level of personality has concentrated on the observation and assessment of constructs such as tasks (Cantor, 1990), projects (Little, 1989), strivings (Emmons, 1986), and life scripts (Tomkins, 1987). Individuals are aware of the reasons for many of their actions and such "self-knowledge" is viewed by many as the "richest of all data" (Allport, 1961). Brown and Canter (1985) write, "Recourse to ordinary explanations of experiences is often made with the admission that people have a rich and elaborate conceptual understanding of what, and why, they do what they do" (p.242). Linked to attitudes and group norms, these goal articulations are explicitly contextualized and change with situational and developmental demands. This information can be studied through qualitative analysis of interview and life history data, but does not necessarily appear on true-false tests of temperamental traits.

Narrative Identity and the Self-Concept

McAdams' third level of personality is the internalised and evolving narrative individuals construct to integrate their pasts, presents and perceived futures into a sort of sustaining identity. Essentially, understanding the person means understanding the person's "story". Overwhelmed with the choices and possibilities of modern society (Fromm, 1941; Manning, 1991), modern individuals internalise this autobiographical narrative in order to provide a sense of coherence and predictability to the chaos of their lives (Giddens, 1991; Sartre, 1964). According to Giddens (1991), in modern society, "a person's identity is not to be found in behaviour, nor - important though this is - in the reactions of others, but in the capacity to keep a particular narrative going" (p.54). Bruner (1987) writes:

> The heart of my argument is this: eventually the culturally shaped cognitive and linguistic processes that guide the self-telling of life narratives achieve the power to structure perceptual experience, to organise memory, to segment and purpose-build the very "events" of a life. In the end, we become the autobiographical narratives by which we "tell about" our lives.
>
> (p.15).

The storied identity can be seen as an active "information-processing structure", a "cognitive schema" (Blackburn, 1994) or a "construct system" (Tagg, 1985) that is both shaped by and later mediates social interaction. Giddens (1991) writes, "Each of us not only 'has,' but lives a biography" (p.14), while Denzin (1987) suggests we are "attached to the world through a circuit of selfness" (p.36). People tell stories about what they do and why they did it. These narratives explain their actions in a sequence of events that connect up to explanatory goals, motivations, and feelings. Moreover, these self-narratives then act to shape and guide future behaviour, as persons act in ways that accord to the stories we have created about ourselves (Ryff, 1982).

These narratives have an "internal logic" (Canter, 1994) and are used to make life understandable and predictable. While our life goals and strategies give us a direction in which to act and our traits give us our behavioural styles; our individual *identities* provide the shape and coherence of our lives (Giddens, 1991). Epstein and Erskine (1983) use this "need to maintain a coherent, integrated conceptual system" or "theory of reality" to explain "behaviour that either is manifestly self-destructive or is maintained in the absence of reinforcement" (p.135). Human subjects, unlike their counterparts in the hard sciences, react differently to stimuli based on how events and constructs are "perceived and interpreted...in line with pre-existing and emerging goals" (Toch, 1987).

Importantly, these "structured self-images" are not created in a vacuum (Kohli, 1981). Identity theorists like Erikson (1959) and Giddens (1991) argue that identity is very much shaped within the constraints and opportunity structure of the social world in which people live. Rather than stripping individuals of community and macro-historical context, therefore, narrative analysis can inform our understandings by illustrating how the person sees and experiences the world around her. Katz (1988) calls this the merging of "phenomenal foreground" with "social background", and theorists like Groves and Lynch (1990) would argue that the two are intricately intertwined. Narratives are also excellent data for the analysis of the underlying sociostructural relations of a population (Bertaux, 1981).

Moreover, whereas personality traits are supposed to be both stable and transcontextual, the narrative identity "has to be routinely created and sustained in the reflexive activities of the individual" (Giddens, 1991, p.52). Unlike stage theorists, McAdams argues that identity is a life-long project that individuals continuously restructure in light of new experiences and information. Individuals change their personality and behaviour by rewriting and restructuring their understandings of their pasts and their theories of reality (Kohli, 1981).

Identity narratives can be analysed to discern the "themes" and roles that guide an individual's behaviour (Agar, 1980; McAdams, 1985, 1993). Verbal and written life histories are not the identity myths themselves, but they "hold the outlines" of these internal narratives. The precise methodology of this thematic analysis varies (see Denzin, 1989; or Tagg, 1985), yet some of the most innovative studies have borrowed constructs from the work of semiotics, linguistics, hermeneutics and psychobiography. Importantly, the accounts and explanations themselves (not the "facts" they contain) are the primary "data" of these studies (Brown and Canter, 1985; McAdams, 1993). These stories represent personal outlooks and *theories* of reality, not reality (Thomas and Thomas, 1928). Rouse (1978) suggests, our autobiographical tales are "much embellished but truthful even so, for truth is not simply what happened but how we felt about it when it was happening, and how we feel about it now" (cited in McAdams, 1993, p.29).

Narrative Applications to Criminological Research

Criminal behaviour is a multidimensional phenomena that requires multiple tools if we are to understand it (Giddens, 1976). Astute critics like Rafter (1990) warn of the "growing insularity" of criminology and point out the need to share and "swap" ideas with those in different disciplines lest we create an (ivory) "tower of Babel" (Groves and Lynch, 1990). I am proposing that criminologists swap the notion of the self-concept or narrative identity process from our colleagues in social and personality psychology.

Criminologists have widely abandoned the notion of understanding identity or personal subjectivity along with other "humanist" and existential concepts in favour of more quantifiable and empirically testable concepts such as reinforced learning. Yet, new psychological conceptions of the "self" (e.g. Bandura, 1989; Epstein, 1994) and recent developments in social science (particularly in postmodernist and symbolic interactionist research) have mounted a challenge to conventional views of the self-interested individual that should not go unnoticed by criminology (Guba and Lincoln, 1994). As Groves and Lynch (1990) write:

> Criminology should take subjective orientations seriously *because people have them*. Experience exists. Hopes, fears, and memories exist. ...If these feelings and experiences are beyond the grasp of some particularistic vision of criminology, so much the worse for criminology.
>
> (p.367)

A narrative perspective can be particularly useful in research concerning developing "criminal careers" (Blumstein and Cohen, 1987), and, as Canter (1994) has shown, the narrative perspective can also inform the field of investigative psychology.

Applications to Understanding Crime

Criminology has had a long tradition of using life history data, especially in the Chicago School of sociology during the first part of the century (Becker, 1966). Discussing life histories like *The Jack-Roller*, for instance, Shaw (1929) writes, "So far as we have been able to determine as yet, the best way to investigate the inner world of the person is through a study of himself through a life-history" (p.6). Scott and Lyman (1968) even argue that stories are intimately connected to behaviour such as crime that is outside of socially approved boundaries. "Since it is with respect to deviant behaviour that we call for accounts, the study of deviance and the study of accounts are intrinsically related, and a clarification of accounts will constitute a clarification of deviant phenomena" (p.62; see also Hartung, 1965).

Nonetheless, the marriage of oral histories and criminology has been rocky, and the method has been all but abandoned by criminologists today (Bertaux, 1981; Thomas, 1983). Lewis and Maruna (in press) argue that this is largely because criminologists have traditionally viewed these documents as purely sociological rather than psychosocial data. Bennett (1981) writes that despite the numerous oral histories collected by criminologists over the last century, delinquent narratives have never been explicitly analysed as explorations of "somatic, psychiatric and psychological regions" of human identity (p.236). He argues that the small amount of non-sociological commentary that was included in the life story research in this time was merely "inserted to placate the psychologists who headed the institute for Juvenile Research" (p.190). Finestone (1976) similarly points out, "Shaw made no attempt to pursue the implications of the Jack-Roller's idiosyncratic point of view for an understanding of his involvement in delinquent conduct" (p.101).

Precisely by drawing attention to these subjective aspects of first-person accounts, narrative psychology can provide a methodological and theoretical framework for exploring many of the concepts and constructs thought to be related to criminal behaviour. As far back as 1926, Bolitho argued that criminal offenders were driven by "personal myths" (cited in Canter, 1994). The "definitions", "attitudes" and "norms" of Sutherland's (1947) differential association theory also could be investigated from a narrative framework, as could Kaplan (1980) and Reckless (1967) "self-factors", or Yochelson and Samenow's (1977) "errors in thinking". Loeber and LeBlanc (1990) point out that labelling theory represents one of the few inherently developmental/longitudinal theories of crime. The labelling process is also, to a large degree, about identity and ("looking-glass") self-concept (Becker, 1963; McGuire and Priestley, 1985), and could be explored further from a narrative perspective (Becker, 1966).

The most developed strain of criminology interested in self-perceptions, the study of offender accounts, attributions and rationalisations, may benefit the most from a narrative framework. Sykes and Matza (1957) describe the various "techniques of neutralisation" delinquents use to absolve themselves from experiencing guilt for their crimes. These include the denial of responsibility, denial of injury, denial of the victim, and condemnation of the condemners (see also Scott and

Lyman, 1968; Landsheer, et al., 1994). In the framework of narrative psychology, these "accounts" or neutralisations have implications for the way that a person views the world around him and his control over that world.

Addressing the Stability/Change Paradox

For many of the issues and concerns of criminological inquiry, there is little need to undergo the considerable work involved in collecting and analysing narrative data. Yet, traits alone cannot explain "the social and cognitive processes" (Graham and Bowling, 1995) and the "complex interplay between objective and subjective contingencies" (Gartner and Piliavin, 1988) that lead to desistance from crime. Only by looking at the "whole person" can we begin to understand this type of change.

Narrative psychologists have started to lay the fundamental groundwork for this study of personal change, and the study of desistance would be an ideal area in which to continue this research. Most identity researchers agree that a person's self-understanding can change over time, though the change needs to "make sense" or be internally consistent (McAdams, 1994a). Epstein and Erskine (1983) compare personal identity change to paradigm shifts in the sciences, where past information is reorganised and understood in a new light. Individuals interpret and assimilate every emotionally salient experience into this evolving and cohesive narrative. When information is processed that does not fit into one's story, the person can either change her story to accommodate the new facts or distort the information to fit her story.

Erikson (1959) and Elkind (1968) argue that people first begin to shape individual identities during adolescence. Consequently, teenagers go through a "psychosocial moratorium" where they "try on" various possible selves "for size". Identity theorists would argue, therefore, that it is no coincidence that these "disorganised" early narratives correspond with high rates of criminal behaviour (Canter, 1994). Canter writes, "Many acts of violence seem to erupt at a time when the perpetrator is searching for identity and personal meaning"(p.326).

To test this, identity stories could be collected for individuals over time, comparing versions of the same incidents constructed at different times in the life course or "criminal career". Cross-sectional designs comparing stories of "unchanged" individuals to another "changed" group have also been designed (Baumeister, 1994; Heatherton and Nichols, 1994; Miller and C'deBaca, 1994). Theorists like Giddens (1991) and Rotenberg (1987) even argue that a person's autobiographic identity can be "reconstructed" in order to act as a "corrective intervention" into the past that can change the course for a person's future.

To date, however, only a few empirical studies have addressed the issue of narrative identity and desistance from crime and delinquency. Greenberg (1981, 1985) and Moffitt (1993) offer extremely potent and testable theories of desistance that centre around adolescent self-concept and identity, yet neither has been qualitatively tested. In retrospective interviews with ex-offenders, Graham and Bowling (1995), Irwin (1970), Maruna (1997), Mulvey and LaRosa (1986) and Shover (1985) have all found indications that a change in identity and self-concept is critical to the process of reform. Similar results have been found in research on the cessation of addictive behaviours such as drug use (Denzin, 1987; DiClemente, 1994; Kellogg, 1993; Stall and Biernecki, 1986; Waldorf, 1983).

Nonetheless, prospective longitudinal research is also needed in order to "dissect maturation into its components" as Glueck and Glueck (1940) suggest. Moffitt (1993), in fact, calls desistance research and delinquency studies in general "woefully ill-informed about the phenomenology of modern teenagers from their own perspective". If policy makers hope to reduce crime rates, it would benefit them to begin to know and understand the young people who commit crimes as well as those who are able to change their behaviours (Lewis, 1990).

Applications to Investigative Psychology

Canter (1994) has been instrumental in outlining how the field of investigative psychology can benefit from this narrative perspective as well. He argues, in fact, that the analysis of self-narratives should be "at the heart of offender profiling" (119). Canter views crime as an interpersonal transaction that involves characteristic and psychologically entrenched ways of dealing with other people. By understanding the stories offenders live by, he argues, investigators can better predict offender behaviour.

Conventional criminological research on offender traits, on the other hand, gives investigators little information about the individuality and uniqueness of specific offenders. As Canter (1994) writes, "The criminology literature is remarkably quiet about variations between criminals, usually preferring to treat them all as one particular kind of person" (p.389). Narrative psychology, based in research on the "whole person", is more individual-based and provides a more comprehensive understanding of a person's unique personality than do trait-based profiles. Alison and Parkinson (1995) write:

> The advantage that the narrative approach has over 'modus operandi' is that in the latter the investigator can only make limited and static inferences about the offender's background. ...In the former the investigator may gain insight into the whole psychological pattern that identifies that individual.
> (21)

Self-narratives, after all, are shaped by experience, and then reflected in behaviour. Therefore, the specific themes and patterns in an unknown person's past *behaviour* can provide important insight into the person's self story. Once reconstructed, this self-story can be used both to predict *future* behaviour as well as other characteristics. Canter (1997) has referred to this as the Actions to Characteristics (A to C) canonical equation. Whereas in most prediction studies in criminology, the characteristics of individuals are used to predict future actions or outcomes, in criminal investigations, the reverse of this process is also necessary. Police investigators try to hypothesise the characteristics of likely offenders based solely on the actions (e.g. styles of burglary or murder) of an unknown offender.

Research in investigative psychology (c.f. Canter and Heritage, 1989) has involved looking for correlations between the themes that an offender exhibits in his transactional styles and the themes and patterns of his noncriminal lifestyle. As this approach grows in profiling, clusters or "categories" of narratives may arise that can improve upon the FBI differentiation between "organised" and "disorganised" offenders (Ressler and Schachtman, 1992). Narrative typologies could also benefit the classification schemes of treatment providers (e.g. Gendreau and Ross, 1987) and aid the development of social policy geared toward high-risk populations (Lewis and Maruna, in press).

Nonetheless, identity is an on-going process, not a tangible or permanent quality of an individual. Any narrative typology needs to be based on the understanding that individuals develop and adapt their stories constantly over time (Giddens, 1991). Though various categories of self-*stories* may be identified, narrative psychology does not seek to divide *persons* into "types" in the way that offender categories based on trait scores might (Harvey, et al., 1961; Megargee and Bohn, 1979; Quay, 1983). Canter (1994) characterises such a misuse of narrative psychology as being based on a "cafeteria view" of life stories, whereby a narrative identity is understood as a permanent "thing" that can be quickly identified and labelled:

> The cafeteria view of life stories pulls the framework back into the realms of static characteristics. Instead of having distinguishing ear lobes, criminals can be recognised by the particular heroes they endorse. Life is not that simple. Narratives are moving targets that change their shape in response to life circumstances.
>
> (p.312)

Efforts to predict future criminal behaviour based on psychological traits and background variables have had mixed results (Farrington and Tarling, 1985), and the "high false-positive" problem (Bottoms, 1977) of these past efforts becomes even more critical when the stakes involve criminal investigation and possible prosecution. Though Canter is right that narrative theory offers a richer method for profiling offenders, he also warns that any application of psychological theory to the investigative process should proceed with extreme caution. Narrative theory is best used as a means of understanding specific individuals in full social and developmental context.

Summary

Trait psychology implies that the "criminal personality" is something stable and permanent. Yet, considerable longitudinal and ethnographic research on crime over the life course indicates that so-called "criminal careers" are sporadic, short-lived, and largely shaped by social and developmental context (Canter, 1994; Currie, 1991; Graham and Bowling,

1995; Katz, 1988; Sampson and Laub, 1992, 1993; Sullivan, 1989). Narrative psychology offers a dynamic, developmental perspective that can be seen as a viable alternative to the positivist paradigm in criminology (Sarbin, 1986). By going beyond traits or simple "modus operandi" and trying to understand aspects of the "whole person", criminologists and psychologists can better understand the change and development in criminal behaviour over time.

References

Agar, M. (1980), 'Stories, Background Knowledge and Themes: Problems in the Analysis of Life History Narrative', *American Ethnologist*, 7, 223-239.
Alison, L.J. and Parkinson, M. (1995), *Criminal Autobiographies: Generating and Extracting the Destructive Life Stories of Adult and Juvenile Offenders*, University of Liverpool, Internal report.
Allport, G.W. (1937), *Personality: A Psychological Interpretation*, New York: Holt, Rinehart & Winston.
Allport, G.W. (1961), *Pattern and Growth in Personality*, New York: Holt, Rinehart & Winston.
Andrews, D.A. and Wormith, J.S. (1989), 'Personality and Crime: Knowledge Destruction and Construction in Criminology', *Justice Quarterly*, 6, 289-309.
Bandura, A. (1989), 'Human Agency in Social Cognitive Theory', *American Psychologist*, 44, 75-184.
Banfield, E.C. (1968), *The Unheavenly City*, Boston and Toronto: Little, Brown.
Baumeister, R.F. (1994), 'The Crystalization of Discontent in the Process of Major Life Change', *Can Personality Change?*, Washington, D.C.: American Psychological Association.
Becker, G.S. (1968) 'Crime and Punishment: An Economic Approach', *Journal of Political Economy*, 76, 169-217.
Becker, H. (1963), *Outsiders*, New York: Free Press.
Becker, H. (1964), 'Personal Changes in Adult Life', *Sociometry*, 27 (1), 40-53.
Becker, H. (1966), 'Introduction', in C. Shaw (ed.), *The Jack-Roller*, Chicago: University of Chicago Press.
Becker, H. (1968), The Self and Adult Socialisation, in E. Norbeck, (ed.), *The Study of Personality*, New York: Holt, Rinehart, and Winston.
Bennett, J. (1981), *Oral History and Delinquency*, Chicago: University of Chicago Press.
Bertaux, D. (1981), 'From the Life-History Approach to the Transformation of Sociological Practice', in D. Bertaux, (ed.), *Biography and Society: The Life History Approach in the Social Sciences*, London: Sage.

Blackburn, R. (1994), *The Psychology of Criminal Conduct: Theory, Research and Practice,* New York: John Wiley and Sons.
Block, J. (1971), *Lives Through Time,* Berkeley, CA: Bancroft Books.
Blumstein, A. and Cohen, J. (1987), 'Characterizing Criminal Careers', *Science,* 37, 985-991.
Bolitho, W. (1926), *Murder for Profit,* New York: Garden City.
Bottoms, A.E. (1977), 'Reflections on the Renaissance of Dangerousness', *Howard Journal,* 16, 70-96.
Bromley, D. (1977), *Personality Description in Ordinary Language,* Chichester, UK: Wiley.
Brown, J. and Canter, D.V. (1985), 'The Uses of Explanation in the Research Interview', in M. Brenner, J. Brown and D.V.Canter. (eds), *The Research Interview,* London: Academic Press.
Brown, W.K. and Miller, T.M. (1988), 'Following-up Previously Adjudicated Delinquents: A Method', in R.L.Jenkins and W.K. Brown, (eds), *The Abandonment of Delinquent Behaviour: Promoting the Turnaround,* New York: Praeger.
Brownfield, D. and Sorenson, A.M. (1993), 'Self-control and Juvenile Delinquency: Theoretical Issues and an Empirical Assessment of Selected Elements of a General Theory of Crime', *Deviant Behaviour,* 14, 243-264.
Bruner, J.S. (1987), 'Life as Narrative', *Social Research,* 54, 11-32.
Buss, A.H. (1989), 'Personality as Traits', *American Psychologist,* 44, 1378-1388.
Canter, D.V. (1994), *Criminal Shadows,* London: Harper Collins.
Canter, D.V. (1997), 'Psychology of Offender Profiling', in R. Bull and D. Carson, (eds), *Handbook of Psychology in Legal Contexts,* London: Wiley.
Canter, D.V. and Heritage, R. (1989), 'A Multivariate Model of Sexual Offence Behaviour: Developments in Offender Profiling', *Journal of Forensic Psychiatry,* 1 (2), 185-212.
Caspi, A. and Moffitt, T.E. (1993), 'The Continuity of Maladaptive Behaviour: From Description to Understanding in the Study of Antisocial Behaviour', in D. Cicchetti, and D. Cohenen (eds), *Manual of Developmental Psychopathology,* New York: Wiley & Sons.
Caspi, A., Moffitt, T.E., Silva, P.A., Stouthamer-Loeber, M., Krueger, R.F. and Schutte, P.S. (1994), 'Are Some People Crime-Prone? Replications of the Personality-Crime Relationship Across Countries, Genders, Races and Methods', *Criminology,* 32 (2), 163-195.
Cline, H.F. (1980), 'Criminal Behaviour Over the Life Span', in O.G. Brim and J. Kagan (eds), *Constancy and Change in Human Development,* Cambridge, MA: Harvard University Press, pp. 641-674.
Conley, J.J. (1985), 'A Personality Theory of Adulthood and Aging', in R. Hogan and W.H. Jones (eds), *Perspectives in Personality,* 1, Greenwich, CT: JAI Press, pp. 81-116.

Costa, P.T. and McCrae, R.R. (1989), 'Personality Continuity and the Changes of Adult Life', in M. Storandt and G.R. VandenBos (eds), *The Adult Years: Continuity and Change,* Washington, D.C.: American Psychological Association.
Currie, E. (1985), *Confronting Crime,* New York: Pantheon Books.
Currie, E. (1991), *Dope and Trouble: Portraits of Delinquent Youth,* New York: Pantheon Books.
Currie, E. (1993), 'Shifting the Balance: On Social Action and the Future of Criminological Research', *Journal of Research in Crime and Delinquency,* 30 (4), 426-444.
Dannefer, D. (1984), 'Adult Development and Social Theory: A Paradigmatic Reappraisal', *American Sociological Review,* **49**, 100-116.
Denzin, N.K. (1987), *The Alcoholic Self,* Newbury Park, CA: Sage.
Denzin, N.K. (1989), *Interpretive Biography,* Newbury Park, CA: Sage.
Denzin, N.K. and Lincoln, Y.S. (eds) (1994), *Handbook of Qualitative Research,* Beverly Hills, Ca.: Sage.
DiClemente, C.C. (1994), 'If Behaviors Change, Can Personality Be Far Behind?', in T.F. Heatherton and J.L. Weinberger (eds), *Can Personality Change?,* Washington, D.C.: American Psychological Association.
Elkind, D. (1968), *Children and Adolescents: Interpretive essays on Jean Piaget,* New York: Oxford Press.
Emmons, R. (1986), 'Personal Strivings: An Approach to Personality and Subjective Well-being', *Journal of Personality and Social Psychology,* **51**, 1058-1068.
Epstein, S. (1994), 'Integration of the Cognitive and the Psychodynamic Unconscious', *American Psychologist,* **49 (8)**, 709-724.
Epstein, S. and Erskine, N. (1983), 'The Development of Personal Theories of Reality from an Interactional Perspective', in D. Magnusson and V.L. Allen (eds), *Human Development: An Interactional Perspective,* New York: Academic Press.
Erikson, E. (1959), *Identity and the Life Cycle,* New York: W.W. Norton & Company.
Eysenck, H. (1977), *Crime and Personality,* London: Routledge & Kegan Paul.
Eysenck, H. (1989), 'Personality and Criminality: A Dispositional Analysis', in W.S. Laufer and F. Adler (eds), *Advances in Criminological Theory,* **1**, New Brunswick, NJ: Transaction Publishers, pp. 89-110.
Farrington, D. (1986), 'Age and Crime', in N. Morris and M. Tonry (eds), *Crime and Justice,* 7, Chicago: Chicago University Press, pp. 189-250.
Farrington, D. (1992), 'Explaining the Beginning, Progress, and Ending of Antisocial Behavior from Birth to Adulthood', in J. McCord (ed.), *Facts, Frameworks, and Forecasts: Advances in Criminological Theory,* **3**, New Brunswick, NJ: Transaction Publishers.

Farrington, D.P. and Tarling, R. (1985), 'Criminal Prediction: An Introduction' in D.P. Farrington and R. Tarling (eds), *Prediction in Criminology,* Albany, NY: State University of New York Press.

Finestone, H. (1976), *Victims of Change: Juvenile Delinquents in American Society,* Westport, Conn.: Greenwood Press.

Flanagan, T.J. (1987), 'Change and Influence in Popular Criminology: Public Attributions of Crime Causation', *Journal of Criminal Justice,* **15**, 231-243.

Foucault, M. (1988), 'The Dangerous Individual', in L.D. Kritzman (ed.), *Michel Foucault: Politics, Philosophy, Culture — Interviews and Other Writings, 1977-1984,* New York: Routledge, pp. 126-151.

Fromm, E. (1941), *Escape from Freedom,* New York: Farrar & Rinehart.

Garofalo, R. (1885), *Criminology,* Naples, Italy: N.p.

Gartner, R. and Piliavin, I. (1988), 'The Aging Offender and the Aged Offender', in P.B. Baltes, D.L. Featherman, and R.M. Lerner (eds), *Life-Span Development and Behavior,* 9, Hillsdale, NJ: Lawrence Erlbaum Associates.

Gendreau, P. and Ross, R.R. (1987), 'Revivication of Rehabilitation: Evidence from the 1980's', *Justice Quarterly,* **4**, 349-408.

Gibbons, D.C. (1989), 'Comment - Personality and Crime: Non-issues, Real Issues, and a Theory and Research Agenda', *Justice Quarterly,* **6 (3)**, 311-323.

Giddens, A. (1976), *New Rules of the Sociological Method,* Stanford, CA: Stanford University Press.

Giddens, A. (1991), *Modernity and Self-Identity: Self and Society in the Late Modern Age,* Stanford, CA: Stanford University Press.

Glueck, S. and Glueck, E. (1940), *Juvenile Delinquents Grown Up,* New York: Commonwealth Fund.

Goring, C. (1913), *The English Convict: A Statistical Study,* London: Darling & Son.

Gottfredson, M. and Hirschi, T. (1990), *A General Theory of Crime,* Stanford: Stanford University Press.

Gottfredson, M. and Hirschi, T. (1995), 'National Crime Control Policies', *Society,* **32 (2)**, 30-36.

Gough, H.G. (1965), 'Cross-cultural validation of a measure of asocial behavior', *Psychological Reports,* **17**, 379-387.

Gould, S.J. (1981), *The Mismeasure of Man,* New York: W.W. Norton & Company.

Gove, W. (1985), 'The Effect of Age and Gender on Deviant Behavior: A Biopsychosocial Perspective', in A.S. Rossi (ed.), *Gender and the Life Course,* New York: Aldine, pp. 115-144.

Graham, J. and Bowling, B. (1995), *Young People and Crime,* London: Home Office.

Greenberg, D.F. (1981), 'Delinquency and the Age Structure of Society', in D.F. Greenberg (ed.), *Crime and Capitalism: Readings in Marxist Criminology,* Palo Alto, California: Mayfield Publishing Company.

Greenberg, D.F. (1985), 'Age, Crime, and Social Explanation', *American Journal of Sociology,* **91,** 1-21.

Groves, W.B. and Lynch, M.J. (1990), 'Reconciling Structural and Subjective Approaches to the Study of Crime', *Journal of Research in Crime and Delinquency,* **27 (4),** 48-375.

Hagestad, G.O. and Neugarten, B.L. (1985), 'Age and the Life Course', in R.H. Binstock and E. Shanas (eds), *Handbook on Aging and the Social Sciences,* New York: Van Norstrand Reinheld, pp.35-57.

Hartung, F.E. (1965), 'A Vocabulary of Motives for Law Violations', in F.E. Hartung (ed.), *Crime, Law and Society,* Detroit: Wayne State University.

Hathaway, S.R. and Monachese, E.D. (1963), *Analyzing and Predicting Juvenile Delinquency with the MMPI,* Minneapolis: University of Minnesota Press.

Heatherton, S. and Nichols, H. (1994), 'Personal Accounts of Successful Versus Failed Attempts at Life Change', *Social Psychology and Personality Bulletin,* **20 (6),** 664-675.

Hermans, H.J.M., Kempen, H.J.G., and van Loon, R.J.P. (1992), 'The Dialogical Self: Beyond individualism and rationalism', *American Psychologist,* **47,** 23-33.

Hindelang, M.J. (1981), 'Variations in Sex-Race-Age-Specific Incidence Rates of Offending', *American Sociological Review,* **46,** 461-475.

Hooton, E.A. (1939), *Crime and the Man,* Cambridge, Mass: Harvard University Press.

Huesmann, L.R., Eron, L.D. Lefkowitz, M.M. and Walder, L.O. (1984), 'Stability of Agression Over Time and Across Generations', *Developmental Psychology,* **20,** 1120-1134.

Irwin, J. (1970), *The Felon,* Englewood Cliffs, NJ: Prentice-Hall.

Jolin, A. (1985), *Growing Old and Going Straight: Examining the Role of Age in Criminal Career Termination,* PhD Thesis, Portland State University.

Kaplan, H.B. (1980), *Deviant Behavior in Defense of Self,* New York: Pergamon.

Katz, J. (1988), *Seductions of Crime: The Moral and Sensual Attractions of Doing Evil,* New York: Basic Books.

Kellogg, S. (1993), 'Identity and Recovery', *Psychotherapy,* **30,** 235-244.

Kohli, M. (1981), 'Biography: Account, Text, Method', in D. Bertaux (ed.), *Biography and Society,* London: Sage.

Landsheer, J.A., Hart, H. and Kox, W. (1994), 'Delinquent Values and Victim Damage: Exploring the Limits of Neutralization Theory', *British Journal of Criminology,* **34,** 44-53.

Lange, J. (1931), *Crime as Destiny,* London: Allen & Unwin.

LeBlanc, M., Ouimet, M., and Tremblay, R.E. (1988), 'An Integrative Control Theory of Delinquent Behavior: A Validation 1976-1985', *Psychiatry*, **51**, 164-176.
Lewis, D.A. (1990), 'From Programs to Lives: A Comment', *American Journal of Community Psychology*, **18 (6)**, 923-926.
Lewis, D.A. and Maruna, S.A. (1995), 'Putting the Person in Policy Analysis', paper presented at the Association of Public Policy Analysis and Management conference, Washington, D.C.
Lewis, D.A. and Maruna, S. (in press), 'Person-Centered Policy Analysis', *Research in Public Policy and Management*.
Lewis, O. (1968), *La Vida: A Puerto Rican Family in the Culture of Poverty*, New York: Vintage Books.
Lilly, J.R., Cullen, F.T. and Ball, R.A. (1994), *Criminological Theory: Context and Consequences*, **2**, London: Sage.
Lipsey, M.W. (1992), Juvenile Delinquency Treatment: A Meta-Analytic Inquiry into the Variability of Effects', in T.D. Cook, H. Cooper, D.S. Cordray, H. Hartmann, L.V. Hedges, R.J. Light, T.A. Louis, and F. Mosteller, *Meta-Analysis for Explanation: A Casebook*, New York: Russell Sage Foundation, pp. 83-127.
Little, B.R. (1989), 'Personal Project Analysis: Trivial Pursuits, Magnificent Obsessions, and the Search for Coherence', in D.M. Buss and N. Cantor (eds), *Personality Psychology: Recent Trends and Emerging Directions*, New York: Springer Verlag, pp. 15-31.
Loeber, R. (1982), 'The Stability of Antisocial and Delinquent Childhood Behavior', *Child Development* **53**, 1431-1446.
Loeber, R. and LeBlanc, M. (1990), 'Toward a Developmental Criminology', in M. Tonry and N. Morris, N. (eds), *Crime and Justice*, **12**, Chicago: University of Chicago Press, pp. 375-437.
Lombroso, C. (1911), *Crime: Its Causes and Remedies*, Boston: Little, Brown.
McAdams, D.P. (1985), *Power, Intimacy and the Life Story: Personological Inquiries into Identity*, New York: The Guilford Press.
McAdams, D.P. (1992), 'The Five-Factor Model in Personality: A Critical Appraisal', *Journal of Personality*, **60 (2)**, 329-359.
McAdams, D.P. (1993), *The Stories We Live By: Personal Myths and the Making of the Self*, New York: Willam Morrow & Company.
McAdams, D.P. (1994a), 'Can Personality Change? Levels of Stability and Growth in Personality Across the Life Span', in T.F. Heatherton and J.L. Weinberger (eds), *Can Personality Change?*, Washington, D.C.: American Psychological Association.
McAdams, D.P. (1994b). *The Person: An Introduction to Personality Psychology*, Fort Worth, Tx.: Sage

McAdams, D.P. (1994c), 'A Psychology of the Stranger', *Psychological Inquiry,* **5**, 145-148.
McGuire, J. and Priestley, P. (1985), *Offending Behavior,* New York: St. Martin's Press.
McGuire, J. (ed.) (1995), *What Works: Reducing Reoffending,* New York: Wiley & Sons.
Magnusson, D. and Bergman, L.R. (1988), 'Individual and Variable-Based Approaches to Longitudinal Research on Early Risk Factors', in M. Rutter (ed.), *Studies of Psychosocial Risk: The Power of Longitudinal Data,* Cambridge: Cambridge University Press.
Mak, A.S. (1990), 'Testing a Psychological Control Theory of Delinquency', *Criminal Justice and Behavior,* **17**, 215-230.
Manning, P.K. (1991), 'Critical Semiotics', in B.D. MacLean and D. Milovanovic (eds), *New Directions in Critical Criminology,* Vancouver, Canada: The Collective Press.
Maruna, S.A. (1997), 'Going Straight: Desistance from Crime and Self-Narratives of Reform', *The Narrative Study of Lives,* **5 (1)**.
Matza, D. (1964), *Delinquency and Drift,* New York: John Wiley & Sons.
Megargee, E.I. and Bohn, M. (1979), *Classifying Criminal Offenders: A New System Based on the MMPI,* Beverly Hills, CA: Sage.
Merton, R.K. and Montagu, A. (1940), 'Crime and the Anthropologist', *American Anthropologist,* **42**, 384-408.
Miller, W.R. and C'deBaca, J. (1994), 'Quantum Change: Toward a Psychology of Transformation', in T.F. Heatherton and J.L.Weinberger (eds), *Can Personality Change?,* Washington, D.C.: American Psychological Association.
Moffitt, T.E. (1993), 'Adolescence-Limited and Life-Course-Persistent Antisocial Behavior: A Developmental Taxonomy', *Psychological Review,* **100 (4)**, 674-701.
Mulvey, E.P. and LaRosa, J.F. (1986), 'Delinquency Cessation and Adolescent Development: Primary Data', *American Journal of Orthopsychiatry,* **56 (2)**, pp. 212-224.
Murray, C. and Herrnstein, R.J. (1994), *The Bell Curve: Intelligence and Class Structure in American Life,* New York: The Free Press.
Neugarten, B.L., and Neugarten, D.A. (1986), 'Changing Meanings of Age in the Aging Society', in A. Pifer, and L. Bronte (eds), *Our Aging Society,* New York: W.W. Norton.
Quetelet, A. (1833), *Recherches Sur le Penchant au Crime aux Différents ages,* Belgium: Hayez.
Rafter, N.H. (1990), 'The Social Construction of Crime and Crime Control', *Journal of Research in Crime and Delinquency,* **27 (4)**, 376-389.

Rafter, N.H. (1994), 'Eugenics, Class, and the Professionalization of Social Control', in G.S. Bridges and M.A. Myers (eds), *Inequality, Crime and Social Control,* Boulder, CO: Westview Press.

Rand, A. (1987), 'Transitional Life Events and Desistance from Delinquency and Crime', in M. Wolfgang, T.P. Thornberry, and R.M. Figlio (eds), *From Boy to Man: From Delinquency to Crime,* Chicago: University of Chicago Press, pp. 134-162.

Rathus, S.A. and Siegel, L.J. (1980), 'Crime and Personality Revisited: Effects of MMPI Response Sets in Self-Report Studies', *Criminology,* 18, 245-251.

Reckless, W.C. (1967), *The Crime Problem,* New York: Appleton-Century-Crofts.

Reed, A. (1992), 'The Underclass as Myth and Symbol: The Poverty of Discourse About Poverty', *Radical America,* 24, 21-40.

Ressler, R.K. and Schachtman, T. (1992), *Whoever Fights Monsters,* New York: St. Martin's Press.

Robins, L.N. and Rutter, M. (1990), 'Introduction', in L.N. Robins and M. Rutter (eds), *Straight and Devious Pathways, from Childhood to Adulthood,* Cambridge, UK: Cambridge University Press, pp. xiii-xix.

Rotenberg, M. (1987), *Re-Biographing and Deviance: Psychotherapeutic Narrativism and the Midrash,* New York: Praeger.

Rouse, J. (1978), *The Completed Gesture: Myth, Character and Education,* New Jersey: Skyline Books.

Rowe, A. and Tittle, C. (1977), 'Life Cycle Changes and Criminal Propensity', *Sociology Quarterly,* 18, 223-236.

Rutherford, A. (1992), *Growing Out of Crime: The New Era,* Winchester: Waterside Press.

Rutter, M. (1989), 'Age as an Ambiguous Variable in Developmental Research; Some Epidemiological Considerations from Developmental Psychopathology', *International Journal of Behavioral Development,* 12, 1-134.

Ryff, C.D. (1982), 'Self-Perceived Personality Change in Adulthood and Aging', *Journal of Personality and Social Psychology,* **42 (1)**, 108-115.

Sampson, R.J., and Laub, J. (1992), 'Crime and Deviance in the Life Course', *Annual Review of Sociology,* 18, 63-84.

Sampson, R.J. & Laub, J. (1993), *Crime in the Making: Pathways and Turning Points Through Life,* Cambridge, Massachusetts: Harvard University Press.

Sampson, R. J. and Laub, J. (1995), 'A Life-course Theory of Cumulative Disadvantage and the Stability of Delinquency', in T.P. Thornberry (ed.), *Developmental Theories of Crime and Delinquency: Advances in Criminological Theory,* 6, New Brunswick, NJ: Transaction Publishers.

Sarbin, T.R. (1986), *Narrative Psychology: The Storied Nature of Human Conduct,* New York: Praeger.

Sartre, J-.P. (1963), *Search for a Method,* New York: Alfred Knopf.

Sartre, J-.P. (1964), *The Words,* New York: Braziller.

Schuessler, K.F. and Cressey, D.R. (1950), 'Personality Characteristics of Criminals', *American Journal of Sociology,* **55**, 476-484.
Scott, M.B. and Lyman, S.M. (1968), 'Accounts', *American Sociological Review,* **33 (1)**, 46-61.
Shaw, C. (1929), *Delinquency Areas,* Chicago: University of Chicago Press.
Sheldon, W.H., Stevens, S.S., and Tucker, W.B. (1940), *The Varieties of Human Physique,* New York: Harper & Row Publishers.
Shover, N. (1985), *Aging Criminals,* Beverly Hills, CA: Sage Publications.
Stall, R. and Biernecki, P. (1986), 'Spontaneous Remission from the Problematic Use of Substances: An Inductive Model Derived From a Comparative Analysis of the Alcohol, Opiate, Tobacco and Food/Obesity Literatures', *International Journal of the Addictions,* **21**, 1-23.
Stevens, D.P. and Truss, C.V. (1985), 'Stability and Change in Adult Personality Over 12 and 20 Years', *Developmental Psychology,* **21 (3)**, 568-584.
Sullivan, M. (1989), *Getting Paid: Youth Crime and Work in the Inner City,* Ithaca: Cornell University Press.
Sullivan, M. (forthcoming), 'Developmental Transitions in Poor Youth: Delinquency and Crime', in J. Graber, J. Brooks-Gunn and A. Petersen (eds), *Transitions in Adolescence,* Hillside, NJ: Lawrence Erlbaum.
Sutherland, E.H. (1947), *Principles of Criminology,* 4th edn, Chicago: University of Chicago Press.
Sutton, J.R. (1994), 'Children in the Therapeutic State: Lessons for the Sociology of Deviance and Social Control', in G.S. Bridges and M.A. Myers (eds), *Inequality, Crime and Social Control,* Boulder, CO: Westview Press.
Sykes, G.M. and Matza, D. (1957), 'Techniques of Neutralization: A Theory of Delinquency', *American Sociological Review,* **22**, 664-673.
Tagg, S.K. (1985), 'Life Story Interviews and Their Interpretation', in M. Brenner, J. Brown and D.V. Canter, D. (eds), *The Research Interview,* London: Academic Press.
Tennenbaum, D.J. (1977), 'Personality and Criminality: A Summary and Implications of the Literature', *Journal of Criminal Justice,* 5, 225-235.
Thomas, J. (1983), 'Book Reviews', *American Journal of Sociology,* 770-773.
Thomas, W.I. and Thomas, D. (1928), *The Child in America,* New York: Knopf.
Thorne, A. (1989), 'Conditional Patterns, Transference, and the Coherence of Personality Across Time', in D.M. Buss and N. Cantor (eds), *Personality Psychology: Recent Trends and Emerging Directions,* Washington, DC: American Psychological Association, pp. 223-253.
Toch, H. (1986), *Psychology of Crime and Criminal Justice,* Prospect Heights, Illinois: Waveland Press.
Toch, H. (1987), 'Supplementing the Positivist Approach', in M. Gottfredson and T. Hirschi (eds), *Positive Criminology,* Beverly Hills, CA: Sage Publications.
Tomkins, S.S. (1987), 'Script Theory', in J. Aronoff, A.I. Rabin and R.A. Zucker (eds), *The Emergence of Personality,* New York: Springer, pp. 147-216.

Trasler, G.B. (1979), 'Delinquency, Recidivism and Desistance', *British Journal of Criminology,* **19**, 314-322.

Waldo, G.P. and Dinitz, S. (1967), 'Personality Attributes of the Criminal: An Analysis of the Research Studies, 1950-1965', *Journal of Research in Crime and Delinquency,* **4**, 185-202.

Waldorf, D. (1983), 'Natural Recovery from Opiate Addiction: Some Social-Psychological Processes of Untreated Recovery', *Journal of Drug Issues,* 13, 237-280.

West, D. (1982), *Delinquency: Its Roots, Careers, and Prospects,* London: Heinemann.

Wilson, J.Q. (1975), *Thinking About Crime,* New York: Random House.

Wilson, J.Q. and Herrnstein, R.J. (1985), *Crime and Human Nature,* New York: Touchstone Books.

Wolfgang, M.E. and Ferracuti, F. (1967), *The Subculture of Violence,* London: Tavistock Publications.

Wooton, B. (1959), *Social Science and Social Pathology,* London: George Allen & Unwin.

Yochelson, S. and Samenow, S.E. (1977), *The Criminal Personality Volume II: The Change Process,* New York: Jason Aronson.

10 Destructive Organisational Psychology

DAVID CANTER

It is argued that organisational psychology theory and findings can be used in the context of criminal teams, groups and networks, as a guide for how these criminal activities can be weakened and possibly destroyed. Drawing on the many studies of legitimate organisations it is proposed that there are many difficulties inherent in maintaining formal, well-structured criminal organisations. As a consequence most criminal networks are characterised by being fluid and much more anarchic than their non-criminal counterparts. Law enforcement attempts to destabilise these criminal networks should therefore include challenges to the satisfactions and morale of their members as well as taking advantage of the vulnerabilities that organisational analysis will reveal, rather than focusing solely on the identification of apparently significant individuals in the criminal process.

David Canter is Director of the Centre for Investigative Psychology at the University of Liverpool. He has published widely in Environmental and Investigative Psychology as well as many areas of Applied Social Psychology. His most recent books since his award winning *"Criminal Shadows"* have been *"Psychology in Action"* and with Laurence Alison *"Criminal Detection and the Psychology of Crime"*.

10 Destructive Organisational Psychology
DAVID CANTER

Criminal Teams, Networks and Organisations

Most crime involves people dealing with each other at some stage in their criminal activity. It is most common in property and commercially driven crime, although that can include activities as varied as vice, paedophile networks and fraud. Furthermore, these interactions between people may be as casual as a person selling a stranger in a pub some CD's he has pirated; as formal as a gang leader giving instructions to his team on how they will rob a bank; or as structured as a criminal Triad organisation initiating noviciate members and training them up through their ranks. All these transactions are in one sense or another aspects of criminal organisations.

Of course, some forms of crime are integrally linked to the existence of legitimate or illegal organisations. The world-wide distribution of illegal drugs, for example, the smuggling of contraband goods, unlawful trading in banned or controlled products, or international fraud and corruption, all depend upon networks of contacts that have, in various ways, to be managed and controlled. Offenders in prison are also often part of networks that can be used to weaken the prison authority. To investigate and undermine all these activities it is often as important, if not more important, to understand the organisational frameworks that support them rather than to focus entirely on the key individuals who carry out the illegal activities.

The task of law enforcement agencies the world over is to reduce the effectiveness of criminal networks and organisations and, wherever possible, to destroy them or to prevent their emergence in the first place. In order to do this it is necessary to understand how organisations work, what makes them productive and efficient and enables them to continue to exist? This will then provide the insight to reduce their productivity and make their existence problematic.

There is considerable understanding in the psychological and sociological literature of the processes that keep organisations working. The proposal here is to turn that knowledge on its head. Usually organisational psychologists are concerned to strengthen the businesses and networks they are studying, but in the context of criminal investigations the objectives are the very opposite. Police officers and detectives want to destroy the organisations they are examining in order to reduce or remove the criminal activities that they support. This may be thought of as the development of an 'anti-organisational psychology'. A destructive organisational psychology that seeks to find the vulnerabilities in the teams and networks that make up criminal transactions and then exploit those weaknesses to serve the objectives of the legal process.

From the perspective of a destructive organisational psychology there is a vast literature to be raided for insights into how normal, legal organisations work and the difficulties they have in maintaining their activities. Most of this literature provides pointers to what can go wrong with even the most efficient, legitimate group of people trying to earn their daily bread. Many of the problems that non-criminal organisations face are also faced by illegal ones. Indeed, the nefarious nature of the organisation can often aggravate their problems, making criminal organisations even more vulnerable to the difficulties all organisations face.

The Essence of Organisations

The nature of organisations, their very essence, is a product of why they exist and of the mathematical consequences of a number of people working together. Therefore any organisation, legitimate or illegitimate, will share this essence and have many characteristics in common. Of course, no two organisations are identical and there will be many important differences between criminal organisations and between them and non-criminal ones. For simplicity, though, in what follows it will be the similarities they all share that will be emphasised.

These similarities stem from two central aspects of all organisations. One is their objective. The second is their structure. In other words, first, the reasons why the organisation exists, what it is there for, and secondly, how it goes about achieving those objectives, its component parts and how they are related.

Organisational Objectives and Job Satisfaction

If a person can achieve a task or set of tasks on his or her own without the assistance of anyone else then no organisation is necessary. A lone rapist or a murderer killing his spouse can often achieve their goals without recourse to any help from other criminals. But as soon as a task is identified that requires two or more people the basis for an organisation exists. This may be as few as two offenders setting out to rape a victim together because they can control her better that way, or hundreds of people around the world involved in a paedophile network.

If the group is to continue in existence at all as an entity its members must have some shared objective and an understanding that their objective is shared. This may be a confused and poorly articulated objective and may well have many levels and aspects to it. For example, the two rapists may share an objective of showing each other how determined and 'masculine' they are, and be very unclear about a particular victim. But they will not achieve anything if one of them assumes they are going to rob a bank and the other thinks they are going to frighten girls in the park.

A crucial aspect of these objectives is that the members of the organisation gain some benefit from their involvement. There are always personal objectives as well as organisational objectives to keep people with at least the minimal level of involvement in an organisation. In the psychological literature these have often been referred to as 'morale' or 'job satisfaction' or job motivation. These are the basic reasons people have for continuing to be part of an organisation and to function within it. An important discovery from decades of study of legitimate organisations is that, contrary to popular belief, financial benefit is not the sole, or evens necessarily the primary, motive for people being part of any organisation. Social benefits from mixing with others, status benefits from being recognised as part of a group, or sheer interest in the job itself, have all been shown to be more powerful as job motivators in some jobs than the financial rewards on offer.

The debates in the literature as to the essential motives for staying and working in an organisation are very relevant to considering illegal organisations because in many of them the financial benefits are small and short lived, especially when set against the risks involved. There may often also be huge disparities in distribution of financial gain between different members of a criminal organisation that could cause great disaffection. Thus although there has been little systematic study of the clarity of objectives and motives for being part of criminal organisations, it seems very likely that many people stay as part of them because they are coerced to do so, usually by fear and intimidation. It may also be the primary way in which they gain any social standing and any sense of belonging to a community or family.

Structure and Leadership

The second inevitable component that is the essence of an organisation is that it will have some structure. The people who make it up will have different, but related roles within the activities of the organisation. These roles may be fluid and each may carry out the full range of activities in which the group or network engages, but at any point in time the various tasks that the organisation needs to have done in order to achieve its objectives will have to be divided amongst its members. This process gives rise to differentiation within the organisation and often to the emergence of different groups and sub-groups.

Such differentiation itself requires management and guidance. This may be achieved through group discussion and the emergence of a consensus but it often requires some direction from one or more individuals, in a word, leadership. The notion of leadership, like that of motivation, is a complex and hotly debated one within the realms of organisational theory. But the relevance of these debates to considering criminal organisations lies in the attention they have drawn to the many different forms of leadership that any group, team or network requires. Leaders are not required merely to issue instructions. They are needed to devise plans, to obtain knowledge and information as well as to keep people participating in the organisation. Criminal groups, like non-criminal ones, are likely to have different people taking these different leadership roles. This, of course, has important implications for how such an organisation may be disabled. Removing the person who has the important information, or who coerces the other members to stay within the group may be more effective than arresting the person who plans and gives instructions, who may be the most difficult to convict in court.

Organisational Vulnerability: Communication

An Organisation is nothing without communications between its members and with its suppliers and 'clients'. Communications are fundamental to the two aspects explored earlier, objectives and structure. People need to be informed of what the objectives and tasks of the organisation are and to be kept involved in its activities. The assignment of roles and the processes of leadership all depend not only on communications between the different individuals and groups but also on some of those individuals having knowledge of the communication process itself.

Non-criminal organisations constantly battle to maintain and improve the efficiency and effectiveness of their communications. Weaknesses in this aspect of their activities are frequently chronic problems with which they struggle. This is almost invariably their Achilles' heel. For criminals this vulnerability is more parlous. They have to keep their contacts confidential and secret wherever possible. This makes them less effective and more prone to confusion and misinterpretation. Therefore many of the vulnerabilities of criminal organisations can be traced to the various weaknesses that emerge from problems generated in aspects of their communication processes.

The Vulnerability of Size

The organisational psychology literature is replete with studies that show that, broadly speaking, the larger an organisation the more problems it has. Larger organisations are less efficient than smaller ones. Their staff is less satisfied with their working situation and more likely to indicate this through high turnover and absenteeism rates. Many explanations have been put forward for these consistent findings but some of the most obvious have direct implications for the investigation of criminal organisations - communications, control and alienation.

The Vulnerability of Size 1. More Communication

As messages are passed between more people there are more opportunities for confusions to occur. As a consequence the larger an organisation the more likely are its communication processes to be weak. For a criminal organisation this also means the more opportunity there is for unwanted leaking of information. The implications for law enforcement therefore are to establish the extent of a criminal network as fully as possible. The larger a network the more likely are there to be weak, in the sense of confused or ambiguous, communications between aspects of it. These weak links can be utilised for intelligence sources or as opportunities for disruption.

The clandestine nature of the communication process creates more possibilities for confusion. A person buying an illegal drug has no way of determining who the supplier is to their dealer nor where the supplier's stock originates. The country of manufacture that is required by law to be marked in all products sold legally has no place in illegal market. One interesting consequence of this is that criminal networks probably rely much more on published accounts of matters of relevance to them than is often realised. A notable example is the way the upsurge in the use of particular recreational, illegal drugs often follows very public banning of them. It is only through the public outcry against the drugs that illicit users find out about their existence. Conventional television advertising campaigns are not an option for the producers of 'ecstasy' or 'crack cocaine'.

These communication problems will also mean that misinformation, rumour and superstition will be rife amongst criminal networks. They will be very prone to misinterpreting what has happened and exposed to misleading information. A fact that well-informed police officers around the world have always taken advantage of.

The Vulnerability of Size: 2. Less Effective Control

Along with the problems of extended communication any increase in size also puts greater demands on the mechanisms of control. This is particularly problematic for criminal organisations both because of their need to keep their activities secret and because of the importance that coercion often has in maintaining those activities. Knowing who is doing what is the key to control and clandestine communications make this much more difficult to determine.

The problems that increase in size poses for effective control can be better understood by recognising that leadership requires an understanding of who is communicating with whom. The mathematical implications of this are that the more people involved the more of the organisational effort that is required to monitor communication processes themselves.

Consequently the less time and energy there is available for the directly 'productive' activities of the organisation.

As criminal networks grow, therefore, the greater the possibility that 'maverick' offshoots will form who are not strongly under the power of any 'boss'. These may be the downfall of the central group or may be the source of new criminal activities. This proliferation and growth has particularly important policy implications for international law enforcement agencies as it can help them to predict the forms of growth that crime will take as well as providing them with strategic opportunities for intervention.

The Vulnerability of Size: 3. Individual Alienation

As the communication networks grow longer and the messages become more ambiguous and less reliable there is a growing possibility that the concerns and goals of particular individuals are not being catered for by the organisation. This is the recipe for some members of the organisation not to feel involved with it or committed to it. These will typically be people who are the ends of communication chains and whose contacts with other members of the network are low in frequency. They are the people who are most likely not to follow the instructions given to them or to provide information to people outside the organisation. Such people are good targets for intelligence activities and have potential as informants, even though their position in the communication network may mean that they have little detailed information.

The Vulnerability of Structure:

Although two people may share tasks out evenly and play very similar roles in their dyad such equality is rare. Certainly the larger the group the more likely is it that the individual members will each have different functions and that the group as a whole will therefore have some identifiable sub-groups that each interact with each other in different ways. The most notable feature of these differences in interaction is that there will be unevenness in the distribution of communications. Some people will send and receive more than others.

The simplest way to consider organisational structure is the degree of hierarchy it exhibits. In a strongly hierarchical structure the chains of command are long and a very small proportion of individuals carry responsibility for the actions of the organisation as a whole. This can lead to a strong direction for the organisation, including careful monitoring of the actions of everyone within it. It is the classic structure for a military organisation that needs to be able to respond to complex, challenging situations with all the resources available to it in a focused and concerted way. But the long chains of command, or communication routes that such a hierarchy requires is enormously vulnerable to breakdowns and ambiguities in those communications. There is therefore a tendency for these hierarchies to become very 'flat' when the communications are under pressure, through the need to keep them secret or because of the risks of confusions. 'Flat' in the sense that few people keep in touch with as many people in the network as possible, so that the layers of command are reduced.

This 'flattening' of an organisation can have further problems. The people in the key, 'central', positions become bombarded with information and demands for contact. The flow of information therefore becomes very uneven because the people in the central positions do not have the time or resources to deal with every contact. They hoard the information they receive and people at the periphery do not know what is happening. This can add to confusions and the generation of alienated groups outside of the central leadership.

One way of attempting to deal with these difficulties is to create a more open organisation in which everyone can keep in contact with everyone else. But such open structures can cause further problems for criminal organisations. They increase the risk of secret information leaking from the network and of the loss of control by the central figures as other individuals and groups have more opportunity to influence the course of affairs.

The sorts of problems that criminal organisations have which derive from aspects of the organisational structure therefore often can be understood in terms of the demands on the criminal 'leaders'. Indeed, this is undoubtedly one reason why notorious criminal leaders become of such interest to the factual and the fictional media. They can be readily portrayed as tragic heroes. If they are able to survive for any length of time they must have some remarkable management skills, but these skills are doomed to lead them to eventual failure as the forces of law eventually overtake them. The great demands on the individuals who 'lead' criminal groups or steer nefarious networks stem from the many different capabilities that are required of them. They need to have enough background knowledge to understand what their group or network is doing and to have enough specific information to be able to give effective instructions. However, they also need to be able to motivate their subordinates in some way, whether negatively through coercion or positively through promised rewards. Demands for trust and loyalty are only likely to be successful in very tight knit groups that have long established family ties or ethnic minority connections.

On top of these direct management skills leaders need to be aware enough of what is going on within their group to maintain the secrecy and focus of the group. To some extent, of course, the criminal nature of the activities facilitates this in the same way that a known enemy keeps an army on its toes. Pressure from law enforcement can strengthen the resolve of a criminal group and increase the power of its leadership. However, the overload that can be placed on the leadership by the structural processes can be the major cause of the group or network collapsing.

To deal with these demands leaders in many groups of any size will have recognised lieutenants who help them to cope. These individuals may be trainee leaders themselves or people who have specific functions to do with the control of the group. By understanding these processes police intelligence analysts may be able to identify the potential vulnerabilities inherent in a criminal organisational leadership. For example if the network has grown rapidly in recent weeks it is very likely that the leaders are not fully aware of all that is going in within the network and that any central figure is very dependent on the information given to him by his 'lieutenants'. It is also likely that many of the more peripheral people feel very separate from the 'core' of the group and are either attempting to gain admittance or seeking ways of becoming more separated. Police contact with such individuals could therefore take advantage of these vulnerabilities.

Reciprocal Anarchy as an Organisational Strategy

The many difficulties that face criminal groups, teams and networks in forming effective organisations and maintaining effective leadership does have the consequence that very few criminals are really part of organisations in any formal sense. The clear management positions, strict chains of command and specific roles that would be expected of a legitimate organisation are far less likely to be found amongst criminals than a shifting set of loosely knit allegiances and changing patterns of communication. The much publicised criminal organisations such as 'Hells Angels' and 'Chinese Triads' and the 'Mafia', so enjoyed by Hollywood, are very rare indeed against the general mass of much more anarchic criminal activity. Even when they do exist they are likely to survive only for a relatively brief period as recognisably structured organisations. All the pressures considered above will lead to change and collapse and reconstruction in relation to changing demands.

Indeed, it is this anarchic, network quality of criminal organisations that can make them so difficult to investigate and destroy. A strictly structured organisation can be readily understood and described and can be destroyed by removing crucial individuals in the network, but a fluid, flexible, opportunistic pattern of activities can easily be reconstructed if some of its members are removed. Also no one will know exactly what the network does or how and so obtaining clear intelligence on the network can be very difficult indeed.

Destroyers of Morale

One approach to a destructive organisational psychology of crime is to tackle the reasons people have for being part of criminal organisations rather than only using the more conventional law enforcement approach of seeking to destroy the organisation directly. This has some parallels to the psychological warfare strategies that are used to undermine enemy populations. This approach does require some understanding of why people join and continue membership of criminal networks and of the weaknesses within those networks that can lead to their members being confused or misinformed about their network or its activities.

If people only remain within a criminal group because of pressures that are brought upon them then removal of those pressures are crucial. This is widely recognised by law enforcement agencies throughout the world in their witness protection programmes. But can also be extended by ensuring that rapid police action will minimise the risk of coercive violence. Once an area of a city becomes a 'no-go' area for the police or other forms of protection from violence, whether it is in shanty towns in South America, or caused urban guerrillas in Europe, then scene is set for organised crime to emerge.

A further mechanism for reducing morale and commitment to a criminal organisation is to reduce any self-esteem that members may gain by belonging to it. This requires that the status and kudos of the criminal organisation be challenged at any opportunity. If its members see themselves as a heroic team of freedom fighters attempts should be made to change the perception to a gang of callous thugs. This may be done in one to one contact with the criminals as they come into police contact or through the accounts of their activities that are portrayed in the media. The confusions in the communication process can be utilised here, as many criminals in the organisation will not have first hand knowledge of the actions of other people in the group.

The third process is to encourage feelings of alienation and separateness from the other members. Reducing the ability of criminals to communicate with each other will increase the likelihood of some of them feeling less involved with the organisation and will also feed the confusions in their communications with others. Out of this process, sub-groups of more isolated offenders may be identified who can then help to undermine the whole criminal organisation.

Myths of Organised Crime

In conclusion the points made in this essay can be summarised as challenges to a number of myths that seem to circulate amongst police officers about organised crime.

Because police officers themselves usually have only limited experience of how organisations work, namely experience of police forces, they have a tendency to assume that any other network of people will be managed in a similar way. But many studies of criminal groups, including those reviewed in the present volume, show that whilst there is often some element of organisation to criminal networks, in that there is some degree of role definition and rules of how to carry out activities, this is usually far less rigid or stable than for legal organisations. In general then it is a myth that large networks of criminals are 'organised' in anything like the same sense that a police force or university is organised.

The Hollywood image of a clear set of levels and chain of command is difficult to defend from detailed case studies of many criminal networks. Besides the problems such frameworks can create for criminals as discussed in this essay it is also often the case that criminal culture shies away from notions of authority and control. If images are to be drawn from fictional accounts the indications are that criminals far more often operate within structures illustrated in 'Lock, Stock and Two Smoking Barrels' than those illustrated in 'The Godfather'.

Bibliography

This essay is offered as a set of hypotheses about criminal organisations. They are derived from a wide reading of the organisational psychology and the criminology literature as well as more popular accounts of criminals and their activities. Formal citation of reference sources has therefore not been included. The following bibliography is offered as a basis for further study and as an indication of some of the published literature that has either been drawn on for this essay or provides more detailed information that will support or challenge the views offered.

References

Abadinsky, H. (1983), *Organised Crime*, 2nd edn., Chicago: Nelson-Hall.
Chell, E. (1987), *The Psychology of Behaviour in Organisations*, London: MacMillan Press.
Conklin, J.E. (1973), *The Crime Establishment: Organised Crime and American Society*, New Jersey, Prentice-Hall.
Decker, S.H. and Van Winkle, B. (1996), *Life in the Gang: Family Friends and Violence*, New York: Cambridge University Press.
Fincham, R. and Rhodes, P.S. (1992), *The Individual, Work and Organisation: Behavioural Studies for Business and Management*, New York: Oxford University Press.
Greenberg, J. and Baron, R.A. (1997), *Behaviour in Organisations: Understanding and Managing the Human Side of Work*, 6th edn., New Jersey: Prentice Hall.
Vecchio, R.P. (1995), *Organisational Behaviour*, 3rd edn., Florida: Harcourt Brace.
Watson, P. (1980), *War on the Mind,* London: Penguin.
Whyte, W.F. (1993), *Street Corner Society*, 4th edn., Chicago: University of Chicago Press.